MR ISHERWOOD CHANGES TRAINS

Christopher Isherwood and the search for the 'home self'

VICTOR MARSH

'Christopher Isherwood sustained a long project of spiritual self-fashioning, a fact often overlooked, or even denigrated, by his many biographers, critics and reviewers. In this original reappraisal, Dr Marsh makes a convincing case for the centrality of the spiritual in Isherwood's life. In addition, his interrogation of the contingencies that have accumulated to separate homosexuality from spirituality strikes me as being of more general and profound importance. … written with admirable lucidity.'

Professor Stephen Muecke,
School of English, Media and Performing Arts, University of New South Wales

'Dr Marsh gives the most nuanced reading of Christopher Isherwood and his principled self-disclosure that I have read, astutely placing the meaning of Isherwood's sexuality in relation to seeking and living a spiritual life. The historicizing and critical review of Isherwood is excellent and contributes an important and necessary corrective to much of the literary misunderstandings and ignorance that has been extant about Isherwood. The author gives expert and original readings into Isherwood's life narratives, discovering valuable connections that provide insights into core metaphysical concerns about the nature of the self (where homosexuality can be read as a crucial means of spiritual wholeness).

This book is an important and relevant addition to the field of sexuality studies and the nascent area of the convergence between Eastern and Western approaches to homosexuality and spirituality. Dr Marsh makes an eloquent and rigorous case to reclaim the validity, coherence and necessity of a spiritual life not predicated on the denial of one's sexuality, but rather on its celebration and significance.'

Associate Professor Baden Offord, School of Arts and Social Sciences,
Southern Cross University; Co-Director, Centre for Peace and Social Justice

MR ISHERWOOD CHANGES TRAINS

Christopher Isherwood and the search for the 'home self'

VICTOR MARSH

Clouds of Magellan | Melbourne

First published 2010
Clouds of Magellan
www.cloudsofmagellan.net
Melbourne, Australia

ISBN: 9780980712056

A Cataloguing-in-Publication for this title is available from the National Library of Australia

Images used with kind permission of the artist, Don Bachardy:

Colour portrait of Christopher Isherwood on his 76th birthday, 26 August 1980.
Acrylic on paper. Don Bachardy.

Portrait of Christopher Isherwood, 17 November 1968.
Pencil and ink wash drawing. Don Bachardy.

Contents

Acknowledgments

In the long evolution of this work, I have several people to thank for their encouragement. I must acknowledge my gratitude for the close critical reading given the text at various stages by Amanda Lohrey and Ruth Blair, Stephen Muecke and Baden Offord. The faults remain entirely my own. Thanks go to the School of English, Media Studies and Art History and the University of Queensland, which made it possible for me to research this project under a UQ Postgraduate Research Scholarship

I must also thank Gordon Thompson, my gracious publisher at Clouds of Magellan, for taking on a difficult book, and Helen Bell for her meticulous editing.

In Los Angeles, I am indebted to the following people: to Dan Luckenbill of the UCLA library for his suggestions for further reading, his personal reminiscences of Christopher Isherwood, and introducing me to Don Bachardy. To Don Bachardy, for the portrait art included in this volume, for his insights and feedback, and for kindly submitting to a lengthy interview. To Romaine Ahlstrom and the staff of Reader Services at the Huntington Library in San Marino and especially to Sue Hodson, the curator of the Isherwood collection, who gave me access to important papers, lecture notes, and correspondence. To Nirvana—Bob Adjemian—Publisher of the Vedanta Press, Pravrajika Vrajaprana, and other members of the Ramakrishna Order of Southern California, for helping me understand Isherwood's relationship with the Society and with Swami Prabhavananda.

Elements of the discussion have been canvassed previously in *Life Writing*, *Ariel*, *Theology & Sexuality*, *White Crane*, and *Postscripts: The Journal of Sacred Texts and Contemporary Worlds.*

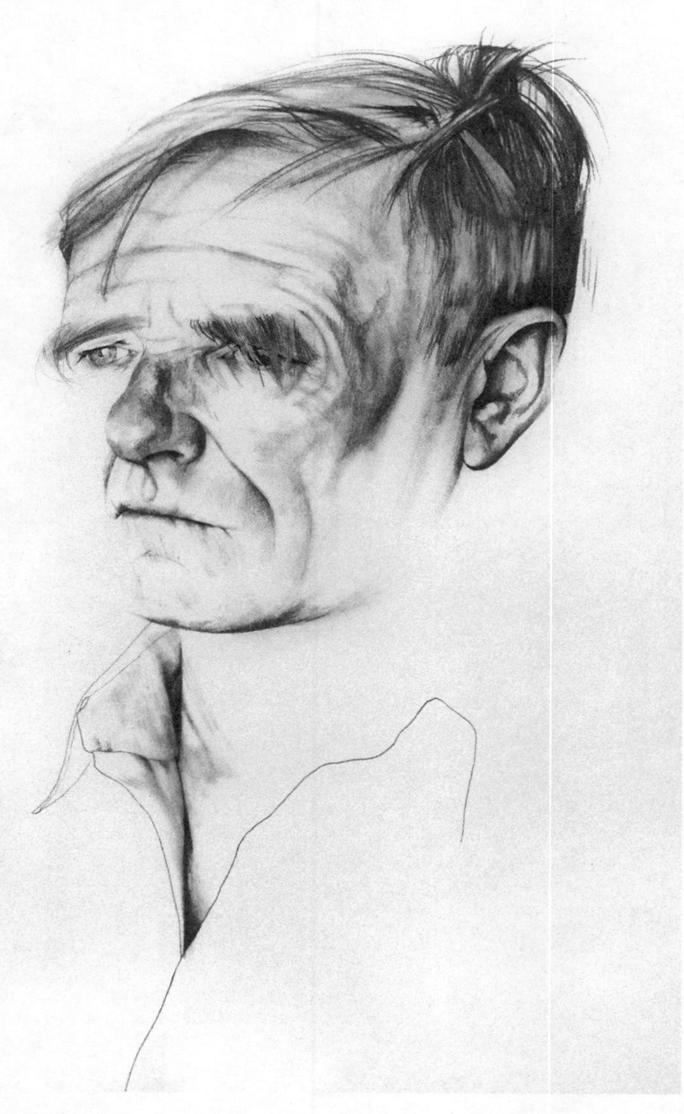

Christopher Isherwood by Don Bachardy

1
Introduction

> *The critique of what we are is at one and the same time the historical analysis of the limits that are imposed on us and an experiment with the possibility of going beyond them.*
>
> —Michel Foucault, 'What is enlightenment?'

This book comes out of research undertaken for a doctorate. When people would ask me, 'In what field?' my response—'spiritual autobiographies by queer men'—would produce a range of surprised reactions: from outright astonishment bordering on disbelief, to (from the more subtle) a wry smile. In any case, the next question would be, 'You mean … there ARE such things?' with the not always vocalised subtext, 'There can't be very many!' and I was supposed to join in the joke. Of all the things that queer men are about, it couldn't be religion, or 'spirituality', the assumption goes. Queer = gay = homosexual = they're all about sex; religion and sexuality have always been mutually exclusive—*homo*sexuality is officially labeled as an abomination by the churches. Ergo, these represent two mutually exclusive possibilities for being and knowing.

In my early research I was fascinated, then, to find a cache of autobiographical writing by queer men who, in spite of the common misconception that an authentic religious life could only be pursued if based upon a repudiation of their 'deviant' sexuality, had engaged sincerely with various forms of religious belief and practice. This rich corpus of texts, narrating spiritual journeys both within and without mainstream religious groups, gives voice to experience otherwise discursively silenced by the conventional religious narratives that dominate public perceptions, narratives that privilege normative constructions of identity. As they concern themselves with an area of human spirituality usually ignored by mainstream commentary, these writings have proved worthy of close attention.

Among this group, the British expatriate writer Christopher Isherwood, who lived more than half of his life in southern California, stands out as being of exemplary interest. Isherwood was born in Cheshire, England, in 1904. He was the son of an army officer who was killed near Ypres, in the First World War. Isherwood knew from an early age that he wanted to be a writer and, frustrating his mother's wishes for him to be a don, he dropped out of Cambridge. Adding to his mother's disappointment, he studied medicine only briefly before moving to Berlin on the recommendation of his close friend, the poet WH Auden, whom he had known since prep. school. On the eve of the Second World War, with the memory of his father's death still with him, he and Auden migrated to the United States, declaring themselves to be pacifists. Isherwood died in Los Angeles in 1986.

There have been calls for Isherwood to be re-evaluated as a serious religious writer (Wade 2001), yet the proposal has met with a certain amount of scepticism, as I will show, for this possibility does not square with the standard view of Isherwood, which is dominated by a set of stereotyped views that pays little attention and even less respect to his religious life.

In what follows I provide a reading of Isherwood's life and work based not so much on the early writing—dating from his time in Berlin during the 1930s—nor from the 'out' gay autobiographical texts of the 1970s, but from the neglected religious writings of the intervening years that culminated in the modest classic *My Guru and his disciple*, his last major book, which was published in 1980 just a few years before his death. This element of the life and work recommends him as being of exceptional interest into the twenty-first century, yet it has been given scant attention by the literary commentariat until very recently (the rare exceptions coming among the collection of essays edited by James Berg and Chris Freeman in 2004—*The Isherwood century*—

and a rather muddled attempt from Antony Copley, in his book *A spiritual Bloomsbury*, 2006).

I will analyse factors contributing to the entrenched scepticism around the allegedly irreconcilable ways of being and knowing—'queer' and 'religious'—to challenge the limitations that are commonly thought to apply in the domain of queer men's spiritual lives. The analysis raises issues to do with the social and political construction of knowledge, and it is within this wider context that I will offer my reading of Isherwood's contribution to contemporary thought. While postmodern interrogations of gender have destabilised conventional notions of masculinity, and feminists have challenged the patriarchal constructions of religion, queer men are presumed to have abandoned the field of spirituality and religion altogether, to focus solely on civil rights. The struggle for equal rights before the law is unquestionably important, yet too often it rests on the untested assumption that queer folk have no interest in the religious life, and no right to contest the hateful constructions of their identity emanating from religious institutions.

I take my lead here from the feminist theologian Lucy Reid, who has had to work hard to break through the entrenched patriarchal resistance within her (Anglican) church to her vocation to be a priest. Early in her studies Reid sought to discover the 'feminine face' of God:

> To describe God with maternal attributes is a radical departure from the norm of patriarchal, male identified language, but it is not merely a feminist gesture; it is an attempt to use the best metaphors available to talk about certain aspects of the Divine. (Reid 2005, p. 17)

Reid drew inspiration from many of the mystics of the Christian tradition. Discussing the writings of Julian(a) of Norwich (1342–ca 1416), she writes:

> The traditional models of divine fatherhood and judgement are inadequate (even destructive) containers for her understanding of God, and so she gently but firmly redefines them with a radically new, feminine model. (p. 15)

Reid reached back into church history for support but I propose that this notion of 'inadequate containers' is particularly relevant to my study of recent queer explorations of the possibilities of a spiritual life. Contemporary interrogations of the politics of gender have de-stabilised rigid frameworks of knowledge and re-opened possibilities of knowing otherwise closed off by orthodox constructions. Reid insists—also 'gently but firmly'—that 'if we do not use images from female experience, we impoverish and restrict our ability to imagine God' (p. 17) and I think the point holds good for the life pathways opened up by queer religious experience.

Christopher Lane, in his remarkable book, *The ruling passion: British colonial allegory and the paradox of homosexual desire*, discusses 'homosexual' desire in the context of British colonial culture, describing the effect of non-conformist desire as a 'counterforce that shatters national allegory by introducing unassimilable elements' (Lane 1995, p. 2) into the narratives of Empire. He recognises that homosexual desire—and its textual manifestations—disrupted the allegories of empire by introducing 'sexual ambivalence, political contention, self-antagonism, and national and racial disputes' (p. 2) into the imperial project. Queer folk recognise that colonialism is a project operating *within* as well as across political cultures, and their life experience gives them insight into how such a project outlaws identity positions that do not conform to the dominator model that 'colonises' possibilities of meaning. To investigate the power and influence of the coloniser, and interrogate its ruling principles, the colonised subject (in this case, the putative 'homosexual') needs to become aware of the infiltration of the colonising power within the internal infrastructure of his/her own sense of self. This inquiry, according to Michel Foucault, should be 'oriented toward what is not or is no longer indispensable for the constitution of ourselves as autonomous subjects'; otherwise, he asks, 'do we not run the risk of letting ourselves be determined by more general structures of which we may well not be conscious, and over which we may have no control?' ('What is enlightenment?' p. 47). To Foucault, criticism, then,

> is no longer going to be practiced in the search for formal structures with universal value, but rather as a historical investigation into the events that

> have led us to constitute ourselves and to recognize ourselves as subjects of what we are doing, thinking, saying. (pp. 45–6)

In contrast to the search for 'formal structures with universal value', Foucault prefers

> the very specific transformations that have proved to be possible in the last twenty years in a certain number of areas that concern our ways of being and thinking, relations to authority, relations between the sexes, the way in which we perceive insanity or illness. (pp. 46–7)

Foucault characterises what he calls 'the critical ontology of ourselves' as 'a historico-practical test of the limits that we may go beyond, and thus as work carried out by ourselves upon ourselves as free beings' (p. 47).

I read Isherwood's work against this broader context of interrogating the (im)possibilities of knowledge embedded in the dominant mythology that colonises meaning and proscribes freedom in the social and political context in which he lived. The discomfort he experienced with the prevailing expectations projected onto him after the death of his father in WWI, as well as his growing awareness of the implications of his differently ordered sexuality within Edwardian society, brought these issues uncomfortably into focus for him as he moved away from unquestioning allegiance to the values and expectations of Empire. By choosing to embrace rather than deny his difference Isherwood, as a citizen born at the centre of colonial power, effectively renounced the privileges of birth. A man without a country, he left himself in the existential dilemma of being without a pre-ordained, 'authorised' identity, which he had to 're-author' himself.

While Britain continued to refuse 'to relinquish its historical and psychic investment in its empire' (Lane, p. 232), Isherwood's dissident opinions and life choices disrupted the embedded values underpinning British society, and his life and work are emblematic of a culturally and politically significant period of shifting allegiances. The resources he was to draw on in his personal reconciliation process point forward to developments that are highly relevant beyond the end of the 'Isherwood Century' (Berg/Freeman) and the shift into a new millennium. Otherwise, why would one want to resurrect another dead, white, male writer, who originally rose to prominence in the 1930s?

Some readers will know already that Isherwood lived in Berlin during the rise of the Nazis and wrote the famous stories on which the musical (and movie) *Cabaret* was based. Liza Minelli played Sally Bowles. Wasn't there a 'Christopher' character there, among the other roles? These are the mnenomic prompts I resort to in order to jog people's memory, when they ask me who Isherwood was. But even among literary types who have heard of the Berlin stories and who could recall a *Mr Norris changes trains* (1935), a *Goodbye to Berlin* (1939), or the collected *Berlin stories*, or even the play *I am a camera* (adapted for the stage by John van Druten, 1955), there is less awareness of what happened to the writer after he de-camped to California in 1939. 'Herr Issyvoo', as he was called by his German landlady, slipped off the literary radar after the early works, yet he kept writing and continued to do so until just a couple of years before his death in 1986.

I want to draw attention to the reasons why Isherwood abandoned Europe on the eve of War, what drove his peregrinations across Europe (and to the Far East), and what it was that he found in southern California that satisfied the deeply felt need that I characterise—using Isherwood's own terminology—as the search for the 'home self'.

Other readers will be more familiar with Isherwood's later work, when he became a standard-bearer for the gay liberation push in the 1970s, especially with the publication of *Christopher and his kind* in 1976. But the work Isherwood produced during the intervening period—roughly from 1945 through to the 1970s—is often ignored, or dismissed outright by literary commentators. In what follows I hope to untangle the complex of prejudicial attitudes bound up in the refusal to give that mid-life work serious attention.

Apart from the intrinsic interest of his intellectually independent and courageous, non-conformist journey through periods of exceptional cultural and political upheaval, there are broader issues here to do with the sometimes unstated ideologies embedded within the supposedly incompatible categories—'queer' and 'religion' (the latter has come to represent a normative social force, the former a strictly 'post religion' phenomenon)—that this analysis of the life, the work, and the historical contexts will examine. If a self-confessed (and unrepentant) 'homosexual' were to engage seriously with religion, an entire moral universe would be threatened, for the 'homosexual' needs to remain a pariah in order for orthodox constructions of morality to remain stable (and in power). To step outside the parameters necessary to maintain the moral universe in its coercively policed configuration would destabilise the very basis of a normatively constructed reality.

In my view, too often there is an unchallenged set of binarisms at work in the reading of Isherwood's life, one that would separate 'the life of the body' and the 'life of the spirit', typically assuming that a man can't be serious about one if he is engaged with the other, and this deeply rooted assumption is simply not flushed out or challenged. Few commentators are ready to consider how one might, rather, *inform* the other and therefore miss the integrative effect of the *Advaita* (literally 'not two') philosophy he studied with his guru, Swami Prabhavananda (which will be the focus of chapters 4 and 5). Not recognising crucial elements of the particular spiritual practices taken up by Isherwood, many commentators continue to beat up the straw man they have tended to make of him.

Isherwood in aspic

For, in the case of some emblematic writers there develops an entrenched cultural investment in certain modes of assessing them. In a sense, a culture can become over-invested in such constructions, resistant to any other way of reading, to the extent, even, of ignoring evidence to the contrary. Accordingly, Isherwood's reputation is suspended in aspic, limited to perpetual fame as either the chronicler of pre-war Berlin or, much later, as a literary mentor during the days of Californian gay liberation, during the 1970s and early 80s.

By the time of his first visit to Berlin, at age 24, Isherwood had published a first novel (*All the conspirators*) and was working on *The memorial*, which would be published in 1932. His first autobiography *Lions and shadows* was published in 1938, but it was really the Berlin stories, with the characters of the Novaks, Sally Bowles, Mr Norris, and Herr Issyvoo himself, that were the basis of Isherwood's early rise to fame. Somerset Maugham described him as the most promising novelist of his generation to Virginia Woolf, and the Woolfs' Hogarth Press was one of his early publishers. However, when Isherwood and Auden emigrated to the US on the eve of the Second World War, they were pilloried as virtual traitors by the British literary and political establishments. (Benjamin Britten and Peter Pears made the same move, but were forgiven upon their return to the motherland.)

Literary critics in Britain found cause to lament the subsequent decline in Isherwood's literary output, for only one novel, *Prater Violet* (1945) came out of the early years in California. *Prater Violet* was followed by the novels *The world in the evening* in 1954, *Down there on a visit,* 1962, and *A single man*, 1964, but it was really the autobiography *Christopher and his kind* in 1976 that produced the second wave of interest in Isherwood that brought him out of virtual cultural exile. A long-standing member of the American Civil Liberties Union, Isherwood supported the work of the One Institute, an offshoot of the early Mattachine Society in Los Angeles, and he mentored several younger writers. Having acknowledged his sexuality directly in this text, however, his life and work were subjected to reductive pathological readings, tethered to a mid-century pseudo-psychoanalytic discourse that would diagnose a 'homosexualist' (Savage 1976) as a developmental failure, with the attendant glib characterisation of the homosexual as narcissist—a term much in vogue among literary critics at the time, who liked to propose psychoanalytical readings of authors from their texts.

Isherwood lived through a period when the classification of 'the homosexual' as a case suitable for medical attention was in full swing. The medical model was supposed to have liberated such men from the attention of the law courts but it was common practice in the second half of the twentieth century for certain medical and psychological procedures, such as shock treatment, and so-called 'aversion' therapy, to be applied to 'cure' men of their alleged sickness. Worse, medical discourse was adopted to work in tandem with religious constructions to rationalise continuing, deeply rooted prejudice, adding psycho-pathology to the already established moral perversity of such a 'type'. As William Turner notes, according to the common scientific explanations of the 1950s and 1960s, 'to ask after the stories of "homosexuals" as anything other than a compilation of case studies for psychological purposes would have been a waste of time; such stories possessed no other edifying value' (2000, p. 61).

In what follows I will use the terms 'homosexual' and 'gay' reluctantly, and with distaste, for I find the whole project of classifying people according to their sexuality problematical—an insufficient basis around which to construct an identity. The reader will see—at least by the final chapter—that I insist, ultimately, on a more radical understanding of subjectivity than is offered by these narrowly conceived categories. I will probe the question: who is a 'homosexual' when he is not having sex? To develop an answer, I have focused on life-narratives where 'spirituality' emerges as a central preoccupation alongside sexuality.

Interrogating sexual identity

For men who have been marginalised by the hostile discourses produced by religion, medicine and the law, the problematised issue of identity takes on critical importance at the very time when the study of subjectivity—probing what constitutes the 'I'—has become the focus of intense theoretical debate, as highlighted by Mansfield (2000). There has been a notable shift in thinking about what constitutes a 'self' across a wide range of disciplines, and this is another of the broader theoretical contexts that applies in my reading of Isherwood. In the next chapter I will look at how such theoretical discussions have forced a radical revision of commonly assumed understandings of the self as knowable, predictable and controlled, a discussion that problematises the notion of the subject as 'a self-contained being that develops in the world as an expression of its own unique essence,' in the words of Nick Mansfield (p. 13). In the modernist view, 'self' was regarded as a single solid entity set against an objective world, but this construction has been under challenge, as Phillip Lucas describes:

> In the emerging *post*modern condition, the self is seen as a series of successive identities, each characterized by an interminable series of experiments and explorations. The postmodern self is always in process, eclectically drawing elements and images from both the old and the new in its search for 'meaning'. (Lucas 1996, p. 149)

Lucas was reviewing Robert S Ellwood's book *The sixties spiritual awakening*, for the journal *Church History*, and was not entirely sympathetic to the shifts that Ellwood was describing, but the whole issue of the relative instability of the 'self' is something that queer men face early in their lives and is not only of theoretical concern.

In postmodern analyses 'identity' is increasingly positioned at the intersection of issues such as class, race, gender, sexuality, and religion, all of which influence the fashioning of a self. In fact, as the whole notion of self as a fixed, locatable entity has become problematised, postmodern scholarship often declines to use the term 'identity' altogether, preferring the notion of 'subject positions', focusing more on how people constitute themselves differently at different moments in time, in different contexts and in different relationships. After Foucault proposed the notion of 'technologies of the self' (Foucault 2000, p. 177), scholars have begun to use various words to translate his term '*assujettissement*', in French, employing 'subjection', 'subjectification', 'objectification' and 'subjectivation' to denote the possibility not only of alienated manipulation by external forces but also the more positive, active identification with certain subject-positions through their own volition (see Luckhurst 2008, for example). As Felicity Nussbaum describes it:

> Postmodern theory recognizes that the self is less a reified thing than an ideological construct articulated in the language available to the individual at a particular historical moment. The coherent and stable human self who originates and perpetuates the meaning of experience and history is the construct of modern philosophical thought. (Nussbaum 1988, p. 131)

According to Nussbaum, postmodern theory helps us recognise that ideas about the 'self' are 'constructs rather than eternal truths' (p. 128). To recognise that the truth status of commonly held beliefs about identity is relative to particular historical circumstances has enabled the work of dissident queer politics to move boldly forward on several fronts in recent decades, but much work still needs to be done with regard to deconstructing the prescriptive set of meanings produced by conventional religious teachings.

Nick Mansfield writes that the focus on the self 'as the centre both of lived experience and of discernible meaning has become one of the—if not *the*—defining issues of modern and postmodern cultures' (2000, p. 1). This is very important to any discussion of queer experience but is especially appropriate in any discussion that examines religious versions of identity positioning. I look at this more closely in the next chapter, where I will analyse how representations of the 'self' are canvassed in the scholarly literature about subjectivity (more specifically, in the fields of life-writing and autobiography), and I will compare these representations with notions of the self found in the discourse of mysticism—a comparison which, I believe, is rarely drawn. I will differentiate two models of the self, contrasting the orthodox model derived from the discourse of psychology—in which the individual is privileged, in the best Western humanist tradition—with the notion of a 'self' derived from non-dualistic Eastern mystical traditions such as Buddhism, Taoism and the discourse of *Advaita Vedanta*, which I will show has common features with the postmodern analysis that has destabilised the standard modernist assumptions about the nature of personal identity.

In much writing on cross-gendered identities, the psycho-spiritual potential in those who 'walk between worlds' (de la Huerta) is usually ignored in favour of descriptions of sexual behaviour as the authentic basis for positioning identity, whether the writing is fictive or auto/biographical. Cross-cultural studies—from anthropology, for example—indicate more positive pathways for gender variant types than that allowed for by familiar negative constructions such as the 'religious abomination'/'medical pathology'/'social criminal'/'sexual outlaw' models. My discussion of Isherwood (in chapters 3, 4 and 5), then, will be framed within a review that challenges conventionally produced notions of subject positions that rely too heavily on the figuration of the homosexual as either a religious pariah, or psychopathological misfit, or both (chapters 2 and 6).

My study has restricted itself largely to texts by a male writer, not because I find work by women any less interesting, but because in discussions with my sisters I have learned that it is better not to speculate about their experience—women tend to do a rather better job themselves, writing about reconfigured identities liberated from patriarchal assumptions. It is for that very reason that I am indebted at many points in my discussion to the penetrating theoretical insights offered by a number of scholars who are women. Also, as far afield as my theorising wanders in the following discussion, I have tried to focus my discussion on this one particular case study, rather than reach too far after universalist claims.

Versions of the life

A massive biography of Isherwood, by Peter Parker, was published in British and American editions for the hundredth anniversary of his birth in 2004. There have been others (by Jonathon Fryer, for example, in 1993) with Claude J Summers' in 1981 probably the best, to my mind; and Katherine Bucknell, who has edited two collections of the diaries to date—1996 and 2000—has written insightful introductions to those editions, which are particularly well informed by her close reading of the source material. Bucknell is preparing the final two volumes of the diaries for publication in 2010 and 2011.

In his biography Parker says Isherwood's life reflects 'the upheavals, the fragmentation and the deracination of the twentieth century' (Parker 2004, p. 832). I want to take up this claim—both the man and the works as exempla of fragmentation, deracination and the de-centred self—and explore a terrain that too many commentators neglect, with special reference to Isherwood's spiritual writings.

Parker spent twelve years working on his biography, and the detailed research is rich and impressive, making it very useful as a reference work. He had unprecedented access to more sources than any earlier biographer, especially the diaries from Isherwood's mother, Kathleen, and his brother, Richard, plus material provided by Isherwood's surviving life partner, the artist Don Bachardy, as well as correspondence now archived in the Huntington Library and several other collections, and the writer's own published documentation of his life. Isherwood's personal preoccupations, friendships, and the chronology and the genesis of his various texts, are thoroughly accounted for in Parker's narrative.

However, while he records the events of the life exhaustively, and with more historical detail than any previous biographer, Parker's opinion is not always sympathetic. Scepticism is undoubtedly a valuable trait in a biographer, but there are critical points where it masks a lack of understanding. While for the most part Parker maintains a detached and aloof stance, the points at which he abandons that stance to offer out-and-out judgments are significant, for they suggest something about the biographer's own blind spots. Unfortunately, this has the effect of contributing to, and reinforcing, entrenched prejudicial attitudes towards the writer, which have dominated

Isherwood scholarship until recently. This is especially the case in Parker's depiction of the relationship between Isherwood and his guru, Swami Prabhavananda, an issue I will return to in chapters 3 and 4.

I have tracked the reception of the Parker biography as it has been reviewed around the world and it is clear from this informal survey that many prejudicial attitudes are extant today that have contributed to a profound and continued mis-reading of Isherwood's life and literary output. I will argue that a re-appraisal of Isherwood as a serious spiritual writer is, indeed, overdue and show how both unconscious and conscious cultural prejudices continue to cloud evaluations of important aspects of his life and work. Isherwood was a precursor of many trends that had become prominent by the close of the 20th century, and my discussion will review the influential writer through a new lens, focusing on issues to do with the role of spirituality as a source of knowledge even for those minority types whose sexuality runs against majoritarian norms.

The encounter with Vedanta

Between the Berlin years and the later period in the 1970s, Isherwood continued to write, even if British critics tended to regard his work rather frostily, or ignored it altogether. In addition to the novels, diaries and autobiographical work, it was during this period that he wrote influential texts arising out of his engagement with the teachings and practices of Vedanta, an interest he pursued from 1939 until his death in 1986.

'Vedanta' is the most highly developed presentation of the religious philosophies based on the study of the ancient Indian scriptures, the 'Vedas', and subsequent commentaries including the 'Upanishads'. These texts included translations into English, with his guru, Swami Prabhavananda, of key Vedanta texts such as the Bhagavad Gita (their title: *The song of God*, published in 1944), Shankara's *Crest jewel of discrimination* (the *Viveka Chudamani*, 1947) and the *Yoga sutras* of Patanjali (which they titled *How to know God*, 1953). Isherwood also wrote explanatory guides to Vedanta for Western readers (*An approach to Vedanta*, 1963, for example) and an official biography—still widely read today—of the 19th century Bengali mystic Paramhans Sri Ramakrishna (*Ramakrishna and his disciples,* 1965) for the headquarters of the Ramakrishna Vedanta Society, the Belur Math in Calcutta.

But even as he was emerging as a kind of cross-cultural translator for a new Western readership, this whole corpus tended to further alienate the literati, especially in Britain. Isherwood notes some of the bitchy reviews that the biography of Ramakrishna received, marked among other things by 'predictable sneers' towards southern California. Isherwood quotes from one review in his own autobiography, *My Guru and his disciple:* 'I have always been slightly suspicious of Indian sects who choose to establish themselves in this, the "crank belt" of southern California' (p. 288). Even his friend WH Auden was inclined to dismiss it all as 'mumbo jumbo'. Isherwood visited Auden in New York in 1951, when the play *I am a camera* (adapted by John van Druten from the Berlin stories) was in rehearsals, and he and Auden were happy to see each other again:

> We talked a great deal about Wystan's Christian beliefs without getting into any arguments. And I showed him entries in my diary describing my life at the Vedanta Center. He shook his head over them, regretfully: 'All this heathen mumbo jumbo—I'm sorry my dear, but it just *won't do*.' Then, in the abrupt, dismissive tone which he used when making an unwilling admission, he added: 'Your Swami's quite obviously a Saint, of course.' (*My Guru and his disciple*, p. 204)

Such exotic pursuits drew down upon Isherwood the ethnocentric prejudice commonly held towards the religious practices of a subject people (especially in colonialist Britain), but Isherwood was considered risqué for several other reasons: because he was unapologetic about his sexuality—more so after having taken a young male partner, thirty years his junior—and because he lived in California (regarded suspiciously as the 'Left' coast of the United States). In addition, he worked as a writer for the Hollywood movie studios. How could he be taken seriously as a literary figure if he persisted in working in that ersatz profession? (The fact is that Hollywood was an entrepôt for an elite European émigré community of artists, composers, writers and filmmakers, and Isherwood was a friend and colleague to many of the most prominent of them.)

The tenuous division of the 'worldly' from the 'spiritual' can hardly be sustained in any reading of the life and work of this complex man. In spite of the glamorous life—mixing with the stars, getting drunk with Charlie Chaplin, picnicking with Greta Garbo—under the guidance of his unusually non-judgemental guru Isherwood persisted with religious study and spiritual practices that, after a short-lived attempt at the renunciate life, were carried out within a lifestyle that was certainly not predicated on a denial of his sexuality.

So, there is a complex tangle of knots in standard accounts which, if I can unravel them, will lay bare a great deal about the prejudices—informal and institutional—that have clouded evaluations of the life and work of an exceptionally independent writer and thinker: unchallenged assumptions that mask Isherwood's surprising contribution to contemporary reversionings of the religious life. I will also draw attention to certain factors that Isherwood may be said to have contributed himself in this regard. This study is in no way intended as a new biography, but it does aim to review and revise some of the standard readings in the light of his ignored or much misunderstood religious praxis. As it is not a biography, in what follows (chapters 3, 4 and 5, particularly) I will not stick to a chronological account of the life. As I follow certain thematic threads I will often work forward in the life events, then circle back to pick up on other threads left dangling.

The Third Wave

If calls for Isherwood's religious life to be taken seriously are to be responded to, there are certain issues that need to be addressed. Foremost among these is the dominant cultural expectation that spirituality must be based on the denial of sexuality, especially *homo*sexuality. 'My personal approach to Vedanta was, among other things, the approach of a homosexual looking for a religion which will accept him', he wrote in his (yet unpublished) diary in 1970 (Bucknell 2000, ix). It is this aspect of the life and work that has provoked a revival of interest in Isherwood today and what follows should be read as part of this 'third wave' of interest (the 'first wave' coming with the Berlin stories, and the 'second wave' with the 'out' gay texts). I will interrogate several of the issues contributing to widespread disrespect from the literary establishment that has amounted to an effective occlusion of his religious life and writings that continues even today (with the exceptions already noted).

This renewed interest in Isherwood surprises literary scholars who have been inclined to write Isherwood off as a figure of minor interest in the British literary canon. Such interest is driven by people dissatisfied with what I might call the 'baby and the bathwater' problem; for, while recognising that religion is one of the major sources of homophobia, many queer folk, in their struggle for insight into the nature of the self, have not been content to eschew the rich resources available from diverse religious traditions that have opened up as the world's cultural traditions increasingly intermingle. In fact, as Peter Savastano describes, they may even become 'virtuosi in the holy art of bricolage' (2007, p 9).

In addition to the pathologising discourse of psychological medicine that promulgated a construction of 'homosexuality' as developmental failure—an idea adopted rather too readily by Antony Copley (2006, p. 251), but interrogated most effectively by Jamie Carr in her study of Isherwood (2006)—there is also the problem of an unreconstructed colonialist prejudice towards religious practices associated with a subject people. For a lapsed Anglican atheist and former socialist to investigate Vedanta, and take on a guru, was anathema in 1939, and it contributed to the feeling in Britain that Isherwood was, once again, 'letting down the side' after his virtual betrayal of the home country by his conscientious adoption of pacifism. As we will see in chapters 3 and 4, Isherwood was seeking out not only a rationale for his newfound pacifism, but a differently ordered array of 'technologies of the self' than those provided by either the Anglicanism of his upbringing, or the political slogans of his Socialist period. In Vedanta he found useful transformational tools among an otherwise 'subjugated knowledge' system (to borrow Michel Foucault's terminology; see 1980, p. 82) that allowed him to move beyond the boundaries of his culturally ordained subject positioning—not only as a Briton, but also as an unrepentant 'homosexual', and a religious pariah.

The politics of knowledge

In spite of the customary prejudices emanating from the churches there is strong testimonial evidence, in the form of autobiographical texts, that many men and women whose sexual orientation tends towards same-sex couplings have engaged vigorously with the religious life, and continue to do so, even when the discourse emanating from their own faith traditions continues to slander them. I position Isherwood's work among the first rank of these testimonies.

Even when not writing formal autobiography (such as in *Lions and shadows*, *Christopher and his kind*, *Kathleen and Frank*, *My Guru and his disciple*) Isherwood worked up material from his own life for his fiction, often drawing from his diaries. The various sub-genres of literary form now more commonly grouped under the rubric of 'life-writing'—memoir, biography, autobiography, diaries, letters and so on—offer a set of writing and reading practices for radical resignifications of the hostile meanings ascribed to the differently ordered sense of being and becoming that queer folk live. Within the newly identified (sub)genre 'queer spiritual autobiography' (Stewart 2002) such a writing praxis defends itself against what French scholar Didier Eribon calls the 'culture of insult' (2004) that repeatedly attacks queer modes of knowing, of representation and of subject positioning.

Meaning and power are inextricably related in contemporary constructions of identity, so resistance to culturally prescribed identification has important political dimensions. Both psychological medicine and conventional religion can be seen as operating within an economy of power that restricts diverse possibilities for exploration and expression in modern culture. The authorised forms that identity—and meaning itself—may take are prescribed by a dominant, privileged class in order to 'normalise' its majoritarian practices and shore up the shared beliefs that provide the foundation for complex interlocking systems of domination. As JF Lyotard insists: '[K]nowledge and power are simply two sides of the same question: who decides what knowledge is, and who knows what needs to be decided?' (1986, p. 9).

To re-open the possibilities for newly ordered subject positions entails a struggle with entrenched political and epistemic constructions, then. The privileged forms of (hetero)sexuality authorised by religious doctrine, and rendered as 'scientific facts' by medicine, become legitimating norms that 'justify themselves', as scholar Kathleen Sands puts it, 'by claiming ontological priority over that which they regulate' (2008, p. 2). In this system, 'heterosexuality' is presented 'as natural, eternal, or God-given, and this supposed ontological priority provides the warrant for compelling people to enact it'. Moreover, Sands continues:

> The type of power that courses through sexuality is *normative power*. The regime of sexuality delimits how people may conceive and represent themselves, how they construe their desires, the regulations to which they are subject, the economic rewards they may receive, the neighborhoods or nations in which they may live, the laws that will or won't apply to them, the medical treatment they'll be given or denied. (p. 2)

Sexuality is 'never just there', writes Sands, 'it is never just a reality; it is always already a set of prescriptions and proscriptions that define what may and may not present itself as real' (p. 1).

Italian Marxist Antonio Gramsci adapted the use of the term 'hegemony' to signify the dominance of one group or class over others; not only between nations (as in its original Greek usage) but *within* a society. Gramsci focused his analysis on the ideological machinery through which the dominator class is able to project and institutionalise its own meanings. Such 'machinery' operates using an array of cultural processes that typically involve advertising, education and the media, as well as the more overt backing of police and the army. In order to succeed, the set of meanings promulgated and enforced by the ruling group (the 'hegemon') involves the willing and active consent of those subordinated, who may come to accept that configuration of meaning as 'common sense' and 'natural'. But what is taken as 'common sense', suggests Geoffrey Nowell-Smith, could be understood as 'the way a subordinate class lives its subordination' (cited in Alvarado & Boyd-Barrett 1992, p. 51). 'Common' sense, then, comes to reflect accepted, normative assumptions, rather than a real awareness of equality, of being 'as one' (French: '*comme un*'). Writing practice that asserts possibilities for being and knowing differing from those provided for in the politically privileged hegemonic representations has distinctly political repercussions, then.

The majoritarian and conformist hegemony of normative heterosexuality relies heavily on defining itself as distinct from (and morally superior to) the despised and stigmatised 'Other', the *homo*-sexual. Subjects who wish to resist such constructions, finding themselves discursively and politically marginalised within this economy of power, may choose to step outside the epistemic control of the systems of meaning produced and authorised by such forces. Rather than tamely living out their subordination, following scripts prescribed by these normative systems, such disobedient subjects may choose instead to rewrite the narratives prescribed by dominant systems of meaning and power that prove hostile to their unconventional identities. In such cases, writing texts in first person voice produces testimony that has the power to re-configure the significance of the life and may assert entirely different constructions of meaning and value than those authorised as 'natural' by the normative constructions of the hegemon.

This applies equally to religious constructions of meaning. By withholding from non-conformists the possibility of an engagement with 'the divine', certain dominant institutionalised voices within conventional Western religious discourse operate within what Foucault calls 'regimes of truth'—power/knowledge relations that constitute 'a set of rules by which truth is produced'. That is to say, in this analysis, the production of truth forms part of a complex economy of power that denies religious knowledge as unavailable to those folk whom it discursively positions outside the field of moral respectability. Foucault argued, in *The history of sexuality volume one*, that any strategy aimed at resisting the mechanisms of power must involve a transgression of laws, a dismantling of prohibition and an 'irruption of speech' (Foucault 1978, p. 5). In his personal search and his textual interrogation of notions of what constitutes a 'self', Isherwood produced versions of subjective identification that disrupted authorised views of masculinity, and confronted the exclusivist modeling of the religious life as it was framed discursively within his own historical and cultural context.

My discussion draws upon Peter Berger's analysis of the functioning of 'plausibility structures' in the sociology of knowledge systems, and the mechanisms by which different sources of knowledge and information are accorded 'differential plausibility', with 'deviant' views marginalised or excluded. 'The threat to the social definitions of reality' writes Berger, with

Thomas Luckmann, is neutralised by 'assigning an inferior ontological status, and thereby a not-to-be-taken seriously cognitive status, to all definitions existing outside the symbolic universe' (Berger & Luckmann 1966, p. 133). These 'definitions of reality' are instruments of power, de-authorising that which is not in accord with their models, and according to which Isherwood—as a notorious 'homosexualist'—should not have anything to say about religion; neither, in the same analysis, should insights drawn from a training in an 'alien' religious tradition be considered plausible, or of an equivalent ontological status to that accorded the privileged constructions of the Abrahamic—in Isherwood's case, specifically the Christian, Anglican—traditions.

Isherwood had stepped away from the religion of his upbringing and regarded himself as an atheist. Giving himself permission to rehearse different, independent possibilities for selfhood, he moved restlessly through different national and cultural settings, in the process of investigating and re-inventing himself. Ultimately he found effective tools for his searching and often painful self-inquiry from within a completely different religious tradition that was not at all 'fashionable' at the time, in spite of the assertions of some recent commentators (see Sutherland 2004). His late autobiography *My Guru and his disciple*, although modest in its tone, inscribes strikingly original testimony into the cultural record and models new possibilities for courageous spiritual research that reaches beyond his personal experience, and forward into the twenty-first century, as a model of successful integration.

Isherwood drew tools for his personal transformation from an Eastern tradition, exemplified by a tolerant guru who did not regard his student's sexuality as an insurmountable obstacle to his spiritual practices. Yet critical response to his work sometimes suffers from the reflex tendency of a Christianised worldview to deem its superior epistemological status as self evident, and its application universal; a tendency that has worked not only to 'naturalise' the assumptions of one particular *Weltanschauung* but also, in some cases, to paralyse the intelligent exploration of the religious life by queer men and women. In this context, life-writing texts assertively 'talk back' (as bell hooks would have it) to dominant cultural narratives, becoming sites for staging what Judith Butler calls 'unforeseen and unsanctioned modes of identity' (Salih/Butler 2004, p. 10). They disrupt authorised versions of masculinity and femininity and destabilise the construction of the homosexual-as-religious-pariah, or as psychopathological specimen, or both.

Isherwood's insistence on maintaining both aspects of his life—his spirituality and his unconventional sexuality—makes him of exemplary interest today, then, as queer thinkers research ways of re-connecting with systems of meaning and identification that integrate all aspects of their being, beyond the familiar and conventional divisions produced by the stigmatising culture of shame. With the help of his guru, Isherwood was able to re-assess his life experience without the shame-based constructions common within Christianity. Australian scholar Rosamund Dalziell has written about the issue of shame in contemporary autobiography and shown how shaming is related to an exercise of power whereby 'the economically and socially powerful maintained a "discourse of respectability" by shaming those who did not conform to their mores' (Dalziell 1996, p. 132).

The autobiographical self

Dalziell posited that 'the confessional origins of autobiography as a literary genre lend themselves to the revelation of hidden and shameful aspects of the self' (p. 132). Dalziell was writing specifically about the shaming related to the issue of 'illegitimacy' of birth but, clearly, autobiography can do more than reveal the 'hidden' and the 'shameful'. Felicity Nussbaum writes that 'marginalized and unauthorized discourse … holds the power to disrupt authorized versions of experience, even, perhaps to reveal what might be called the randomness and arbitrariness of the authoritative and public constructs of reality' (Nussbaum 1988, p. 136).

Writing autobiographically becomes a resistant strategy for re-narrativising the self, then, an assertive recontextualisation that wrests control of ascribed meanings away from the toxic narratives embedded within hostile discourses. In this assertive re-narrativisation, the 'subject' changes place from being an 'abject' subject—a product of a discourse of subjugation—into an assertive agent of self-signification. This might now be regarded as standard practice in relation to feminist and even queer re-visions of life narratives, but I want to take this work further, to show how other areas of experience considered out of bounds for queer folk—in this case, the religious life—can also be reclaimed by this dissident and assertive narrative practice.

I read Isherwood as a precursor, then, not only of the turn to the East that would gather momentum among new generations of 'seekers' (Roof 1999) in the latter part of the century, but also of the assertive autobiographer moving beyond conventional views and the entrenched political and ideological conventions of his time to explore new possibilities for being and becoming. Isherwood's example is of particular interest in a secular age where many people seek out transformational techniques from religious and spiritual practices previously regarded as culturally (and politically) unavailable—even 'alien'.

The later chapters will analyse how his investigation and embrace of Vedanta philosophy and practice confronts the standard views of what is possible for a 'gay' man to know (and finally, *en passant*, perhaps de-stabilise this 'gay' figuration as well).

As a student of a non-dualist (*Advaita*) Vedanta tradition, Isherwood was able, also, to think past the dichotomising which casts Western religious practice within a reified 'rationalist' discourse, one which is positioned in opposition to 'Hindu' beliefs and practices which it must, perforce, characterise as 'superstitious'.

Guru *bhakti*

Isherwood's religious training was conducted over several decades by his guru, Swami Prabhavananda. But the role of the guru within the *bhakti* (devotional) expression of yoga is commonly misunderstood outside of the Vedanta traditions. 'Devotion is not easy, it is not for the casual', wrote Kabirdas in the 12th century. 'Joyous for the dedicated, it is bewildering for the curious' (Kabirdas 2006). To fail to recognise, or respect, the focalising power of the guru-student relationship, as many Western commentators continue to do (e.g. Altman 2004), is to miss a great deal in Isherwood's controversial life.

In *The Tibetan book of living and dying* (1994) Sogyal Rinpoche, who has done much to popularise Tibetan Buddhist teachings in the West, writes insightfully of the Western suspicion of 'masters', and what he calls 'the alchemy of discipleship' (p. 133–4). Western thinkers who value their independence rankle at hints of submission in the teacher/disciple relationship, assuming suspiciously that the spiritual preceptor must be intent on rendering the student utterly passive and subject to the guru's will. The Rinpoche writes:

> It is essential to know what real devotion is. It is not mindless adoration; it is not an abdication of your responsibility to yourself, nor undiscriminating following of another's personality or whim. Real devotion is an unbroken receptivity to the truth. Real devotion is rooted in an awed and reverent gratitude, but one that is lucid, grounded and intelligent. (p. 136)

The master focalises devotion, and forms a bond with each student that is unique among all other forms of human relationships, guiding them into zones of awareness of which the master is already aware:

> When the master is able to open your innermost heart, and offers you an undeniably powerful glimpse of the nature of your mind, a wave of joyful gratitude surges up in you toward the one who helped you to see, and the truth that you now realize the master embodies in his or her being, teachings, and wisdom mind. (p. 136)

To miss this, at the core of the practice, or to interpret it only suspiciously, is to eclipse a significant factor in the life, then, and leaves the superficial commentator focusing on relatively unimportant externals.

This mode of religious practice is one of several factors that need to be examined as part of the recuperation of that aspect of Isherwood's work that has been shut out by prejudice and stereotypical misrepresentations. In the interests of full disclosure I should say that my discussion draws partly on insights from work done with my own guru over more than thirty-five years. I hope that this experience—although one from a different tradition, and with different meditation practices from Isherwood's—rather than being a drawback, will provide useful insight into certain aspects of the guru/disciple relationship, and the integrative potential of the Advaita teachings, which are sometimes misunderstood in Isherwood studies.

Although he might be shocked to hear it, I have taken Dennis Altman's lead here. In 'Writing the Self' (2002), Altman questions the claims of 'objectivity', saying that 'the failure to acknowledge the personal stake in an intellectual position becomes a form of dishonesty', with claims to 'objectivity' 'revealed for ideological pretense' which is, he says, 'less honest than an attempt to state one's own position' (p. 318). An author needs 'to engage in a certain degree of self-revelation', he writes, and 'to be willing to explore openly the reasons which have led them to a particular subject or study' (p. 318).

I will draw attention to testimony about the application of certain principles of (Advaita) Vedanta that allowed Isherwood, the erstwhile atheist, to continue to engage with spiritual practice even as he was trying to explore and discover the nature of his sexuality, and his *dharma* as a writer. Isherwood persevered with the practices over many decades and, after a long journey, he was able to exceed the discursive parameters that supposedly constituted him, even to himself. In learning how his finite personal 'ego' self related to the deepest stratum of the universal 'Self' (what in Vedanta would be called *Param Brahman*; what Aldous Huxley called the 'Divine Ground'; what Paul Tillich termed the 'Absolute Ground of Being') Isherwood came to recognise a continuity of being realised within an integrative experience of unity that subsumed even the identification as 'homosexual'.

Isherwood was a central figure among a group of Western intellectuals and writers, including Aldous Huxley, Alan Watts, Marco Pallis and others who, in very different ways, would usher in an intelligent re-appraisal of approaches to the religious life radically re-configured from the versions provided by the hegemony of exclusivist colonial Christianity.

Before I plunge into a closer discussion of Isherwood's own journey, I want to step back and take a chapter-long look at ways in which the standard, culturally privileged, 'authorised' approaches to the religious life, and the meanings of identity, might be reconfigured to re-open the possibilities of spirituality even for queer folk, and provide a fresh context within which to recognise the importance of the life and work of this exemplary border crosser. I will return to focus more directly on Isherwood in chapters three, four and five.

2

Reclamations: *reframing the possibilities of the religious life*

It is no longer sufficient merely to go back over the Christian and European cultural traditions. The horizons of the world are no longer confined to Europe and America. We have to gain new perspectives, and on this our spiritual and even our physical survival may depend.

—Thomas Merton, *Mystics and Zen Masters*

'My personal approach to Vedanta was, among other things, the approach of a homosexual looking for a religion which will accept him', Isherwood wrote in his diary in 1970. Yet even today a young queer man looking at all the world's major religious traditions might find it hard to recognise a hospitable environment in any of them. In 1993, Arlene Swidler published a collection of essays that surveyed hostile attitudes towards homosexuality in the various major traditions, producing a bleak picture for anyone identifying as such. Jeffrey Siker has published a more recent encyclopedia on the same topic (in 2007). But such surveys remain problematical for several reasons. As Cynthia Cavalcanti pointed out in a review of the Swidler collection, there is the difficulty in defining what is meant by 'homosexuality' and, further, in determining the appropriate term within any of those traditions that might most closely fit our current understanding of the troubled notion. This raises the issue whether 'homosexuality' can be discussed as occurring within different cultures and different historical periods, at all.

The historical evidence for such behaviour is very patchy in some religious traditions, in any case. Even *within* one tradition, attitudes about what we might call homosexuality vary according to period and location (see Cabezon on Buddhist traditions, in Swidler 1993, and Cabezon 1992). Arvind Sharma, in his study of Hinduism for the Swidler collection notes that, in Sanskrit, certain terms describing sexual acts do not specify whether those practices are homosexual or heterosexual. Terms for anal intercourse and for oral-genital contact do not differentiate whether they apply to same-sex encounters or to those between a man and a woman. (See Arvind Sharma, in Swidler 2003.)

As Cavalcanti points out, because early religious literature has predominantly been the work of celibate monks, pronouncements may have a particularly monastic slant. Cavalcanti finds that traditional teachings against same-sex liaisons usually have not been framed in terms of 'homosexuality' contrasted with 'heterosexuality', but rather in terms of sexuality viewed as against celibacy, but while that might hold true in traditional teachings on sexual ethics I think she would agree that trend has been somewhat re-appraised with the rise of born-again, evangelical Christianity.

Such surveys will always suffer from the inappropriateness of transferring twentieth-century categories—from a taxonomy of types based on sexual behaviour—across different cultural and religious traditions and histories. I agree with Cavalcanti that these surveys represent conventional ways of thinking, and that what is needed is a new lens through which to view the phenomenon of religion and the existence of the problematical notion of 'homosexuality' as a marker for identity therein.

Queer folk trying to map subject positions freed up from toxic, homophobic constructions find that the field is hotly contested—a site where warring discourses struggle to maintain the higher ground—and religion, rather than assisting them with useful tools for self-discovery, seems to be one of the major sources of shame-based figurations. Yet, rather than abandoning the field altogether, some have found that certain aspects of the religious life can expand the possibilities for researching the nature of the self and, indeed, offer new ways of thinking about it.

I mentioned in my introduction that what constitutes the 'I' is the focus of intense theoretical debate. Recognising that notions of the self are specific to particular historical contexts allows us to go beyond the prescriptive formulations produced by our own particular culture to reconnoitre new fields of experience and 'identity'.

In this chapter I wish to explore a fresh way of approaching the issue of what might constitute a spiritual life, then, and how that has a bearing on the sense of personal identity, before I bring the focus back to Isherwood in the subsequent chapters.

Sexuality and 'identity'

According to Michel Foucault's analysis, 'in the space of a few centuries, a certain inclination has led us to direct the question of what we are, to sex' (1978, p. 78):

> The notion of 'sex' made it possible to group together, in an artificial unity, anatomical elements, biological functions, conducts, sensations, and pleasures, and it enabled one to make use of this fictitious unity as a causal principle, an omnipresent meaning, a secret to be discovered everywhere. (p. 154)

Following Foucault's lead, I question what has been occluded by the practice of seeing things only through that lens, and what other knowledge sources are denied in the positioning of identity strictly around the axis of sexuality.

There is a great deal of textual evidence that many queer men have active spiritual lives. Mark Thompson's two influential collections (*Gay spirit: myth and meaning*, 1987 and *Gay soul: finding the heart of gay spirit and nature*, 1995) are largely in the form of transcripts of interviews with queer 'writers, healers, teachers and visionaries'. David Shallenberger's 1998 study, *Reclaiming the spirit*, is distilled from dozens of interviews with queer men and lesbians, and recounts his own experience of 'church shopping' for a congregation that would nurture him and his 'covenant'. Catherine Lake's *Recreations* (1999) is a collection of first person accounts, and includes poetry and essays. Brian Bouldrey's *Wrestling with the angel* (1995) is a collection of essays by different writers that gives first-person accounts of their experiences in various religious settings. Dino Hodge did the same for the Australian context with *The fall upward*, in 1996. Winston Leyland's *Queer dharma: voices of gay Buddhists* (1998) is a collection of historical essays and personal accounts of queer men's Buddhist practice. Robert Barzan's *Sex and spirituality* (1995) is a collection of his own essays under various headings. Peter Sweasey's 1997 book, *From queer to eternity*, is a long essay structured around various themes and illustrated by anecdotes, quotes and personal expression extracted from taped interviews with other conscientious queer folk. Sweasey comments:

> Because the existing forms of religion have so often been barred to us, we have been forced to emphasise the inner life. Religion is sometimes our enemy, but our spirituality cannot be colonized. (pp. 12–13)

Sweasey finds that queer spiritual life is more likely to emphasise the personal and the 'spiritual' rather than the doctrinal and organisational, and this finding is borne out by Andrew Yip's sociological study, 'The persistence of faith among nonheterosexual Christians' (2002).

The case is sometimes made for a uniquely 'gay' or queer form of spirituality, one related to the operation within the psyche of a proposed archetype of androgyny, for example, although this is not the only model proposed. Early work by Wayne Meeks (1973) and Daniel Boyarin (1994) has a bearing on this, and would figure in a longer study. Rollan McCleary's *A special illumination: authority, inspiration and heresy in gay spirituality* (2004) offers a thorough and detailed overview of the field, and Randy Conner's 'mythopoetic' account *Blossom of bone* (1993) attempted to weave a queer mythology drawing together accounts of gender-variant shaman figures, priests and artists—across cultures, and from widely different historical periods—'to reclaim the connections between homoeroticism and the sacred'.

Rather than following that lead, however, I suggest that the common queer experience of marginalisation can precipitate a search for an 'authentic' selfhood which in itself marks the beginning of spiritual inquiry, as I define it. Toby Johnson, a former Catholic monk, begins his discussion of queer spirituality from a similar point. In Johnson's words, 'Gay enlightenment comes, in part, from seeing the world from the perspective of an outsider' (2004, p. xi).

'Spirituality' and 'religion'

For the purposes of my discussion I will separate the term 'spirituality' from 'religion'. I read 'religion' as referring to a sociological phenomenon, entailing inclusion/exclusion from socially and politically valorised faith communities which produce and support what Peter Berger terms the 'plausibility structures' that anchor the sense of belonging in community. 'One of the fundamental propositions of the sociology of knowledge', writes Berger in *A rumour of angels*, is that the 'plausibility' of views of reality 'depends upon the social support these receive' (p. 50). According to his analysis, 'we obtain our notions of the world originally from other human beings, and these notions continue to be plausible to us in very large measure because others continue to affirm them' (p. 50). 'Plausibility structures' are produced by networks of people 'in conversation', as Berger puts it, who hold to a common world-view and set of moral commitments that help to maintain belief. Berger acknowledges that 'it is possible to go against the social consensus that surrounds us', but reminds us that there are 'powerful pressures (which manifest themselves as psychological pressures within our own consciousness) to conform to the views and beliefs of our fellow men' (p. 50).

Hans Mol has a related perspective, discussing various propositions with regard to theories of identity that define it not as an individual thing alone but as also strongly social. Mol cites Erik Erikson's work, in which identity connotes 'both a persistent sameness within oneself and a persistent sharing of some kind of essential character with others' (Mol 1976, p. 57) and notes Berger and Luckmann's construction that identity is 'a phenomenon that emerges from the dialectic between individual and society' (Berger & Luckmann 1966, p. 174). Mol also cites Soddy's earlier (1957) definition of identity working 'as an anchorage of the self to the social matrix' (qtd in Mol, p. 58) to argue that religion provides the mechanism 'by means of which on the level of symbol systems certain patterns acquire a taken for granted, stable, eternal, quality', thus 'sacralising' identity (Mol, p. 5). (See Carden 2006 for a fuller discussion of this.)

For a sub-set of queer men who feel rejected by the religion of their upbringing, the 'plausibility structures'—these anchorage points to the social matrix—whether held together by ritual, mythic and symbolic functions, or as institutionalised discourses of meaning and power (in Foucault's analysis) are not inclusive of them unless they renounce their sexuality. The normalising functions of social cohesiveness and 'sacralised' identity that create a web of belonging and cohesiveness for some people, then, work to position others 'outside the fold'.

There are notable exceptions, of course. I refer to the work of Michael Bernard Kelly (2007), and memoirs by priests as varied as John J McNeill (1998), Bernard Duncan Mayes (2001), and earlier, Malcolm Boyd (1978, 1986), as vigorous examples of men struggling with the 'angel' *within* the Church. (Rabbi Steven Greenberg's *Wrestling with God and men*, 2004, is less strictly autobiographical and more concerned to make a case for same-sex relationships in a dialogic conversation with Orthodox Judaism.) The point remains, however, that in these contexts they are engaged in a struggle for a 'place at the table', to use Bruce Bawer's term (1994). Chris Glaser's *Uncommon calling: a gay man's struggle to serve the Church* (1975), which recounts his struggle to be accepted as a minister within the Presbyterian churches, is notable on this front.

The slanderous misrepresentation of queer people by the Church has hardly subsided in recent times. Amanda Lohrey's study 'Voting for Jesus: Christianity and politics in Australia' (2006), features an account of her interviews with young university students who identify as 'evangelical' Christians and whose attitudes towards homosexuality still reflect unreconstructed moralistic and heteronormative assumptions. Catholic theologian and priest James Alison has become a welcome and more inclusive voice in recent years, but the struggle to reclaim equal rights at the altar has not been entirely won: as the power play between the Catholic Archbishop of Brisbane, John Bathersby, with the priest he sacked, Father Peter Kennedy and the congregation of the parish of St Mary's church in South Brisbane, demonstrated more recently (see Fraser 2009, and Pearson 2009, for opposing accounts of this case).

A homophobic 'God'?

Alan Watts points to the nexus between the spiritual and the social in the Judaeo–Christian tradition, which 'identifies the Absolute—God—with the moral and logical order of convention', contrasting this against the 'way' of Zen (1957, p. 11). Watts describes the conflation as 'a major cultural catastrophe', and critiques the manner in which 'it weighs the social order with excessive authority' (p. 11). If Watts's analysis is correct, his corollary is particularly telling for people marginalised by this kind of construction:

> It is one thing to feel oneself in conflict with socially sanctioned conventions, but quite another to feel at odds with the very root and ground of life, with the Absolute itself. (p. 11)

We may be disposed to defining who we are according to powerfully and institutionally authorised notions of what it is to be 'well' rather than sick, law-abiding rather than criminal, 'normal' rather than pathological, 'sane' rather than 'mad' (Foucault 1984, p. 50); but 'God' is a very big stick to wield against others.

Some churches, finding their power to authorise acceptable—and de-authorise deviant—ways of being somewhat diluted within an increasingly secularised society, have attempted to ally their discourse with psycho-medicine and bolster their moral positioning with the authority and mystique of science. In California, the Rev. Donald Wildmon, of the American Family Association, likes to use terms such as 'gender dysphoria' to identify his target. And two days before Christmas 2008, Pope Benedict XVI tied his campaign against homosexuality to environmentalist causes, calling for a 'human ecology' to protect the species from self-destruction. The Pope averred that 'saving humanity from homosexual or transsexual behaviour is just as important as saving the rainforest from destruction'. Reuters (23 Dec 2008) reported that Pope Benedict recommended that humanity needed to 'listen to the language of creation' to understand the intended roles of man and woman.

Of course, if the Pope were really drawing his teaching from observing the natural world, he would have noticed, along with zoologists, that so-called 'homosexual' acts have been observed among literally thousands of species, from insects to mammals, even birds. In fact, such acts are recognised increasingly as normal variations of sexual behaviour (see Bagemihl, *Biological exuberance: animal homosexuality and natural diversity*, 1999). We could ask what kind of 'nature' Pope Benedict would be referring to, then. It could be argued that the Pope was deploying a construction that manipulates the trope of the 'natural' world in the service of the ideologies of his church, promulgating the cruel and toxic teachings of an apparently homophobic 'God'.

I recall phrases such as 'nature's mistakes' and 'biological errors' being deployed during the so-called 'culture wars' in the US, where I lived during the 1990s. These surfaced, most notably, on a talk radio program (with a huge listening audience) hosted by an advice-giving doctor of physiology (Dr Laura Schlessinger) who claimed at one stage that the moral authority for her advice came from her study with Jewish rabbis. A huge controversy erupted when she (allegedly) referred to 'gays' as 'biological errors'.

'God hates fags!' screams the placard, in a blunter protest. A group of Christians pickets the funerals of queer men who have died of AIDS, and they are led by a Baptist minister, the Reverend Fred Phelps, who quotes biblical chapter and verse as his authority. A schedule of picketing opportunities is posted on an internet website. Conservative churchmen on both coasts still operate in an unholy nexus with 'reparative therapists'. When a team of such therapists was invited to Sydney in 2007, a consortium of churches hosted their visit. Thus, antique religious bigotry has been given a new lease on life with the not always unwitting support of psycho-medicine. 'It was as if,' says Graham Robb, in his social history *Strangers: homosexual love in the nineteenth century*, 'the terminology had been invented to allow prejudice and superstition to survive in a modern idiom' (2003, p. 47).

Steven Greenberg notes a similar approach adopted by the rabbinate of Orthodox Judaism:

> There is a great temptation for rabbis to believe that sexual orientation is largely chosen or, at very least, susceptible to therapy. Gay people who approach rabbis are routinely told that change is possible and that homosexual desire is a test. (2004, p. 15)

According to Greenberg, rabbis will often advise young men troubled by same sex attraction that, after sexual experience in marriage, 'aberrant desires' would disappear (p. 171).

The violence of exclusion

Commenting on Judith Butler's critical work on gender, Sarah Salih notes how 'the violence of exclusion narrows the categories by which subjects "qualify" for full human status' (2004, p. 12). This manoeuvering for the high moral ground has serious consequences in the lives of people trying to come to terms with their sexuality, so there are quite pragmatic reasons why these institutional normative discourses need to be interrogated.

In her essay, 'Religion vs. spirituality', Sandra Schneiders acknowledges that:

> [r]eligious exclusivity has been a source of hatred and violence which many contemporary believers find so scandalous that they can no longer associate with the sources and purveyors of it. (p. 174)

Although writing from within the Catholic tradition, and arguing for 'religion' as 'the appropriate context for spirituality' (p. 176), Schneiders recognises the link made by both Michel Foucault (in *The history of sexuality, volume 1)* and Hanna Arendt, (in *The human condition)*, between 'control of divine forgiveness and control of society' (p. 185).

Thus, many conscientious queer men and lesbians will continue to find that religion is irremediably tainted by homophobia and sexism, even finding my own study problematic in this regard, and this is one of the reasons why I pursue a distinction between 'spirituality' and 'religion'. I follow an Eastern model to deploy a usage of 'spirituality' as concerned particularly with a searching inquiry into the nature of being. The distinction is somewhat artificial, with some obvious overlapping, but has been widely adopted, from 'high' to 'low' culture and, is characterised by a distinct shift away from some of the traditional religious constructions, to the point where the terms 'spirituality' and 'religion' are increasingly used to signify different kinds of practice. (Perhaps this goes some way towards explaining why Buddhism is the fastest growing form of 'religion' in the West, where it is usually associated with empirical meditation practices and rather less allied with highly charged moral judgements.)

At the level of popular culture, for example, hip-hop artist and rap musician Wanda Dee, of KLF, describes it this way:

> Spirituality is the uninterrupted knowledge of God within self. Religion is man-made. I pride myself on being spiritual and not at all religious. ('Good Weekend'magazine, *The Sydney Morning Herald*, 5 June, 2004, p. 13.)

Theologian Anna King suggests that the term 'spirituality' is often used nowadays to *avoid* the use of the term 'religion', which is increasingly associated with more traditional (and oppressive) ideas. King cites Jeremy Carrette, who compares this usage with Artaud's 'non-religious use' of the term 'spirituality' to signify 'an escape from the unnecessary confines of religion into the more inclusive realm of our common humanity, rendering any necessary reference to the transcendent obsolete' (qtd in King 1996, p. 343).

Historically, in the West 'spirituality' has not been distinguished from 'religion', but under the impact of secularisation (that much debated term) more and more people who have found themselves in cognitive dissonance with the meta-narratives supplied by religious doctrines, and increasingly dissatisfied with the politics of the institutions with which such doctrines have been associated, have begun to insist on a similar distinction. When Peter Berger let the secularisation cat out of the bag in the early 1960s, he claimed that religion itself was becoming marginalised. He was later to regret the way the secularisation thesis was being deployed but, in his *A rumour of angels* (1969), he identified it as happening not so much to social institutions—given the increasing separation between church and state—but as applying 'to processes inside the human mind, i.e. a secularisation of consciousness' (p. 16).

At that time Berger felt that the expansion of the state meant that religion was losing its primary role as the 'legitimator' of social life, and this was producing a trend towards pluralisation of beliefs and practices. Berger claims this was predicted as early as 1915 by Max Weber, who foresaw that capitalism would produce a rational (and scientific) worldview leading to secularisation and the 'disenchantment' of the world. (I will pick up on a different usage of this term 'disenchantment' in a Buddhist context later.)

When 'church' religion was undergoing a noticeable membership decline, Berger's colleague Thomas Luckmann wrote (in *The invisible religion*, 1967) that religion itself had moved to the margins of society because 'the internalisation of the symbolic reality of traditional religion is neither enforced nor, in the typical case, favoured by the social structure of contemporary society' (p. 37). This dis-location of religious discourse from the privileged centre of social value systems has produced outcomes too complex to be analysed here, but it is still difficult to quarantine prevailing moral and ethical norms on sexuality from traditional religious teachings.

A case could be made, though, that this secularisation process (although manifesting differently in different regions—comparing say, Europe, with the United States, as examples) has had the effect of liberating conscientious men in search of spiritual connections from being confined to one exclusivist pathway for discovery, and contributed to a 'border crossing' phenomenon whereby they have felt freer to seek out tools for transformation from traditions that would have been negatively sanctioned in earlier political conditions.

Some critics are suspicious of a queer man talking about spirituality at all, especially within the academy, where it is sometimes presumed that capital E 'Enlightenment' was exclusively an event in European cultural history that liberated humans from God-centred constructions, and that small e 'enlightenment', for a modern man of any persuasion, must perforce be thoroughly secularised. (Yet John McClure makes the case for the persistence of spiritual preoccupations in contemporary literature—see his 1995 article 'Postmodern post-secular: contemporary fiction and spirituality'.)

Queer academics in particular have been suspicious of my intentions, presuming that all talk of spirituality represents a kind of Trojan horse for the stealthy return of a lot of anti-sex, anti-body religious rhetoric that they have already thoroughly discredited. (Belgian philosopher and Lacanian analyst Luce Irigaray is one feminist thinker who insists on the centrality of the physical in an incarnationalist approach to yoga/religion.)

The roots of homophobic rhetoric *can* be traced to church teachings, it is true, at least in the context of the culture in which I grew up (see Nelson &

Longfellow 1994), but the slander was picked up enthusiastically by psychiatry, and has long been enshrined in criminal law. (For the slow dawning from the dark ages of psychiatric prejudice, mention must be made of Evelyn Hooker's landmark study from 1957 that demonstrated the operation of a priori prejudice in clinical evaluations of the psychological health of homosexual men. See too recent journal articles by Gary Greenberg, 1997, Peter Butler, 1999; and Drescher and Merlino's 2007 oral history account of the sorry saga of psychiatric medicine's weighty Diagnostic and Statistical Manual—the DSM, in its various revisions.)

Some experts dispute that homophobia is as prevalent in non-Abrahamic religious cultures. Yet even in India, where pre-colonial attitudes towards variant sexualities were not universally hostile, the portcullis dropped resoundingly with the introduction of the British Penal Code. The anti-sodomy law of 1860 was a relatively progressive move in Britain, insofar as it reduced the punishment for sodomy from execution to ten years' imprisonment. However, when introduced in India in 1861, as Section 377 of the Indian penal code, it was a retrogressive step. Similar laws were introduced in other colonised countries in the same year. (See Ruth Vanita & Saleem Kidwai, *Same-sex love in India: readings from literature and history*, 2000, for a full discussion of this history.) In 2009, there are indications that the laws may, finally, be changed after the voices for 'gay liberation' have gained confidence and emerged from the silence of one hundred and fifty years of colonialist shame.

So why (to continue with the complaints my project engenders) would a postmodern, queer man want to lend any support to the totalising grand narratives of religion, after post-structuralists have worked so effectively to demolish them? Isn't it perfectly clear by now that there is a nexus of power relations between capitalism, the law, and the cosy heteronormative teachings of the church, and isn't this power oppressively deployed against men of my 'type'?

I recall the motto that Carl Jung had carved into the lintel above the doorway to his house in Küsnacht: *Vocatum atque non vocatum, deus aderit,* which in translation from the Latin would read: 'Whether invoked or not invoked, the god will be present.' (The same motto is also on his gravesite.) The persistence of this spiritual or religious urge, depending on your acceptance of the terms—even as the forms it takes undergo a radical re-evaluation in post-secular society—is what motivates my attempt to reconfigure ideas of what might constitute 'spiritual', and my attempt to bring attention to the interesting, alternative pathways that queer folk such as Isherwood have pursued.

Living on the margins

Let me track back a little to take a look at a poignant depiction of finding oneself a virtual stranger in one's own culture. This is from Robert Dessaix's *A mother's disgrace*:

> [I]t was stressful coming face to face with a world which fundamentally disagreed with you about absolutely everything—disagreed and patronised. If you're a Hindu in Budapest, you at least have the protection of your cultural cocoon, woven over millennia, but I had no cocoon: my culture was basically everyone else's culture, only my ideas were different. Lunatic some must have said. (1994, p. 120)

There is in this statement a sense of detachment, even exile, from the dominant cultural mythologies:

> I coped, as I do now, mainly by treating all the world-views we were served up as tales that were told, to be understood on their own terms, as you might study the koran [sic] and even become learned in it—or a Brief History of Time, or Derrida, for that matter—without either espousing or rejecting the doctrines you're encountering. It was like studying the street maps of cities you never expected to visit. (p. 120)

(In the image of 'street maps' we meet, once again, Peter Berger's 'plausibility structures'.) In any re-construction of a queer identity, or subject position, it will be crucially important to confront and re-draw these 'maps' to re-locate selfhood in life-affirming spaces.

A young queer man, as often as not, faces suspicion and even hostility within his own family. He may have bruising encounters with the teachings of the Church, where he or his desire nature are slandered as an 'abomination'—Hebrew 'toevah', the punishment for which should be death, according to Leviticus 20:13. (See Greenberg 2004, especially 79ff., for a full discussion of all the nuances of the term in translation.) Often he has a problematical relationship with a Law that casts him as a criminal, and with a Medicine that pathologises as a 'condition' what he feels to be natural. This nexus of social forces conspires to deny him the opportunity to form affectionate relationships and carry them to fruition in officially recognised, longstanding unions. Caricatured as 'promiscuous', any attempt by such folk to create a legal basis for long-term, stable partnerships shakes up stereotypical expectations and is vociferously voted down—witness the history of Proposition 8 in California, for a recent (2008) example. You're damned if you do, damned if you don't.

Such a hostile climate often contributes to a *disillusionment* that reaches deep into his sense of self and undermines his sense of ontological security. However, rather than merely reinforcing a sense of victimhood, I suggest that this very disillusionment may work, paradoxically, as an early initiation into the kind of process that I have re-framed as an authentic pathway for spiritual inquiry and, ultimately, of transformation. In Buddhist terms, this would be called 'dis-enchantment'—a kind of breaking the spell, a 'de-programming' from the discourses that hold the world (of meaning) in the particular discursive configurations in which we encounter it. The disappointment and suffering produced by the discrepancy between our idealised expectations and the way things are, produces a kind of awakening, with disenchantment as a quality of mind to be actively cultivated in the service of liberation process. Hence this extract from the Buddhist monastic code (the 'Vinaya'):

> concentration for the sake of knowledge and vision of things as they are, knowledge and vision of things as they are for the sake of disenchantment, disenchantment for the sake of dispassion, dispassion for the sake of release, release for the sake of knowledge and vision of release, knowledge and vision of release for the sake of total unbinding without clinging. (Thanissaro Bhikkhu, *Buddhist Monastic Code Dhamma-Vinaya. Pitaka: Parivara XII.2*)

In the religious context, for example, men in this situation learn from personal experience to read the discrepancy between the official rhetoric—'we love everyone'—and the homophobic cultural practices stemming from, and authorised by, leading institutional figures (Cardinals, Archbishops, Rabbis, Mullahs etc.) in much the same way, I suggest, that women might recognise a similar dissonance between the misogynistic subtext in a discourse framed entirely within, and authorised by, patriarchal practice and the contrary claims that we are all equal in the eyes of 'God'.

To ignore the subtext and take the rhetoric at face value, I might add, can be an error fraught with real danger for a naïve and trusting queer child who might miss the hostility masked by the rhetoric. Gay men become acutely aware of a range of possible attitudes towards them: ranging from a sort of uneasy liberal tolerance, all the way through to death by stoning. The murder of Matthew Wayne Shepard in Wyoming in 1998 was a tragic reminder that homophobia has real-world consequences. (Shepard was left hanging on a fence to die by his attackers. In her radio commentary Laura Schlessinger allegedly implied that Shephard had brought his fate upon himself.)

Queer bashings are often justified, post hoc, with invocations of bogus religious morality. I remember an interview by broadcast journalist Connie Chung in which she profiled a prisoner convicted of murdering a queer man with whom he had consented to have sex. His contention that his victim was surely going to 'Hell', while he was going to 'Heaven' (because he had repented), was particularly striking. Bigotry loves to dress itself up as righteousness; that is its favourite disguise.

In this version of moral discourse, ethics is confined to a certain construction of morality which is framed by and contains an often unacknowledged political power, and conscientious choices practised outside the discursive framework are ruled 'out of bounds' because of the status of the Church as the custodian of morality, its 'default' role in a secular age. As Franciscan friar Richard Rohr said in a radio interview: 'When religion doesn't move to what I … call the mystical level, almost always the substitution for mysticism is morality' (ABC Radio National *Religion Report*, 15 Nov 2006, p. 5). Andrew Harvey has gone so far as to say the Church has 'squandered' its power by abandoning its mystical heritage—its ability to lead its adherents into direct perception of the divine (interview with Lauren Artress, 2000).

(Rohr uses the term 'mysticism' simply to mean moving 'beyond external belief systems to inner experience'. [p. 5])

John Carroll's recent essay 'Jesus, the Essence of Being' (2007), which presents a revisioning of Jesus through a reinterpretation of the Gospel of Mark, speaks of the 'popping' of illusions, 'like a soap bubble' (p. 14) and describes Jesus' transformation initially as a 'sequence of negations' (p. 15). (Carroll develops his thesis more fully in his book, *The existential Jesus*.)

My point is that this stripping away of illusions can serve as an initiation into a spirituality that has less to do with belonging to socially privileged institutional structures and adhering to the dogmas which undergird their ideological discourse, and more to do with an inquiry into the nature of being made urgent by a disorientation which, in this case, becomes as much ontological as psychological. Marginalised by the kinds of political forces I have sketched, queer men have often felt detached from the core myths and practices of their immediate cultural environment, and rather than finding this an entirely negative experience have found themselves free to construct subjectivities using different knowledge bases from sources in other cultures. Like free electrons, changing 'shells', some among this group have been inclined (whether 'authorised' or not) to seek out beliefs and, more importantly, practices, from other traditions that empower them to reclaim an authentic subjectivity on their own terms. They become 'border crossers', to use Gloria Anzaldùa's term. 'Borders', writes Anzaldùa, 'are set up to define the places that are safe and unsafe, to distinguish us from them' (*Borderlands/La Frontera*, in Rivkin and Ryan, 2001).

Show me your original face

In my model, if the stigma of a maligned sexuality dis-locates one from a comfortable sense of belonging, thus precipitating a search for authentic selfhood, the dis-illusionment may act as a kind of stripping-away process (a 'via negativa'). I suggest this is akin to the interrogatory of the pivotal Zen koan 'Show me your original face, before your parents were born'. Koan practice is a technique originally developed in early Chinese Buddhism, and refined in Zen practice in Japan. Used in conjunction with rigorous meditation sessions, the struggle to solve the impossible question proposed by the teacher pushes the student's mind beyond logical conceptual thought into a deeper (at the same time simpler, and more direct) apprehension of conscious awareness.

'Before your parents were born.' One might ask what forms of personal identification can survive an interrogation that aims to penetrate the matrix of linguistic, social, political and personal history that we usually take as a 'self'. While on the surface the interrogation may appear to be an invitation to gather a cluster of facts—a detailed genealogy of 'identity'—or provoke a flurry of windy conceptualisations, practitioners refer to a stripping away effect, a return to a simpler state of mind uninflected by metaphysical speculations, which tend to collapse into an existential 'now'.

There are similarities here with postmodernism and deconstructionist practices. To track the evolution of notions of the self in Western epistemologies as they shifted focus over centuries is like watching a mind struggling with a koan interrogation, in extreme *slo-mo*. Let me unpack this a little. If the Enlightenment project freed up the personal self from being defined in relation to theistic constructions of a God-centred universe, the increased self-consciousness paved the way for a (rationalist) re-versioning of individual meaning. Kim Worthington puts it this way:

> Through self-reflection—the ego, the subject—is put on its own feet, set free from all unmediated relation to being. In giving priority to the human being's determination as a thinking being, self-reflection marks the human being's rise to the rank of a subject. It makes the human being a subjectivity that has its center in itself, a self-consciousness certain of itself. (1996, p. 1)

But, according to Felicity Nussbaum, even that entity was problematised by philosophers, at least as early as Locke and Hume, who started to lay the groundwork for an interrogation of the notion of a discrete and stable self. Nussbaum zeroes in on the 'public debate over the issue of personal identity' that she locates as occurring between John Locke's *An essay concerning human(e) understanding* (1690) and David Hume's *Treatise of human nature* (ca. 1739–40).

In the *Treatise*, Hume indicated that he was 'having trouble making his ideas on identity consistent' and she cites him: 'It is certain there is no question in philosophy more abstruse than that concerning identity and the nature of the uniting principle, which constitutes a person,' he wrote (Hume, qtd. in Nussbaum p. 132). If Hume assumed that such a principle existed, he found himself unable to name it and, as Nussbaum points out, the question took on 'new significance in the uncovering of an important debate on identity' (p. 133). Locke defined personal identity as 'a thinking intelligent being, that has reason and reflection, and can consider itself as it self, the same thinking thing in different times and places' (p. 133).

But if 'it is consciousness that constitutes the self, and the same self, in past, present, and future', according to Nussbaum Locke's radical idea was that it is 'not a self that takes shape but many selves'; further, that perhaps there is no 'self' at all 'but only a collection of moments of consciousness, many of which may be contradictory to each other' (p. 133). (This idea was also being floated across the Channel, by Denis Diderot, 1713–40.) Nussbaum could have gone further back, to Montaigne, in the 16th century, for the encounter with an unstable self: 'There is no constant existence, neither in our being, nor in that of objects. And we, and our opinions, and all things mortal, go on turning and unfolding incessantly', wrote Montaigne (*Essays*, p. 680).

However far back the roots of this de-stabilisation might be traced (and Montaigne went back to Heraclitus) this is a crucial insight, which has wide-reaching ramifications for our discussion. After a number of assaults on its coherency as a 'unified, rational, and intentional subject' (Nussbaum p. 132), current post-structuralist practice would redefine self 'as a position, a locus where discourses intersect' (p. 152).

The destabilisation of notions of a coherent, unified self has been carried forward on several fronts in the so-called 'West', and we can't ignore the impact of psychoanalytic theory as a major contributor in that shift. Although he was not the first on the scene, Sigmund Freud's introduction of the unconscious into the equation was a landmark in the challenge to earlier notions of self. In one of the 'Introductory lectures on psychoanalysis' Freud identified three 'great outrages' upon what he termed 'naïve self love' (p. 285). He saw the first of these being thrown down by the Copernican revolution, which forced us to realise that 'our earth was not the centre of the universe, but only a tiny speck in a world-system of a magnitude hardly conceivable' (p. 285). The second 'transvaluation' of self, as he calls it, came at the hands of Charles Darwin et al., 'when biological research robbed man of his peculiar privilege of having been specially created, and relegated him to descent from the animal world, implying an ineradicable animal nature in him' (p. 285). In Freud's analysis, these represent two rather significant strikes on 'naïve self-love'. But he doesn't stop there:

> [M]an's craving for grandiosity is now suffering the third and most bitter blow from present-day psychological research which is endeavouring to prove to the 'ego' of each one of us that he is not even master in his own house, but that he must remain content with the veriest scraps of information about what is going on unconsciously in his own mind. (p. 285)

Freud continues, almost modestly, to acknowledge antecedents of this insight, but it is obvious that he is aware of the historical importance of this new field:

> We psycho-analysts were neither the first nor the only ones to propose to mankind that they should look inward; but it appears to be our lot to advocate it most insistently and to support it by empirical evidence which touches every man closely. (p. 285)

Freud was proposing a radically decentred view of the (ego) self and, even if some of his followers were more prepared 'to give the ego a greater executive authority in the management of the self', as Turkle puts it (1995, p. 178), selfhood would never settle into the same configurations again. If, as in Freud's formulation, the ego 'is not even master in his own house', then the question arises: how an idea of 'self' is to be re-formulated. Psychoanalysis provides one way, but there were other traditions and practices pre-dating it that have addressed the same question and come up with different methods to find an answer.

The probing interrogatory of the illusory nature of identity common to Asian philosophy and spiritual practice is profoundly deconstructive of the storying of the self. The Zen 'riddle' typically pushes past the patchwork of facts, the personal history—even social and family history—to insist on the recovery of another level of being and awareness that is existentially and radically simplified; neither constructed, nor even mediated by rational (nor irrational, nor pre-rational) thought. Rather than finding the roots of the self in the complex social and political networks of place, class, and gender, or in the narratives which emanate therefrom, or in the inherent constructedness of language itself, the question becomes, then: what is 'I' when the predicates fall away? I don't have the space to trace the fascinating 'history of the self' any further here, but for many queer folk, and certainly for a pioneer like Isherwood, the destabilisation—even disintegration—of the familiar 'personal' self is a serious issue, with some surprising outcomes.

'Self *versus* 'God'

I should draw attention to another broad subtext working behind the noticeable resistance to the veracity and value of Isherwood's spiritual research. Some commentators worry about what is presumed to be the self-centred nature of meditation praxis, fretting about issues to do with religious authority and heresy, wondering how an authentic spirituality can exist without the cumulative benefit of thousands of years of tradition (not entirely lacking in the guru tradition, of course) and membership within one or other culturally heavyweight religious institutions. Rachael Kohn, for example, is particularly wary of 'the promotion of the self as an absolute value' in some of what she identifies as the 'therapy cults', with their 'claims about the extraordinary empowerment of the self' (*The new believers*, p. 134). Kohn tends to sneer at any form of spiritual psychology that would turn 'the spiritual life into a love affair with one's soul' (p. 134). Paul Heelas, who shares some of Kohn's scepticism, is prepared to allow some validity for new forms of spirituality, within what he terms the 'massive subjective turn' of modern culture (2006, p. 223) but his view is circumscribed by focusing mostly on the so-called 'New Age' phenomenon that until recently has been characterised largely by the trope of the 'spiritual supermarket' (Roof 1999), in which beliefs and practices derived from 'Eastern' religious praxis are regarded as 'interchangeable elements' to pick and choose amongst, 'within a larger set of globally derived spiritualities available to the contemporary western seeker' (Phillips & Aarons 2007, p. 327). The pejorative presumption operating within this trope is that such research lacks focus or discipline: that practices derived from such sampling are rootless, cut off from the cultural contexts that give them meaning. That suspicion probably carries some truth.

As I will show in my discussion of Christopher Isherwood, it is quite possible to engage with a disciplined spiritual practice over time even if it is rooted in another cultural tradition. Practitioners submitting to the disciplines of a school, who follow through in a sustained practice over decades, might even share the same suspicion towards the spiritual 'consumer' culture. John Yale records Swami Prabhavananda's discomfort with the erroneous equation between psychedelic visions and the serious philosophy of Vedanta. The Swami (who was Yale's guru, as well as Isherwood's) ruefully compared notes with the great DT Suzuki, who was very influential in the introduction of Zen practice and philosophy to the West, about what might today be referred to as a 'flakey' or superficial interest in other traditions. Suzuki complained to Swami Prabhavananda of the lack of rigour among the early adherents to Zen, and both teachers were uncomfortable with Alan Watts on that front. Ken Wilber amusingly refers to this as a form of 'hippie dharma'. In an interview with Mark Matousek for the *Utne Reader* (1998) Wilber describes it thus:

> Hippie dharma was the basis of the laissez-faire approach many people took in the '60s. For example, a lot of people were initially attracted to the Beat version of Zen, which said, basically, "Get laid as often as you can, do as many drugs as you can, and call it being beyond good and evil." The real Zen people came along and said, "I don't know what you people are doing. Here's what Zen is: Fold your legs, follow your breath, do that for five years, we'll talk about it." 'Hippie dharma' is all about "Be here now," "Go with the flow," "We're all one," and in an absolute sense that's correct. But it's only correct after you've gone through all the stages of disciplining the body-mind to get to that point. Otherwise, you're just making a lot of prerational noise and calling it transcendence. (Matousek 1998, p. 55)

Scholarship in the area has seldom recognised the idea of 'dedicated involvement with eastern spiritual systems in western settings' which, sociologists Phillips and Aarons show, invoking Weber's famous notion: 'disenchantment of the world' ('Entzauberung der Welt'), may derive explicitly from disenchantment with the West.

Rather than seeing such a choice as an expression of Orientalism, then, which constructs an 'Orient' as an 'object of colonial discourses of knowledge and power' (Turner 1989, qtd Phillips & Aarons, p. 326), personal engagement with such sources could be read as a strategy in the development of new religious identities, and Phillips and Aarons raise the question of how, in utilising such resources, individuals could be seeking to 'resolve the manifest psychic tension between feeling disenchanted with "the West"' even while holding 'formal membership of a western society' (p. 328). Disenchantment, rather than reproducing the familiar narratives of alienation, can be a spur for seeking liberation from spent, outmoded systems of thought associated with Western political and ideological exploitation, and this would include the exclusivist hegemonic grip of religious colonisations of spiritual inquiry tainted by their implication in such exploitation. 'Colonisation' occurs not just across cultures but *intra*culturally as well, prescribing and proscribing authorised forms of spiritual inquiry.

Those working within unquestioned theistic models of representation often express anxiety about the ego self moving in to fill the vacuum if a 'God' figure is not present, with the presumption that self-inquiry is a narcissistic practice that must lead to self-aggrandisement (the so-called 'inflation' trap; or what some like to describe as the 'infinitisation' of the self). But in the case of Christopher Isherwood the guru/disciple relationship operated with its own traditions for re-training the ego.

Clearly it is difficult for many of those indoctrinated within the Abrahamic traditions to recognise and validate systems of thought operating outside those traditions. Pope Benedict XVI is a prominent exponent of this point of view. He has expressed concern that: 'We are moving toward a dictatorship of relativism which does not recognize anything as for certain and which has as its highest goal one's own ego and one's own desires' (qtd in Craig & Fennell, p. 70). Significantly, Craig and Fennell were writing for the journal *New Atlantis*, which, despite its 'New Age' title, is actually a publication of the Washington DC 'Ethics and Public Policy Center' which, as their website proclaims, 'was established in 1976 to clarify and reinforce the bond between the Judeo–Christian moral tradition and the public debate over domestic and foreign policy issues' (http://www.eppc.org).

I propose that once people reject the ready-made interpretation of the meaning of the form their sexuality has taken, and question the way this problematises their relationship with one or other of the 'god'-figures presented by religion, they may be inclined to question what is real, and begin to ask themselves: if not that, then what am I? The psychological distress presages an ontological challenge, precipitating an inquiry that may, in some cases, draw on spiritual resources for resolution, so that—even as they stray beyond the fold demarcated by institutionalised religion—queer folk are motivated to respond to a profoundly existential challenge not ameliorated for them by conventional religious nostrums. I have suggested that to pursue such an inquiry is the first initiation into the differently ordered practice of 'spirituality', which I see as an inquiry into the nature of being itself, often precipitated by a shocking rejection in the name of religion.

In historical terms you could say this is an ancient form of inquiry, with echoes emanating not only from Heraclitus, say, or the oracle at Delphi, but also from the Vedas and the Upanishads (1500 BCE), and elsewhere. Responses to the same inquiry at different times in human history have been constructed in many different ways.

When loosened up from a close identification with the hostile rhetoric of the churches of their immediate cultural context, in recent times many people have turned to other spiritual traditions, with Asian religions figuring prominently. The same process may apply to people dissatisfied with a religious ethic seemingly obsessed with a sexualised construction of morality, whatever their orientation. Despite the risks of 'exoticisation' and recent charges that such interest tends to ignore the availability of similar resources within Western religious traditions, this 'turn to the East' is a contemporary historical fact. There is already a large body of work analysing the trend within the disciplines of sociology, including the sociology of religion (see Ellwood 1994; Roof 1998, 1999; Hamilton 2002; Heelas & Woodhead 2005). Among other chronicles of the trend, Jeffery Paine's *Re-enchantment: Tibetan Buddhism comes to the West* (2004) and his earlier book, *Father India: how encounters with an ancient culture transformed the modern West* (1989), provide more sympathetic and insightful accounts of the phenomenon than offered by Rachael Kohn (1991, 2003). Isherwood figures prominently in Paine's discussion, and his recreation of the first meeting between Isherwood and

Swami Prabhavananda catches the nuances of the interplay perfectly (Paine 1989, p. 193ff.).

To those affiliated with traditional Western churches, this is still a controversial resource, in spite of more than half a century of exploration, and the discomfort is no less acute for queers and lesbians struggling to hold ground within Christian and Jewish contexts as they are currently configured. For example, at a Queer Spirituality conference in Adelaide in 2004, a minister from the Uniting Church (Rev. Dorothy McRae McMahon) was disturbed by this line of inquiry into the roots of the self, and the nature of being, as a legitimate pathway for spiritual investigation. 'You are saying that you are God,' she charged—an accusation rather wide of the mark for a queer man for whom the whole notion of a self has become so thoroughly problematised. But this response typifies the kind of blinkered vision I have been talking about. Actually, the mode of inquiry to which Rev. McMahon was objecting has deep roots even within Christian spiritual practice. In his *Thoughts in solitude*, the Catholic mystic Thomas Merton asserted that 'We find God in our own being, which is the mirror of God' (p. 134). For, to pose the question: What is 'I'? is only the beginning of an open-ended inquiry; the question proposed does not dictate the outcome. (Perhaps the search for the root of the self might take one beyond the self.) Merton goes on to develop the notion:

> His presence is present in my own presence. If I am, then He is. And in knowing that I am, if I penetrate to the depths of my own existence and my own present reality, the indefinable am that is myself in its deepest roots, then *through this deep center I pass into* the infinite I am which is the very Name of the Almighty … My knowledge of myself in silence (not by reflection on my self, but by penetration to the mystery of my true self which is beyond words and concepts because it is utterly particular) opens out into the silence and the subjectivity of God's own self. (p. 134; emphasis added)

Merton travelled to Tibet to study the meditation tradition within that form of Buddhism to deepen his own introspective practice (Paine 2004). Even within a conspicuously Christianised tradition, perhaps he, too, could be described as something of a 'border crosser'.

The kind of inner terrain opened up by meditative introspection was described by Merton using formulations that are particularly Christian in tone:

> The eye which opens to His presence is in the very center of our humility, in the very heart of our freedom, in the very depths of our spiritual nature. Meditation is the opening of this eye. (pp. 48–49)

In this model, the route to the 'God' is within and *through* a self realigned in a mystical absorption. In his study of Angela of Forino, Paul Lachance describes how 'her centre of gravity was no longer in herself but in God' (1990, p. 25).

The tradition of deep inquiry into the nature of self, and being, should not seem so 'foreign' then, even to Christian traditionalists, although perhaps as a result of their defence against the onslaught of Rationalism some tend these days to be wary of the associations of such practices with 'mysticism'. That the inquiry can be conducted within other than theistic contexts also gives concern, yet in his little book on Chuang Tzu (1992), Merton certainly recognises the humour and nuanced understanding of a fellow mystic, albeit one not working theistically:

> If St. Augustine could read Aristotle and Averroës (both of them certainly a long way further from Christianity than Chuang Tzu ever was!), and Teilhard de Chardin could make copious use of Marx and Engels in his synthesis, I think I may be pardoned for consorting with a Chinese recluse who shares the climate and peace of my own kind of solitude, and who is my own kind of person. (1992, pp. xv–xvi)

I do understand these concerns about the inflation of the ego but, notwithstanding the reservations noted from Paul Heelas, Rachael Kohn and others, in the twentieth century there was a distinct and widely recognised turn towards spiritual practices from a variety of non-Abrahamic sources, which show deeper insight into the workings of the personal, egoic self and its limitations than is commonly recognised by commentators trained only in one tradition. In disciplined meditation practice it is just as likely that the ego self will, in effect, 'shrink' to make way for an expanded awareness of states of awareness beyond the personal self; that self may (or may not) be re-absorbed into that greater field of which it is already a part (Buddhist 'no self'; Vedanta 'Self').

For anyone wanting more help in resolving the knotted issue of self and its relationship with an overriding 'Supreme' principle, RC Zaehner untangles the problem adroitly in 'Self-deification'—Chapter VI of his *Hindu and Muslim mysticism*, where he deals directly with the issue of 'inflation'. More recently, of course, Luce Irigaray has reconfigured 'God', in contrast to the former static metaphysical categories, as an integral part of the notion of 'becoming' as a mode of human existence: 'Why do we assume that God must always remain inaccessible transcendence rather than a realization—here and now—in and through the body?' she asks (1993, p. 148).

In 2002, the ABC TV program *Compass* broadcast a report on meditation, which it described as 'a practice long associated with Eastern religions' but nonetheless enjoying a revival in Christian churches over the past twenty years as 'The World Movement for Christian Meditation'. The Movement has been under the guidance of a Benedictine monk, Laurence Freeman, and continues a revival begun by another Benedictine, John Main. Main learned the meditation from an Indian Swami in Malaysia in the early 1950s and only later claimed it as a practice similar to that conducted by the early Christian monks known as the 'desert fathers' (ABC TV, 2002).

Hybridity and the issue of cultural appropriation

By resorting to ideas and—more importantly—techniques from supposedly 'alien' cultural and religious traditions, queer writers may be held to account on charges of cultural appropriation. To take up practices from other cultural traditions raises serious questions: do such practices and ideas work when uprooted from their native cultural and philosophical contexts? For example, while finding much to admire in Indian yoga systems, Carl Jung wrote (in 'Conscious, Unconscious and Individuation') they could 'scarcely be recommended anywhere north of the Tropic of Cancer' (*Collected works* 9, p. 288).

There is often a justifiable concern about a neo-colonialist exploitation of other cultures, or about a hybridised lack of cultural 'purity' (as though each tradition had been free of influence from other sources throughout its evolution). Edward Said has criticised the exoticisation of the 'mystic East' as unreconstructed colonialism, of course, but however one theorises the notion and problematises the terms, the fact remains that the traffic moves both ways across cultures, and continues to accelerate. The usage of such crude geographical/cultural terms ('East' is only 'East', of course, from a Eurocentric standpoint) has been problematised by postcolonial theory in the wake of Said's seminal text, *Orientalism*. (I will continue to use the term 'Eastern' because it is still useful currency, but its problematical status is assumed.) Richard King's cross-cultural study, *Orientalism and religion* (1999), re-examines many such antique usages in the light of post-structural and postcolonial thought. While I recognise the possibility of a kind of neo-colonial exploitation at work in plundering other cultures' knowledge resources, in my view the traffic moves in both directions and hybridity can be a useful theoretical tool in understanding cross-cultural influences. Responding to critics of the hybridity concept, Nederveen Pieterse (2000) argues convincingly that the countervailing argument against hybridity might be faulted for 'fetishising' boundaries. Meanwhile, border crossers before and after Isherwood have continued the exchange.

Gloria Anzaldùa's powerful enunciation of 'mestiza consciousness' has been influential in queer studies, and this passage indicates why:

> At some point, on our way to a new consciousness, we will have to leave the opposite bank, the split between the two mortal combatants somehow healed so that we are on both shores at once and, at once, see through serpent and eagle eyes. Or perhaps we will decide to disengage from the dominant culture, write it off all together as a lost cause, and cross the border into a wholly new and separate territory. Or we might go another route. The possibilities are numerous once we decide to act and not react. (2003, p. 187)

Vietnamese American filmmaker Trinh T Minh Ha recognises that while identity is a significant factor in politicising the personal, she chooses to read it more as a 'point of departure' than 'an end point in the struggle' (1992, p. 140). Further, she says:

> Dominated and marginalized people have been socialized to see always more than their own point of view. In the complex reality of postcoloniality it is therefore vital to assume one's radical 'impurity' and to recognize the necessity of speaking from a hybrid place, hence of saying at least two, three things at a time. (p. 140)

Queer intelligence shares aspects of this multi-focalism and, in some cases, makes way for a taking up of techniques of introspection from other cultures in experimental technologies of selfhood.

Peter Savastano provides another way of addressing the issue in a recent paper for *Theology and sexuality*, in which he identifies queer men as what he calls 'virtuosi in the (holy) art of bricolage'. Savastano suggests that, excluded from 'most of the world's religious traditions', and thereby finding themselves in 'a kind of spiritual diaspora', queer men are forced to 'forge a diverse array of spiritual practices, re-interpret or invent alternative sacred myths, produce their own mystical writings, and form diverse intentional spiritual communities' (2007, p. 9). In the process, he says, they may become 'masters of bricolage'.

I think it needs to be recognised that the subjective repositioning that takes place through such practices occurs in a *trans*cultural zone of being/not-being. In such a context, 'self' is a work in progress, and the body becomes a yogic laboratory for the transformation of consciousness. Isherwood, the expatriate Briton living and working in California, who rather enjoyed the status of outsider, persevered with such practices over several decades; so, if there was a reconciliation in his life, I suggest that his 'home-coming' occurred in this 'zone', rather than in the geographical shift to southern California.

'West' meets 'East'

Isherwood was an early example of the turn towards the 'East' that became more common among spiritual 'seekers' in the 1960s and 1970s and he was pleased, in retrospect, to have been part of the opening up of the 'West' to the

'East'. There is a rich literature, especially in the form of memoir, dealing with the encounter of Western trained minds with these Eastern practices. Other British expatriates such as Aldous Huxley and Gerald Heard moved in the same circles as Isherwood in southern California in the 1940s and 1950s, and they made significant contributions in building bridges towards Asian forms of spiritual practice and belief, as did Alan Watts, who roamed more widely abroad.

One can argue that postmodern practice has 'softened up' the Western notions of self to make philosophy in the West more receptive to Eastern notions. Peter Conradi notes this relationship in his memoir *Going Buddhist: panic and emptiness, the Buddha and me* (2004). Conradi acknowledges that post-modernism posits the self as 'a flimsy construct, an illusion, a myth, a fiction' (p. 49). According to Conradi, through meditation, the practitioner discovers the 'flimsy' nature of the self 'as experience, not theory', coming to the realisation 'that life is a stream of becoming, a series of manifestations and extinctions', leading to an awareness that the concept of the individual ego is 'a popular delusion'. Yet:

> [P]ost-modernity diagnoses our condition only to stop short of accurate treatment: few of the modish Western thinkers who argue that subjectivity is unreal, a potent illusion, a mere 'junction for converging discourses', wish to put this piety to the test in meditation. (p. 49)

Jane Hamilton-Merritt *did* put 'post-modern piety' to the test, when she came up against the same idea—that 'the self is not personal, nor permanent, nor static, and consequently that the individual does not exist as a permanent and identifiable entity' (p. 23)—in her encounter with Buddhist philosophy and meditation practice in Thailand in the 1970s. Hamilton-Merritt writes that she 'could easily understand the erosion, decay, and changing features of a mountain' (p. 57), but when her instructor tells her that there is no constant 'I', because everything is constantly changing, including *her*, she has difficulty in managing the concept. Help comes in the form of an article by Alexander B Griswold (1957), in which she reads that the *Buddha Dhamma* maintains that no individual—whether animal, man, or god (if gods exist)—is permanent:

> Each is a compound, a putting together, of elements such as form, matter, and mental qualities; in each individual, without any exception, the relation of component parts, constantly changing, is never the same for any two consecutive moments. No sooner has separateness, individuality begun, than dissolution, disintegration begins, too. (p. 57)

Stephen Batchelor comes up against this notion too, in his record of encounter with Buddhism, *Buddhism without beliefs* (1997):

> [I]nstead of a coherent personality that stretches back in an unbroken line to a first memory and looks forward to an indefinite future, we discover a self ridden with gaps and ambiguities. Who 'I' am appears coherent only because of the monologue we keep repeating, editing, censoring, and embellishing in our heads. (p. 124)

Read in this context, 'self' can be conceived as not so much the 'ghost in the machine' but as a story that is told continuously, a narrative which creates and sustains an idea of self. (I liken this, metaphorically, to 'knitting', with spiritual practice in a sense working to unravel the knitting.)

This is one of the two points where I need to draw attention to key areas of autobiography theory that are of particular relevance to my discussion, as literary theorists have become concerned with the truth status of textual versions of the self, and several strands of late twentieth-century inquiry are converging towards something like this 'Eastern' configuration.

Self as narrative

In the introduction to his collection *The Faber book of gay short fiction* (1991), novelist Edmund White puts forward the following idea:

> Since no one is brought up to be gay, the moment he recognizes the difference he must account for it. Such accounts are a kind of primitive gay fiction, the oral narratives told and retold as pillow talk or in pubs or on the psychoanalytic couch ... acknowledging homosexual desires and

> integrating them into a larger notion of the self is the first bold act of gay fiction, whether written or whispered. (p. ix)

It is a 'bold' act in the sense that it is a form of 'talking back' to the culture, to take another term from post-colonial studies. As bell hooks would have it: 'for us, true speaking is not solely an expression of creative power, it is an act of resistance, a political gesture that challenges the politics of domination that would render us nameless and voiceless' (1990a, p. 338). This narrative, this 'autobiographical act' (the term used by Elizabeth Bruss and others), is in fact something more than a fictive act; it is both creative and politically resistant, a way of re-drawing the maps and relocating the selfhood otherwise dislocated from the anchorage points within the social matrix.

To re-integrate queer desire into one's personal life narrative it is often necessary to reject the negative constructions provided, ready-made, by homophobic discourses, whatever their source, in order to be able to substitute a re-storyed subjectivity that reflects a sense of authenticity personally meaningful to the narrator. Such telling becomes a resistant strategy in which the sexuality is celebrated—rather than elided to be made acceptable within the dominant, hetero-normative meta-narrative (Lyotard's 'discourses of legitimation' [1986])—and the listener, or the 'reader' of the 'text' may become complicit in the narrativisation:

> If gays tell each other—or the hostile world around them—the stories of their lives, they're not just reporting the past but also shaping the future, forging an identity as much as revealing it ... (White, p. x)

It is this re-configuring of identity through narrative that is most relevant to my discussion—the various textual strategies employed in formal life-writing by queer men for locating a 'self' that is true to their sense of personal authenticity, even while it may be in friction with ruling hetero-normative discourses. Subjectivity is created and positioned as narrative, in which the term 'subject' refers to a set of constructed, textual roles which are now re-positioned through a consciously constructed discourse, with its own cultural and ideological values. Rather than taking on a subjectivity that is a passive product of discourses emanating from outside the self, one participates in the deconstruction of hostile versions of the self and its transformative *re*-construction by an assertive re-storying or re-narrativisation of self. In this way, autobiography has become the literary genre par excellence for rehearsing differently ordered constructions of identity. Christopher Isherwood probed and re-worked autobiographical material like few other writers of his generation, and his interrogation of constructions of selfhood is one factor that continues to make him relevant today.

Life-writing texts are now often seen as the site for resignification, in which the assertive subject re-examines and re-cognises the meaning of difference. Joanne Saul, for example, says that such writing praxis will 'foreground the writer's effort to articulate him or her self through the writing process' and will privilege the literary form as 'the very place where the writer … "finds" him or her self' (p. 260). Saul uses the term 'bio-text' to mark the shift away from the notion of a discrete, knowable subject towards a sense of subjectivities that are 'multiple, performative and in flux' (p. 259), even while 'acknowledging the subject's claim for legitimacy' (p. 260). Her recognition of 'flux' marks an important move forward from the tendency of identity politics to defend a newly articulated 'queer' identity, or 'queer' self, against hostile discourses. Rather than presenting finished versions of a life, in the conventional autobiographical sense, these texts, she asserts, focus on the process of writing a life. This description aptly positions the lives and works I focus on, which rehearse different strategies of being and becoming, insisting on less oppressive subject positionings.

Increasingly, there has been recognition, as Laura Marcus puts it (following Barthes), that 'the self does not pre-exist the text but is constructed by it' (1994, p. 180). Once again, Isherwood can be read as an early exemplar of this notion—of the self as a work in progress—and his constant probing of versions of the self as text foreshadows much of this late twentieth-century theorising of autobiography and subjectivity.

In the late 1980s, Paul John Eakin, in *Fictions in autobiography*, began arguing for an autobiographical truth that is not a fixed and stable content, but a complicated process of self-discovery and self-creation, recognising that the 'self' of all narrative autobiography is necessarily a fictitious construct, and that the 'I' that the autobiographer inscribes is no longer himself, but someone with the same name, though another age, surrounded by other circumstances, immersed in other activities and of a different appearance (I thank Isabel Duran, 2003, for this summary). But Eakin, one of the late twentieth century's foremost scholars of autobiography, has moved the theory on from that earlier position to develop the notion of self *as* narrative. In a seminal article (2004) that moved beyond his previous work, Paul John Eakin went on to tackle the narrative identity thesis that is central to my own discussion: viz., 'that we are or could be said to be a story of some kind'. 'Autobiography', he writes,

> is not merely something we read in a book; rather as a discourse of identity, delivered bit by bit in the stories we tell ourselves day in and day out, autobiography structures our living. (p. 122)

Eakin is prompted to pursue the line of enquiry into the equivalence between narrative and identity by a case study from the neurologist Oliver Sacks, and he uses a quote from Sacks as the epigraph for his article:

> It might be said that each of us constructs and lives a 'narrative', and that this narrative *is* us, our identities. (qtd Eakin, p. 121)

Working in the social sciences, Jerome Bruner uses the same notion, writing that: 'the self is a perpetually rewritten story ... in the end we *become* the autobiographical narratives we tell about our lives' (1987, p. 15).

'Narrative' has become a useful tool in many disciplines, including psychology for, if self is a 'story', it can be told differently, and psychotherapists have exploited the therapeutic potential of re-narrativisation. The Australian psychologist Michael White recognised the therapeutic potential of the narrative approach to self and developed what has become known as 'narrative therapy'. If self is a story it can be told differently, and the narrative therapist works to assist the client in locating 'alternative life narratives'. Susan Nicholson says this is a 'deconstructive' process by which 'the dominant restraining narrative is unmasked and re-examined from a new angle' (1995, p. 24).

For a pre-eminent scholar in autobiographical theory such as Eakin to embrace this approach has been quite controversial. His discussion provoked debate in the journal *Narrative* (see Butte 2005, for example, although Butte's response doesn't address this same issue directly). The philosopher Galen Strawson was very unhappy with the narrative identity thesis, dismissing it in *Ratio* as an 'intellectual fashion' in vogue among academics (2004, p. 439) but, rather than backing away, Eakin took up the challenge and re-stated his arguments more fully in a recent book, *Living autobiographically: how we create identity in narrative*, 2008.

Eakin has been probing the constructions of the self in autobiographical texts from his earliest studies but here he turns to the laboratory of neuroscience to probe the roots of the 'self'. It is no surprise that he should cite Oliver Sacks, who he acknowledges has written so accessibly about neurology and identity for a cross-over, popular audience. In *The man who mistook his wife for a hat* (1985), Sacks drew from his case files to tell the stories of people for whom diseases of the brain affected not only their behaviour but also their sense of who they were. Case histories in medicine might trace the natural history of disease in a patient, Sacks says, but they 'convey nothing of the person, and the experience of the person … there is no 'subject' in a narrow case history' (p. x). Sacks plans to 'restore the human subject at the centre', but to do this he needs to 'deepen a case history to a narrative' for only then 'do we have a "who" as well as a "what"' (p. x). 'The study of disease and of identity cannot be disjoined' and will entail a 'new discipline', which he calls 'the neurology of identity' and which will deal with the 'neural foundations of the self' (p. x). He wants nothing less, then, than to map the neurophysiological processes that underpin our personal biographies.

That damned, elusive self

Eakin picks up on Sacks's description of a patient who has suffered from severe memory loss. 'Mr Thompson' cannot retain the memory of who he is for more than a minute or so, and literally has to re-invent an identity to replace the one he has just forgotten. Asking 'what is this man without his story?' Eakin wants to interrogate the 'twin supporting structures' of identity; namely 'memory and narrative' (p. 121) and he turns to the work of a neurobiologist, Antonio Damasio, to re-examine how to approach the reading of autobiography. 'What exactly does an autobiography's 'I' represent?' asks Eakin (p. 124).

> When we say 'I', reflexivity is built into the pronoun, which operates as a textual referent for the biographical, historical person who writes or utters it (p, 124).

Looking at Mary Karr's memoir *The liars' club*, Eakin asks: 'Where exactly are we located? In a text, in the past, in a mind?' Briefly he poses the usual questions about the factual basis of memory to draw out the 'fictional' nature of textual representations:

> [A] special kind of fiction is unfolding here in which memory and imagination conspire to reconstruct the truth of the past. (p. 125)

Eakin's formulation of the 'truth status' of memoir is almost axiomatic:

> [T]he allegiance to truth that is the central, defining characteristic of memoir is less an allegiance to a factual record that biographers and historians could check than an allegiance to remembered consciousness and the unending succession of identity states, an allegiance to the history of one's self. (p. 125)

Eakin sees autobiography as a 'discourse of identity' which, delivered bit by bit in the stories we tell about ourselves day in and day out, structures our living. But he blurs the two elements: is it life narrative as text he is addressing, or narrative as the very root of selfhood—'the unending succession of identity states' (p. 125), and the allegiance to that history *as* the self?

Eakin's next move is to pull back from the social construction of identity to incorporate a 'neurobiological' approach. 'I want to consider a different source of self,' he writes, 'tracing it to our bodies' (p. 125). He draws upon the argument made by Antonio Damasio 'that self is not an effect of language but rather an effect of the neurological structure of the brain' (p. 125); Damasio cites Kant, Nietzsche, Freud, Merleau-Ponty and others to support his view that 'the body is the basis for the self' (1999, p. 347). Yet Eakin also shows that there is *no neurological evidence* to support the existence of some 'central perceiving unity, distinct from the experience perceived' (p. 128). According to the neurological evidence, he says, the *illusion* of unified perception is produced from multiple centres of activity in the brain. So, even at this level of modeling, the 'self' is elusive, de-centred, and begins to resemble the Buddhist 'no self' we encountered with Jane Hamilton-Merritt and Peter Conradi. Damasio puts it this way:

> The story … is not told by some clever homunculus. Nor is the story really told by *you* as a self because the core *you* is only born as the story is told, *within the story itself* … You are the music while the music lasts. (p. 191)

(The phrase '… while the music lasts' is a reference to TS Eliot's *Four quartets.*) Eakin draws from this perception the idea that 'self' inheres in a narrative of some kind and is not entirely the product of social convention (nor of language, he might add); rather, 'it is rooted in our lives in and as bodies' (p. 128).

I find it remarkable that a prominent theorist of autobiography should have moved from textual analysis to come to such a place. Yet perhaps this should not be unexpected. Postmodernist practice has radically questioned constructions of the self to the point where it appears almost entirely as a linguistic fiction, so people might well ask just where this sense of 'I' inheres. Here, the inquiry has come back to the body, an 'I' rooted in the physicalised sensations of existence. Sacks's portrait of the 'disembodied lady' (p. 42ff.), who loses all sense of proprioception, is a compelling case study in this regard. (Proprioception is the ability to sense the position, location, spatial orientation and movement of the body and its parts from stimuli arising from within the body itself.)

Where exactly does a self locate itself, then? Is it somewhere in this complex mass of physiological systems that the phantom self lurks? The locus of its physical existence is assumed to be the brain and its attendant neurological support systems. Yet, if it is the brain that produces language and memory—the record of the history that we take as a self—this self can be altered, lost, affected in various ways by damage to the brain, as Sacks shows; so even this neurobiological model, I suggest, destabilises contemporary thinking about the self in the brain in a way that has similarities with both postmodernism and the introspective inquiry of Eastern mysticism. The body, as we know, dies. To model identity on such an unstable platform may bring its own ontological insecurities, even without physiological damage to the brain. Yet common sense seems to tell us that the elusive self is inextricably, if temporarily, associated with the body, giving it a location in space, time and matter.

How else might this be understood?

Neurobiology and the 'wisdom traditions'

Let me finish this section of my discussion with a brief look at the work of another neuroscientist, Francisco Varela, who has usefully bridged the Eastern and Western models (and the 'scientific' and 'religious' models too). Varela was a neuroscientist interested in theories about cognition (at one time he was head of a Laboratory of Cognitive Psychophysiology in Paris). In *Ethical know-how: action, wisdom, and cognition* (1999) he drew interesting parallels between studying the mind—using the disciplines of neurobiology and cognitive science to develop theories of 'distributed network processes' (p. 60)—and re-thinking the possibility for ethical behaviour on the basis of certain concepts derived from what he refers to as 'wisdom traditions', Confucian, Taoist and Buddhist in origin (p. 63). To build his model he relies on a concept of the 'virtual self' (p. 41) that coordinates the activity of neural ensembles, using Buddhist notions of self and 'no-self' to replace outmoded ideas of a transcendent, stable self (or 'soul'):

> Learning to embody the empty self is certainly difficult, but all these wisdom traditions agree that the acquisition of this expertise is not only progressive and open-ended but also centrally important. (p. 63)

The deconstruction of the fictions of the self, whether from postmodern practice, or from the kind of inquiry we are invited to make in Eastern spiritual traditions, does not, ipso facto, leave us in a heart of darkness, or the self-centred ethical wasteland feared by Pope Benedict. Varela describes how 'the practice of recognizing the emptiness of the self' (p. 65) is the foundation for *ethical* behaviour in the Buddhist traditions. Varela cites the famous statement by 2nd century Buddhist reformer Nagarjuna (McDonaugh 2003), which is often simplified as, 'Emptiness is full of compassion': as the practitioner recognises the illusion of ego separateness, he/she realises 'emptiness' (Varela, p. 67). Presumably this makes 'room', as it were, for considerations beyond the personal. Otherwise, a superficial reading of this concept might provoke charges of nihilism, but, as Peter Conradi clarifies the issue: 'Emptiness, properly understood, is not negation but, rather, openness' (2004, p. 126). In Conradi's reading of Buddhism, 'This self (ego) spends much time trying to establish personal territory, a nest or cocoon, to defend' (p. 80). Meditation is utilised as part of daily hygiene (p. 69).

In a bad panic the void seems the enemy and one does not know or remember who or what one is. In meditation—by contrast—it could be said that one is learning slowly to relax into such not knowing. This void of not knowing here is, by contrast, not hostile (pp. 117–8).

An emptiness, then, that is released from ego fixations, and pregnant with possibilities. Such awareness clears the way for the realisation of the interdependency of all forms.

I heard the Dalai Lama express this idea in Los Angeles in 1999, when he said that what we do to others we are literally doing to ourselves, teaching that we are all part of one continuous being /not being. One of the deepest aims of Buddhist practice is to drop the discriminating mind, lose the distinction between 'self' and 'other', and arrive at an awareness of non-discriminating non-duality, which brings 'self' and 'other' into a close embrace. This is true of other, related wisdom traditions in different parts of South and East Asia, of course, and will be important for my discussion of Isherwood's training in *advaita* principles, in chapter five (although, of course, the Vedantist approach is less likely to use the trope of the 'no-self', or the 'empty self').

Varela draws on current neuroscience to describe the self as 'a virtual person', a 'nonsubstantial self that acts as if it were present, like a virtual interface' (p. 61), and he bridges that understanding with parallel ideas in these 'wisdom traditions' and the ethical practices deriving from them. Coming to terms with this emptiness is *necessary* for an ethics not based on delusional ego:

Ethical know-how is the progressive, firsthand acquaintance with the *virtuality of self* … It is no ground whatsoever; it cannot be grasped as ground, reference point, *or nest for a sense of ego*. (p. 68; emphasis added)

A clear-eyed recognition that no-thing is for certain, this model is quite clearly *not* the kind of pursuit of one's own ego and desires, then, that some fear the deep inquiry into the nature of the self must entail.

Drawing on evidence from neuropsychology, Varela asserts that language is another 'modular capacity', 'cohabiting with everything else we are, cognitively', and he asserts that the sense of a personal self is 'an ongoing interpretive narrative' (p. 61), an idea that has now become axiomatic to my discussion. He draws attention to the constant shifts in forms of attention as 'typical of our microidentities' (p. 61), underlining the fragility of the narrative constructions of this sense of personal self. These ideas are very much in keeping with the notions of the self developed by Eakin (and Damasio) that I outlined earlier, but Varela carries the discussion into the area that I have marked out as the field of spiritual work.

I want to underline that his book is about '*ethical* know how'. And more than an epistemological proposition, Varela describes the acquisition of this first-hand acquaintance as a *practice*, known in one tradition as the practice of 'mindfulness/awareness' (p. 66), or *samatha-vispasnya*:

> Essentially a radical not-doing, it is traditionally understood as a universal practice, but despite having been refined and explored for over 2500 years by over half the world, it was never discovered independently in the West. Instead of a space for the human in the analyst's studio required in psychoanalysis, 'samatha-vispasnya' creates the space through non-action, *which includes nonresponse to language.* (p. 66; emphasis added.)

Beyond reason

Perhaps the cultural convergence to which I referred above is becoming clearer. I am reminded of Michel Foucault's discussion with a Buddhist teacher, during his stay in a Japanese Zen temple in 1978. Responding to the roshi's question about the depth of his interest in Japan, Foucault says that he is more interested in 'the Western history of rationality and its limits'. 'In reality', he says, 'that rationality constructs colonies everywhere else' (in Carrette, p. 111). Foucault's hint that rationalism is another form of colonialism is provocative, and is pertinent to any discussion of how other cultures and practices use the mind, and how subjectivities are differently configured, culturally. Coming at this from an anthropological standpoint, SJ Tambiah unpacks the implications of rationality as a mode of reasoning, and as a process of constructing knowledge, in *Magic, science, religion, and the scope of rationality* (1990).

> Each society has its regime of truth, its 'general politics' of truth: that is, the types of discourse which it accepts and makes function as true: the mechanisms and instances which enable one to distinguish true and false statements, the means by which each is sanctioned, the techniques and procedures accorded value in the acquisition of truth, the status of those who are charged with saying what counts as true. (p. 147)

In his discussion of the resulting 'multiple orderings of reality', Tambiah turns to the philosopher Lucien Lévy-Brühl, who questioned the evolutionary, progressivist assumptions of Victorian theorists, with their embedded assumptions of a civilising progression: from savagery, to barbarism, to civilisation. Lévy-Brühl concluded, early on, that 'the search for universally valid "theoretical moralities" or a universal science of "theoretical ethics" was doomed to failure' and that, 'since moralities do vary with time and place, they should be studied objectively as social formations' (Tambiah, p. 84). The issue has special importance when dealing with translation between cultures, and the means by which scholars from one culture translate phenomena into categories and concepts of their own culture. (Tambiah, p. 111 ff.)

Foucault and the roshi discuss the 'crisis of Western thought' and the priest asks Foucault if he thinks that Eastern thought could 'allow' Western thought to 'find a new way' (Carrette, p. 113). Foucault identifies the crisis as 'identical to the end of imperialism' and agrees that to confront Western thought with Eastern thought could be one avenue for re-examination, the others being 'psychoanalysis, anthropology and the analysis of history', he says (p. 113). He also proposes that a 'philosophy of the future' must be born 'outside of Europe' or, 'in consequence of meetings and impacts between Europe and "non-Europe"' (p. 113). Once again, the life and work of a figure like Isherwood are emblematic of this increasing cross-cultural hybridisation.

If the self is really a construct of language, as some post-structuralists assert, what kind of conscious activity could be going on that does not rely on language? And who is doing the thinking? Western students of Buddhist practice have to go through a kind of 'de-programming' ('disenchantment') to recognise other ways to use the mind and to negotiate states of awareness that depend neither on rationalism, nor on language, nor on the central power of the directing 'ego self', to investigate layers of being/awareness in ways that do not correspond with the usual subject positionings.

'No ground whatsoever'—Varela recognises that this state is a paradox for the mind and could be threatening to familiar constructs. He says that 'it [self/identity] cannot be grasped as ground, reference point, or nest for a sense of ego' (p. 68). This is reminiscent of the Zen koan I cited above—if the student is pressed to discover 'the face before' he or she, or even the parents were born, perhaps the implication is that he or she won't find one, or, at least, not a 'personal' one. If it does not 'exist' (nor 'not exist', I should add—metaphysics exhausted, the student may simply point to his/her own present face) Varela continues, then 'it cannot be an object of mind or of the conceptualizing process' (p. 68):

> When the conceptual mind tries to grasp it, it finds nothing, and so it experiences it as emptiness. It can be known (and can only be known) directly. It is called Buddha nature, nomind, primordial mind, absolute 'bodhicitta', wisdom mind, All Goodness, Great Perfection, That which cannot be fabricated by mind, Naturalness. (pp. 68–9)

Peter Conradi compares the Buddhist view of the self—as 'not a fixed or changeless product, but a dynamic process always seeking an illusory resting-place where it might finally become "solid"'(p. 80)—with the predicament of the characters in Samuel Beckett's play, *Waiting for Godot.* Conradi reads Didi, Gogo, Pozzo and Lucky as examples of:

> the lonely individual struggling to talk into permanent existence, maintain and freeze something essentially fluid and contingent. Neither Godot nor a solid self will come to save us. This self (ego) spends much time trying to establish personal territory, a nest or cocoon, to defend. (p. 80)

Beckett's characters might be 'waiting' for someone or something to 'save' them, but practitioners of meditation are not simply cut adrift in 'the Void'; the practice serves to anchor awareness in deeper layers of being that are not 'contained' in any sense by narrowly focused, constructed identifications. Thus, the characterisation of the 'homeless mind' resulting from the alienating and compartmentalising forces of modern secular society, offered by Berger, Berger and Kellner (1973), is not inevitable. We should recognise the strong contrast with the Western, psychological model, for as Sokefeld (1999) points out, in the constructions of Western psychology, an inconsistent self—as a 'non-identity'—could be regarded as a disturbance, or even as illness.

In contrast, introspective practices common in the 'wisdom traditions' bring the focal length of the lens of awareness back from the personal self to focus on the nature of conscious awareness itself—as a zero-point field—rather than focusing exclusively on individual (apparently separate) entities within that field. Such practices are intended to reveal a *background* layer to the isolated awareness of being that is usually in the *foreground* of awareness, and blocking out the bigger picture, as it were. (This, too, will be important in my discussion of Isherwood.) In Buddhist terms, self lets go to no-self; in Vedanta, the small 's' self dissolves into the great 'S' Self, with the 'Atman' conceived of as having the same nature as 'Brahman'; the individual finds its roots in the 'Ground of Being' (Paul Tillich's term, reminiscent of Vedanta); and so on. Rather than occurring as a single *coup de foudre* awakening, for most practitioners meditation practice sustained over time deepens the ability to re-focus the lens of awareness, shifting more easily between the concerns of the busy mind usually preoccupied with the personal, and the widest aperture setting that releases awareness from the tight grip of individuality. Rather than being the regressive, pathological process that the neo-Freudians would have it be, this can produce, *en passant*, profoundly therapeutic benefits, even so-called 'mystical' insight.

Before I close this chapter, I want to draw attention to the second major development in autobiographical theory that is of particular relevance to my discussion.

Coming out of the silence

I want to refer back to the point I raised in my opening. According to Michel Foucault's analysis, 'in the space of a few centuries, a certain inclination has led us to direct the question of what we are, to sex' (1978, p. 78). But who is a 'homosexual' when he/she is not having sex? Following Foucault's lead, I question what has been overshadowed by the practice of seeing things only through that lens, and point to spirituality as a knowledge source denied by the positioning of queer identity—or any 'identity'—strictly around the axis of sexuality. Even though his analysis of the power relations implicit in the discourse of sexuality goes beyond the 'repression argument', Foucault makes the useful point that repression operates not only as a 'sentence to disappear' but also as 'an injunction to silence, and affirmation of nonexistence and, by implication, an admission that there was nothing to say about such things, nothing to see, and nothing to know' (1978, p. 4). Foucault was concerned to interrogate the inextricable relationship between forms of knowledge and the exercise of power (1988, p. 71), especially how privileged systems of knowledge served the political need of enabling (and justifying) exercises of power (Turner, p. 43). If a subject receives its cultural and epistemological positioning from a normative ideology that defines and strictly prescribes its possibilities for being and becoming only at the margins of meaning, certain ways of knowing are rendered unavailable.

Some recent theoretical work on life-writing takes up these concerns. Sidonie Smith and Julia Watson (1996) build a case for life-writing as a means of critical intervention into post-modern life. They identify autobiographical narrative as a 'performative' display and describe 'the many means by which models of acceptable identity are circulated and renewed in society', analysing 'how state, church, school, corporation, government and the advertising industry secure normative subjects in acceptable social relationships' (p. 12). In specific situations, Smith and Watson say, people may 'choose not to narrate the stories that are prescribed for them', opting instead to 'reframe the present by bringing it into a new alignment of meaning with the past' (p. 12).

Writing autobiographically, then, becomes a resistant strategy for re-narrativising the self, an assertive recontextualising that recovers meaning from the toxic narratives buried within hostile discourses. 'Seizing the occasion and telling the story', say Smith and Watson, 'turns speakers into subjects of narrative who can exercise some control over the meaning of their lives' and this assertion, they say, is 'particularly compelling for those whose personal histories include stories that have been culturally unspeakable' (pp. 13–14).

Nowadays the possibilities for speaking out might seem obvious but, after the blowtorch of post-structuralist and postmodern analysis had been applied to both aspects of 'auto/biography'—interrogating notions of the 'self' (the 'auto'), and the writing (the 'graphos') of the textual subject—the theoretical possibility offered by Smith and Watson marks a move forward, out of what had threatened to become a bleak, almost nihilistic theoretical silence.

Leigh Gilmore notes how 'the postmodernist glee associated with the dissolution of notions of the self' was 'hardly a welcome prospect for those already all too familiar with the social reality of selflessness' (1994, p. 15). This issue of agency in relation to the possibility of autobiographical practice has been a major area of investigation by feminist theorists who have had to show the way out of the fragmentation of post-structuralist analyses—in which the subject is ultimately a *passive* construction—to allow for a sense of effective agency. I would position queer autobiographical narratives, and spiritual autobiography in particular, within the new field of possibilities opened up by this work.

Kim Worthington says that post-structuralism forced us to confront the idea 'that personal authenticity and subjective agency are impossible, given their constitution in the terms of social discourse' (1996, p. 8). But Worthington finds it disturbing that human beings are 'subjected' by the language in which they conceive themselves:

> There can be no private language, no private morality if even the most private, intimate contours of selfhood are written and read in the extra-personal terms of social language. (p. 8)

In this model, human beings are 'made into subjects by language', and are thus 'subjected to the ideological values, the systems of representations, repressions, hierarchies, and stereotypes with which social language is imbued' (p. 8), and she cites Barthes: 'the language I speak *within myself* is not of my time: it is prey, by nature, to ideological suspicion' (Barthes, *The pleasure of the text* pp.

40–1; qtd in Worthington, p. 9). Such an unstable basis for subjectivity has an obvious bearing on the possibility or impossibility of 'auto' biography: just who is doing the writing (the author), and who is the subject that the author is inscribing?

The postmodern interrogation of conventional notions of identity and authority embedded in patriarchal discourses and politics was a welcome tool to many feminists, but while it contributed to the dissolution of notions of the self, it was not always an entirely welcome prospect to subjects who found themselves located on the culturally constructed margins of power. In the essay introducing their collection *Life/Lines (Theorizing women's autobiography)*, Bella Brodzki and Celeste Schenck point out that the struggle for 'the imperative situating of the female subject in spite of the postmodern campaign against the sovereign self' must be carried out without either 'falling back into essentialism … or retreating into a pure textuality that consigns women … to an unrecoverable absence' (p. 14).

Not all scholars were so polite. The most withering attack came from Liz Stanley in *The auto/biographical I: the theory and practice of feminist auto/biography* (1992), where she mocks the position arrived at by Michel Foucault (1977) and Roland Barthes (1977) on the so-called 'death of the author'. Stanley accepts their critique of the 'conventional view of writing as the unique product of a single unique mind', and therefore as 'a piece of realist ideology which masks the social production of ideas', and she does not take exception to their representation of the privileging of the subject as unique as a 'facile presumption' underlying essentialist views about 'the author' (p. 16). But she challenges the unacknowledged power being practised by the authors of this trope (that of the 'death of the author') being put forward by 'white middle class male first world elite self-styled intellectual' theorists, 'latter day prophets of postmodernspeak' who have failed to acknowledge the authorial presence in their *own* pronouncements, as if in their own texts there is only 'referential discourse spoken by no one, by every one' (p. 17).

In Stanley's re-versioning, new voices emanating from the anti-colonial/black/gay/women's movements, who would protest at exclusion, could be rendered *mute*, all too easily, were they to toe this new postmodern party line. If the position, 'the death of the author', were to hold, such protest would 'be treated as a naïve clinging to the wreckage of bourgeois humanist referential essentialism' (p. 18). To claim a self, to move beyond silence to speak your oppression, to name your oppressors, would be caricatured as 'primitive', according to that construction, especially when language itself is seen as treacherous. So these women 'talk back' to the post-modern paradigm, too. Kim Worthington takes up the question:

> Are we truly 'authored' *by* language, simply subjected in the procedural operations of communicative rationality? Is our existential condition truly one of hopelessly mediated inauthenticity? (p. 170)

Worthington goes on to show that even if 'the sovereignty of selfhood' is challenged by Barthes, 'creative subjective presence is not abolished' but rather is 'reconstituted as the site of fictive self-production' and the subject, so conceived, 'vacillates precariously between the roles of (passive) textual product and (active) producer of the text' (pp. 172–3).

The issue, then, is who is telling the story? In this post-structuralist view, am I a passive 'victim', entirely a construct made up by forces outside of myself that disallows any sense of agency? Am I an object, or a subject? One position is disempowering; the other allows for creativity and assertive resignification. So, even if we were to accept the anti-essentialist, poststructuralist position that 'language is prior to being', we are still left with the notion of a producer, as 'instigator of the production process', says Worthington (p. 173). She concludes that poststructuralist theory is sometimes 'unable to accept the logical consequences of its own hardline position(s)' (p. 173).

Recognising that post-modernism can become 'an epithet of fragmentation, loss, and exile', nevertheless Gilmore credits the influence of postmodernism as allowing for the possibility of political re-positioning. With its inspection of the shifting, discursive field of social life, it could be seen as paving the way for feminist theory to recover the 'possibility for human agency' and explore the possible political interventions a subject-in-process may effect in a world of power relations (p. 18).

I locate life-writing practice by queer men within this frame as a way of *speaking* the unspeakable, interrogating the hostile discourses from religion, the law and psychological medicine to assert more authentic reconciliation with their sexuality *and* their spirituality. In the now familiar genre of 'coming out' stories, life-writing became a means of speaking and generating an integrated identity through autobiographical narrative. But, rather than arguing for a fixed identity structure, I am pushing beyond the now familiar tropes of this writing practice to pursue the interrogation further, when I ask: Who is a 'homosexual' when he is not having sex? Is there not a domain of being not adequately addressed through sexual 'liberation', and the social and political identifications that situate gender in the familiar contexts of identity politics? Texts that assert the *spiritual* possibilities of queer lives are also speaking out of the cultural and political silence.

Beyond 'gay'?

Perhaps the notion of liberation can be opened further than the fixed and defended positioning familiar in the identity politics of the 80s and 90s. In the case of Christopher Isherwood we will see the working of a queer intelligence intent on seeking out pathways for growth and continually questioning the constructions of the 'self'. Just as he was able to pursue independent inquiry, using what were for his time highly unorthodox technologies, the search for new forms of subjectivity must continue to be freed from the *new* orthodoxies.

In the East, 'liberation' moves the personal self beyond its narrative formulations, and then beyond again into a freedom from such narratives altogether. From the *Heart Sutra* of Buddhism comes the mantra said to calm all suffering: *gate gate, paragate, parasmagate, bodhi svaha* ... ('gone, gone, gone beyond, gone completely beyond, hail to enlightenment'). If the first instinct of queer intelligence is to interrogate and reject the oppressive prescriptions of strictly heteronormative sexuality, its instinct for freedom might then move beyond mere freedom of sexual expression into a deeply expanded and all-embracing awareness, using more radical tools available from new applications of mystical praxis. (This is not the same move as arguing for a repudiation of our sexuality, mind. But the dislocation young queer folk go through is as much an ontological as a psychological issue or a legal dispute over civil rights.)

In Mark Thompson's collection *Gay spirit: myth and meaning* (1987a) Dennis Altman raises the question why some artists might not want to be labelled as 'gay artists'. The reasons he finds are not limited to the possibility of an 'internalised' homophobia:

> [I]t becomes easy for the postliberation generation [he's writing in 1987] to dismiss resistance as residual self-hate. But there is a sense, too, in which the cult of asserting gayness through art has become a dead end, a refusal to recognize the extent to which sexuality is only one aspect of any human's identity; there is an oppressiveness to emphasizing it to the exclusion of all else as much as there is to ignoring it. Gay liberation implies both that we recognize the importance of our sexuality—and that we transcend sexuality as a category used to divide people. ('What price gay nationalism?' pp. 17–18.)

The paradox of 'recognising the importance of our sexuality' while at the same time 'transcending sexuality as a category used to divide people' is a key issue, then, if we are to reconsider the possibilities of queer spirituality. I suggest that in the deeper levels of a mystical experience all these taxonomies disappear, as superficial fluctuations in a deeper field of unity. (I will pick up this thread again, in my final chapter.)

It should come as no surprise, then, to find that there are illuminating examples of life-writing by queer men in which 'spirituality' emerges as a central preoccupation alongside sexuality in opening up different possibilities for positioning subjectivity. These writers use memoir as part of the reconstructive process of reclaiming subjectivity and reconfiguring the meaning of their lived experience. Such re-storying of the self becomes part of achieving self-actualisation, even bringing personal and community identities into a new, healed relationship. Maps may be re-drawn and subjectivities re-situated through autobiographical practice as the quest for liberty moves past the embattled defensive strategies of identity politics.

In the next three chapters I will focus on characteristic strategies of self-positioning in Christopher Isherwood's oeuvre, with an emphasis on the intertextuality of events in his life and the narrativisation of the life as text. The first of these chapters deals with the dis-locations Isherwood went through in the first half of his life, and how his disorientation was reflected in a progressive disillusionment with his sense of personal identity. The second of these chapters—'Isherwood comes Home'—will analyse the long-term, radically integrative effects of his encounter with the teachings and practices of the Vedanta tradition, in the person of his guru, Swami Prabhavananda, and the third will focus more closely on the non-dualistic Advaita principles and their subtle integration into the late text *A single man*.

I am not suggesting that Isherwood's turn to 'the East' should form a prescriptive template for other (queer) men to follow. But his search (the dis-locations), and his journey 'home' (the re-location), illustrate the issues canvassed in this introduction. In an independent and original life journey Isherwood modeled the possibility of accessing alternative pathways of growth and insight otherwise abandoned in the name of a religious tradition that is unnecessarily exclusivist in its bogus role as a defender of heteronormative constructions of identity, in which, as Charpentier says, 'a heterosexual gender system is produced … as a *sacred order*' (2000, emphasis in original).

3

Dis-locations: *Isherwood's search for the 'home self'*

It is not Home that one cries for but one's home-self.

—Christopher Isherwood, *Kathleen and Frank*

Until recently, appraisals of Christopher Isherwood's work have underplayed the importance of his mature period, especially those by British literary critics, among whom the prevailing view has been that the writing was in decline after the famous Berlin stories and his controversial move to the United States. Gore Vidal, who admired Isherwood's style, was one of the first to comment on the commonplace British reservations, in a review of *Christopher and his kind* (1976). Philip Larkin held similar judgements about Auden, reckoning that the poet had abandoned his audience on the move to the US. In the opinion of Anthony Powell, to emigrate was the act of 'a treacherous shit' (qtd in Dennis 2009, p. 21) and Powell held to that bitter opinion right through to Auden's death (see Hitchens 1997, citing Kingsley Amis).

In the case of Isherwood, what was happening, of course, was that after decamping to California—abandoning Europe on the brink of war to assume the pacifist position—Isherwood, the atheist, had 'got religion', or more to the point, a guru in the Advaita tradition of Vedanta. This was in 1939 (he was thirty-five), and he lived on, continuing to work, until 1986, but the writing dating from the California migration has often been overlooked or dismissed, with the spiritual elements of his life and work from the same period even more likely to be ignored.

The last of his four major autobiographies, *My Guru and his disciple* (1980) (hereafter abbreviated to *My Guru*), documents Isherwood's longest lasting relationship: the one maintained not with any of his male lovers but with his spiritual adviser, a Swami in the Ramakrishna Order, and the head of the Vedanta Society in southern California: Swami Prabhavananda. The relationship continued for almost forty years. This text can now be identified as a watershed for the sub-genre identified by Christopher Buren Stewart: 'queer spiritual autobiography' (2002). In fact there have been calls, by Wade (2001) and others, for Isherwood to be re-evaluated as a serious religious writer. James Berg and Chris Freeman include five essays on Isherwood's spirituality in their collection *The Isherwood century* and Antony Copley's *A Spiritual Bloomsbury* (2006) devotes an entire chapter to a serious discussion of Isherwood's relationship with Swami Prabhavananda; so a correction to the prevailing prejudice has begun to occur.

As I pointed out in my introduction, with some emblematic writers there is an entrenched cultural investment in certain modes of assessing them. In a sense, a culture can become over-invested in that construction, resistant to any other way of reading them, and ignoring evidence to the contrary. Commentators reading only for the sexuality will often brush aside the sustained interest in Vedanta as some kind of aberration. A particular case in point would be Paul Robinson's 1999 study of queer life-writing, *Gay lives: homosexual autobiography from John Addington Symonds to Paul Monette*, which devotes some sixty-seven pages to Isherwood, yet mentions *My Guru* only in a footnote. So, the occlusion is not restricted to one side of the Atlantic.

In such a view, Isherwood is limited to perpetual fame as either a chronicler of pre-war Berlin—the raucous bad boy of the Weimar Republic who went to Berlin to chase boys (almost inadvertently capturing the *Zeitgeist* of Berlin in the critical period of the Nazis' rise to power)—or later, with the flowering of queer writing, as a prominent figure in the revolution of gay liberation, living unapologetically 'out' with a much younger partner (thirty years his junior), and really into sex. Neither of these constructions allows for an engagement with spirituality.

I will pay particular attention to two representations in this entrenched mode of reading: one, dating from 1979, written by the literary critic, academic and poet DS Savage, and the other the recent, seemingly authoritative biography of Isherwood by Peter Parker (2004). Between them they exemplify most of the occlusive features of this fixed way of reading him.

Isherwood lived from 1904 until 1986. In many ways, his life and texts encapsulate important elements of the entire period. Berg and Freeman regard him as the pivotal writer of his generation. In addition to the fiction, he wrote for the theatre (three plays with his longtime friend WH Auden, and later adaptations for the stage in Los Angeles); screenplays for the Hollywood movie studios (at different times with MGM, Paramount and Warner Brothers); autobiographies (four in all); travel books (*Journey to a war,* covering a visit to China with Auden during the early days of the Japanese occupation, and *The condor and the cows*, from travels in South America with his lover, the photographer Bill Caskey); as well as biographies of his parents (*Kathleen and Frank*), and of Ramakrishna, the 19th century Bengali saint, in whose memory the Ramakrishna Vedanta Society was formed (*Ramakrishna and his disciples*). He also wrote short apologia on his interest in Indian Vedanta philosophy and practice, contributed introductions to collections of talks and essays by Swami Vivekananda (edited by John Yale) and, with his own guru, Swami Prabhavananda, published translations of three key texts in that tradition (*The Bhagavad Gita*, Shankara's *Crest jewel of discrimination*, and the *Yoga aphorisms* of Patanjali). Two volumes of his extensive diaries have been published (one, *The lost years*, the 'reconstructed' coverage of the period 1945–1951, is given as a 'memoir') and two final volumes are in preparation under the editorship of Katherine Bucknell.

But let me now go back to the beginning.

The contexts of class

Born into privilege among the landed gentry in Cheshire, in 1904, and christened Christopher William Bradshaw-Isherwood, Isherwood lived out his adolescence during the First World War. The biography of his parents (*Kathleen and Frank*, published 1971) clearly depicts the differential gradations in the class structure in Britain of the time (see especially pp. 82–3). His take on Henry Bradshaw-Isherwood (his father's elder brother, and the family heir) is particularly amusing:

> If Henry were asked why he considers the Bradshaw-Isherwoods socially superior to these merchants, he would reply without hesitation that the Isherwoods are 'landed gentry'. Which simply means they are farmers who made their money so long ago that their origins can be decently forgotten and that they have lived in the same house for three hundred years, on unearned income from rents and investments. (p. 83)

Even though she had protested to her future husband that she had 'no sort of sympathy about the "best people" and that sort of thing' (p. 85), his mother Kathleen's class affectations became a source of annoyance to Isherwood, and he was relieved to leave his 'class' behind, initially with the relocation to Berlin in his early twenties, but even more so on moving to California, in 1939—in his mid-thirties.

After the death of his father, near Ypres, early in the First World War (when Christopher was only 10), Isherwood came to resent the oppressive expectations of his duty as a man, and as a loyal national subject, derived from the patriotic rhetoric of wartime. He reacted to the glorification, both of the Hero Father, and of war itself that was drummed into his generation while still at school. In *An approach to Vedanta* (1963) he writes of this experience:

> My earliest remembered feelings of rebellion were against the British Army, in which my father was a regular officer, and against the staff of my first boarding school, who tried, with the best intentions, to make me believe in a glamorized view of the 1914–18 War and of my father's death in it. (pp. 6–7)

He also rejected his mother's transformation into the Widow figure, living only to keep alive the myth of the Hero-Father. (He fictionalised his resentment in the character Eric Vernon, the protagonist of his second novel, *The memorial*, 1932.)

Are you really a man?

Isherwood explains the significance of the crisis—and the significance attached to it by his masters—in the first of his autobiographies, *Lions and shadows: an education in the twenties* (published by the Woolfs' Hogarth Press in 1935), where it is presented as 'The Test':

> Like most of my generation, I was obsessed by a complex of terrors and longings connected with the idea 'War'. 'War', in this purely neurotic sense, meant The Test. The Test of your courage, of your maturity, of your sexual prowess: 'Are you really a Man?' Subconsciously, I believe, I longed to be subjected to this test; but I also dreaded failure. I dreaded failure so much—indeed, I was so certain that I should fail—that, consciously, I denied my longing to be tested, altogether. (pp. 75–6)

Isherwood reacted strongly to this challenge, which was doubled for him because of his non-conformist sexuality ('Are you really a man?'). Christopher Lane notes the role of the British public school in modeling the ethos of Empire, writing that the 'proximity between Britain's public schools and empire suggests that the first was synechdocic of the second' because the values of the public schools 'flourished in national policy and global management' (Lane 1995, p. 208). By the next stage of boarding school (at Repton, in Derbyshire, January 1919) Isherwood was already struggling to locate a sense of self derived from some other, less oppressive source that would ring true to his emerging sense of self:

> I had arrived at my public school thoroughly sick of masters and mistresses, having been emotionally messed about by them at my preparatory school, where the war years had given full licence to every sort of dishonest cant about loyalty, selfishness, patriotism, playing the game and his honouring the dead. Now I wanted to be left alone. (p. 77)

Gore Vidal describes the period: 'There was a long shadow over the young … of dead fathers, brothers; also of dead or dying attitudes. Rebellion was in the air. New things were promised' (1976, p. 10).

Isherwood's rejection of the oppressive attitudes prevailing at the time laid the ground for a full-scale rebellion against dominant cultural values. Among the significant friends he made at public school was Edward Upward ('Chalmers' in *Lions and shadows*), a co-conspirator in a rebellion against authority, a 'natural anarchist, a born romantic revolutionary' (*Lions and shadows*, p. 18). The friendship deepened into mutual respect when they were at Cambridge together, and the two supported each other's efforts as writers for many years, well beyond Isherwood's 1939 relocation to California, even though Isherwood's commitment to socialist ideals waned while Upward's continued.

Initially, Isherwood was impressed by Upward's refusal to be confirmed into the Anglican Church, which was standard operating procedure at a public school:

> I had been through the confirmation process a few months earlier, working up all the emotions prescribed in my little black leather 'companion' and delighting the master who prepared me by the complexity and ingenuity of my religious 'difficulties'. Now already I had to admit to myself that, as far as I was concerned, the entire ceremony had been altogether meaningless. If only I had been more honest with myself and avoided it, like Chalmers, from the very start! (p. 19)

DS Savage, intent on a neo-Freudian reading of Isherwood as a regressive 'homosexualist' (his term), finds this and similar confessions, while admirable in their candour, as showing 'all the same, a less than complete grasp of the issues involved' (1979, p. 76). But the 'issues' construed as important by Savage were not necessarily seen the same way by Isherwood himself. (More on Savage, below.) Other readings of the text do not fail to recognise the ironic self-deprecation built into it. This particular passage indicates clearly that Isherwood rued going along with the crowd and that he was determined to act from a greater sense of personal integrity in the future. (This would prove to be important later, when, like many young intellectuals of his generation, including Upward, he became involved with Socialism; then, on his own terms, quit it.)

For anyone who assumes that this rebellion against British values was temporary or superficial, John Lehman's notes in his own memoir Isherwood's use (in conspiracy with Edward Upward) of the term 'the enemy' to sum up the brace of attitudes he was rejecting: 'which covered everything he had, with a pure *hatred*, cut himself off from in English life' (*The whispering gallery*, qtd in Vidal, p. 13; emphasis added). While schoolmasters and family fully endorsed the official line, Isherwood was clearly part of an emerging generation that was going to make up its own mind about such values.

1936 saw a constitutional crisis in Britain, when David (Edward VIII), the future Duke of Windsor, opted for life with American divorcee Wallis Simpson, abdicating his throne in favour of his brother, Bertie. Isherwood certainly wasn't a loyal Royalist. In fact, his genealogy included an ancestor who was the judge who issued the death warrant for the execution of Charles I. Whether he admired the Duke of Windsor's choice or not (later, in a diary entry from 1959, he opined 'I only admire talent'), the stuffy, oppressive model of decorum and duty was there on display, acted out for the populace by the new Royal Family as they closed ranks against Wallis and David, modeling perfectly the elevation of duty above the selfish call of personal love.

Regardless of opinions about the behaviour appropriate for the monarchy, Isherwood and some of his generation found that to be an unacceptably hypocritical option in their own lives.

In the gentrified circles in which he grew up, even if his emerging non-conformist sexuality might have been discreetly tolerated, I suggest that duty would have required the display of a second layer of behaviour for public consumption.

It would be helpful at this point to draw attention to certain key influences from the cultural and political context of the time affecting Isherwood's choices that will make it easier to understand how deeply his dissatisfaction with the status quo in Britain ran.

A hostile cultural milieu

By suggesting that there might have been a tacit acceptance of 'deviant' sexualities behind the scenes, I don't want to underplay the risks that came with going against the grain. Katherine Bucknell, following her close reading as the editor of Isherwood's diaries, notes:

> Isherwood was fascinated throughout his life with marginal figures and with minorities. He himself was a member of what was for centuries one of the most oppressed and anonymous minorities in human society: during the first half of his life, the society which raised and educated him also told him that he was a criminal. (2000, p. xxxiii)

Isherwood's depiction of his parents' courtship, in *Kathleen and Frank*, describes the codes of propriety common to his class, and provides an insightful social history from Victorian into Edwardian times, in particular the public values against which his generation was rebelling. Victorian moral attitudes clearly had not yet been eclipsed and the Edwardian period was no more welcoming to his 'type', as a series of scandals illustrate. Homosexuality was against the law in England (and most countries of Europe) and would continue to be held in social and legal opprobrium for at least another half century.

Although he had died in ignominy in France before Isherwood's birth, the notorious figure of Oscar Wilde cast a long shadow into the 20th century. The Wilde affair of 1895 followed another controversial investigation, the infamous Cleveland Street scandal of 1889 which implicated members of the aristocracy—rumoured to include even a member of the highest family in the land—with the activities of a male brothel, and such incidents drew down severe disapprobation upon 'the love that dare not speak its name' (the phrase is from an 1896 poem by Wilde's lover, Alfred Douglas).

Additionally, the Irish rebel Sir Roger Casement—imprisoned for sedition in London—was receiving a lot of support, especially in America, which made it difficult for the authorities to proceed with his execution. But the strategic release and quiet circulation of the so-called 'Black Diaries', which allegedly revealed Casement's homosexuality, was sufficient to undermine that support, winning the public relations battle for the government and paving the way for his hanging on August 3rd, 1916. Colm Toibin (2001) cites a report to the British cabinet indicating the level of disgust aroused—only two decades after Wilde's disgrace—by Casement's alleged 'sodomitical' practices in the colonies. He was executed only six years after being knighted for his investigative reports on imperialist atrocities.

Towards the end of the First World War, hysteria about the demoralising effect of homosexuality was thrown into lurid relief by the bizarre libel trial of politician and aviator, Pemberton Billings, who had fomented paranoia about the infiltration of British society by German spies who were allegedly intent on 'exterminating the manhood of Britain' by luring men into homosexual acts. Billings published an article in his journal, *Imperialist*, based on information provided by Harold Sherwood Spencer, claiming that the Germans were blackmailing 47,000 'highly placed' British perverts for propagating 'evils which all decent men thought had perished in Sodom and Lesbia'. The names of the 47,000 were said to be inscribed in the 'Berlin Black Book' of an Albanian prince, and the judge in the trial was himself implicated as being listed in the reputed Black Book (see Gagnier, 1986).

During Isherwood's adolescent years, a controversy erupted with the publication of Alec Waugh's first novel *The loom of youth* in 1917, which depicted sexual relations between boys at a fictional public school, 'Fernhurst'. Waugh had been disgraced by an incident at his own school, Sherborne, which had led to his expulsion. (He was allowed to finish the term but, in the meantime, the other boys were instructed to shun him.) His novel also exposed the hypocrisy of the school staff regarding sexual relations between the boys. The message was, clearly, that everyone knew what was going on, and that the only crime was to get caught. The book created a major scandal: it was banned in many schools; boys were caned if caught reading it; anxious parents bombarded the school's masters with letters seeking reassurance that their own boys were not subject to such malfeasance; and outraged letters appeared in the London press for many weeks—humiliating Alec's father. However, the novel sold very well. (Waugh's mild account of the book's reception, written for a new edition in 1954, rather underplays the controversy.)

One of Isherwood's most important mentors as a young writer was EM Forster, who showed the younger man the manuscript of his unpublished novel, *Maurice.* Given the book's subject matter—a love relationship between men of different social classes—and its 'happy' ending, Forster was unable to have it published in his lifetime. Writers were worried about arrest and imprisonment after the trial over Radclyffe Hall's *The well of loneliness* in 1928, and there have been suggestions that Virginia Woolf felt obliged to remove lesbian references in her own fiction (although Woolf published her novel *Orlando* in the same year as Hall's book).

Asked if he tried to convince Forster to publish, Isherwood said they talked about it constantly, from the time they first met in the early 1930s (Geherin 1972, p. 154). *Maurice* was finally published posthumously with Isherwood's help in 1971 and royalties from the publication funded a fellowship administered by the National Institute of Arts and Letters for visiting British writers to the US.

In the screenplay for the cinematic version of the novel, filmmakers Merchant/Ivory interpolated an extra sequence that cleverly invokes the Wilde scandal through the fictional trial of young 'Lord Risley'—a 'criminal of the Oscar Wilde sort'—and the sequence works as a major turning point in the movie's plot.

Graham Robb's lively social history *Strangers: homosexual love in the nineteenth century* (2003) documents the widespread underground of homosexual culture in Britain, Europe (and the US) and has been praised for refuting the poststructuralist convention that homosexuality, because it was not then categorised or 'named', could not be said to exist prior to the 1880s (Goodheart 2004). Robb calls into question what he calls the 'blanket influence' of Michel Foucault's theories of social construction (2003, p. 11). Whether he is being fair to Foucault or not, Robb does contribute a detailed social history of a 'homosexual' sub-culture throughout Europe (and the United States) and he points to the rich Victorian vocabulary, ranging from street slang to medical jargon—margeries, mollies, ganymedes, chestnut-gatherers, 'little Jesuses', inverts, unisexuals, androphiles, normosexuals, parisexuals, ghaseligs, Uranians, and so on—as a marker reaching backwards from that time into European social history that indicated a clear public awareness of alternative sexual practices. But awareness of the phenomenon is not the same as acceptance. Robb's case for a widespread, *de facto* tolerance and acceptance is continually undermined by the evidence he provides, to the contrary, of the real difficulties imposed by the considerable pressures to conform, and the ever-present threat of legal processes against those with deviant sexualities. So, while Robb claims 'homosexuals lived under a cloud, but it seldom rained', he does have to acknowledge:

> Most of them suffered, not from the cruel machinery of justice, but from the creeping sense of shame, the fear of losing friends, family and reputation, the painful incompatibility of religious belief and sexual desire, the social and mental isolation, and the strain of concealment. (p. 30)

Writing about an 1891 study of sexuality by Albert Moll, which was based on hundreds of interviews in Berlin, Robb notes that: 'Illnesses suffered by homosexuals were caused, not by mental or physical abnormality but by fear, guilt and sexual deprivation' (p. 82). As he admits, further weakening his case for widespread acceptance: 'the mere absence of persecution hardly amounts to tolerance' (p. 106) and the threat of blackmail hung about these lives like a persistent miasma. Montgomery Hyde's account of the Oscar Wilde trials, written decades earlier than Robb's study, noted that the Criminal Law Amendment Act of 1885—especially its section 11, which made 'indecencies between males' an offence, *even if practised in private* (Hyde 1945, p. 371)—was nicknamed the 'Blackmailer's Charter.'

Matt Houlbrook (2005) also notes the destabilising threat of blackmail in his study of a later period in 'queer' London, *Queer London: perils and pleasures in the sexual metropolis*, pointing to a scandal from 1937 that exposed 'several men of good standing':

> The values of discretion, intimacy and privacy existed in a persistent tension with everyday social practice; respectable homosexual identities were unstable and problematic. (Houlbrook 2005, p. 209)

So in spite of Robb's self-contradictory assurances of widespread awareness of and de facto tolerance towards 'homosexuality', I think we need to acknowledge the political reality of these conformist pressures if we wish to get a sense of the position Isherwood found himself in, just as his reputation as a writer started to rise. While Isherwood does seem to have accepted his sexuality early, he was uncomfortable living it out within his own social milieu.

To find a place where he could live it, as an integrated part of his life, was not easy, given the dissonance with the social and political attitudes of his era.

Isherwood would not have found inspiration in the double lives led by earlier figures in 19th century queer history, such as Wilde and John Addington Symonds, both of whom married, sired children and carried on their same-sex love affairs behind the crumbling façade of their public personae (see Kaplan 2005; Robb 2003; Booth 2002). 'Private vice' might have been 'less disgraceful than a public breach of etiquette', in Robb's telling (p. 95), certainly, but the pressures were intolerable for all parties, and there was the constant fear of exposure. JA Symonds, who is remembered today as a pioneer in the history of 'gay' rights, struggled to come to terms with his sexuality and the conflicting demands of his public life, presented in his words as the 'perpetual discord between spontaneous appetite and acquired respect for social law' (cited Robb, p. 65). The flurry of activity by his literary executor, after his death, to destroy Symonds' correspondence and other papers, at the urging of his wife, makes particularly disturbing reading (Booth 2002). The lives of the wives, struggling to deal with the shame of incipient and actual scandals, is certainly worthy of more attention. (I wonder if Isherwood's almost intolerant criticism of bisexual Stephen Spender's choice to marry, later in the century, was informed by his personal instinct for integration against the great show of two-faced public respectability so evident in British society.)

To do justice to Robb's social history, I should acknowledge that at the same time as these hostile elements maintained their dominance in the wider society, politics and the law, Isherwood was in a real sense heir to a recent, dissident tradition that had mounted a challenge to conventional morality. Sheila Rowbotham identifies 'a culture of resistance that was both theoretical and lived against the grain', in her excellent biography of Edward Carpenter (2008, p. 209). 'Despite fear, ambivalence and mystification, an exploratory sexual culture was nevertheless defying conventional morality in private, unexpected places', she writes of his era (p. 203). Carpenter, the sandal wearing utopian socialist, who was born in 1844 and still publishing in the 1920s, had an early, life changing encounter with Walt Whitman (both through his writings and in person) and campaigned for the love of comrades for many years in a prolific output of pamphlets, books and lectures, endeavouring to inscribe a heroic myth of an 'intermediate sex' to counter the association of 'homosexuality' with 'degeneration', following the setback of the Wilde affair. Rowbotham rightly claims that 'the social meanings woven into the emerging conceptualisations of homosexual identity carried far-reaching challenges to the existing order' (p. 208) but while Carpenter was an adroit and influential propagandist in many campaigns—for changes in the status of women, workers' rights, prison reform and other social justice issues—and was able to form strong and lasting bonds of affection with many men within the alternative lifestyle he managed to forge for himself, it was this aspect of social change—his most deeply felt desire for a wide acceptance of 'homogenic' love—that was never fully realised in the wider society, despite his best efforts.

So, even though he was in a sense heir to this 'exploratory sexual culture' and his life overlapped with Carpenter's (his own mentor, E M Forster, had been mentored by Carpenter), Isherwood would leave Britain to be free of the stultifying ethos that still prevailed at home.

Isherwood sought long and hard to find a personal 'myth' (as Paul Piazza puts it in his study, *Christopher Isherwood: myth and anti-myth*) that would bring coherence to his existence. Denis Altman (2004) would like Isherwood, in retrospect, to have been more overt about his sexuality in his early work but, as Gore Vidal notes, 'the reticences of the Thirties forbade candor' (p. 18). It wasn't until his novel *The world in the evening*, published in 1954, that Isherwood began to explore queer themes in his own published work, and a homosexual character was not moved to centre stage until the short novel *A single man* (published in 1964).

This ease with his own non-conformist sexuality was not easily won, and was preceded by a series of displacements (both psychological and geographical) that put considerable pressure on his developing sense of who he was and what he might become.

Dis-locations

This is the wider social and cultural context for the personal dislocation Isherwood was experiencing—the psychological insecurities that were destabilising his sense of self at the very time he was being heralded by some (Somerset Maugham, for example) as the best novelist of his generation.

The first of these insults to Isherwood's psyche was the shock and depersonalisation that he underwent with his early initiation into boarding school life. Isherwood recalls how he was uprooted from life in the nursery with a doting nanny and transplanted to St Edmund's:

> [T]he images which remained in the memory are not in themselves terrible or rigorous: they are of boot-lockers, wooden desks, lists on boards, name-tags in clothes—yes, the name pre-eminently; the name which in a sense makes you nameless, less individual rather than more so: Bradshaw-Isherwood, C.W. in its place on some alphabetical list; the cold daily, hourly reminder that you are not the unique, the loved, the household's darling, but just one among many. I suppose that this loss of identity is really much of the painfulness which lies at the bottom of what is called Homesickness; *it is not Home that one cries for but one's home-self.* (qtd in Parker 2004, pp. 40–41; emphasis added)

This reminiscence is from the first draft of the biographical study Isherwood did of his parents (Huntington CI 1082: 81). The version published in *Kathleen and Frank* (1971) differs slightly (see Chapter 15, p. 285). As this was written so late in his life, this trope of the 'home self' is worth keeping in mind and I will return to it, for Isherwood's struggle to develop an integrated sense of identity in the face of hostile cultural forces is a central issue in his life, and the unorthodox means he employed to locate such a 'home' went beyond mere geography, or re-situating historical/cultural locales.

The 'loss of identity' expressed in this passage reveals, I would suggest, more than just nostalgia for the nursery; it is the call of an almost primal search for what he calls the 'home-self' that was to drive Isherwood's restless quest—for security, and for subject positions that rang true to his sense of personal integrity—through a series of relationships, and the restless geographical relocations that finally landed him in California in 1939. The written reminiscence dates from the 1960s, by which time, with the help of his guru, the writer had found a comfortable accommodation with the existential dilemma of being in the world, and in his own skin, but that was achieved only after finding his way through a number of powerful disorientations.

If the trope of the poor little boy at boarding school seems trite, it was at that time that his father was killed (near Ypres, in May 1915). Isherwood was still only ten. He had enjoyed an affectionate relationship with his father whose portrait, in the biography of his parents, depicts him as complex and sensitive, a cultivated man with a great fondness for painting and literature, as well as metaphysics. He was not afraid of showing what we might loosely call today his 'feminine side'—his fondness for knitting (even while at war) is endearing—especially in his correspondence with his fiancée, yet he did not hesitate to present himself for the rigours of warfare (he had served in the Boer War as well).

Re-locations

After the dis-location from social class, family and school, and encouraged by his new best friend WH Auden, Isherwood moved to Berlin. What did this re-location represent for him? Yes, there was the unapologetic youthful sexual experimentation: 'Berlin meant boys', as he wrote frankly in *Christopher and his kind* (1976, p. 2). It was also a rebellious slap in the face to Old England for the young writer to make his new home in the country that had brought about his father's death. If Oscar Wilde's exile in disgrace had been forced on him, Isherwood's was a voluntary escape from the pressures of conformity. While his mother was trying to encourage him to find a place in a society whose very values were crumbling, Isherwood resented what he saw as her retreat into the role of the Hero's Widow and her attempt to maintain the values of a world that was, for him, undergoing major renovations:

> [H]er will is the will of Nearly Everybody, and in their will is my death. *My* will is to live according to my nature, and to find a place to be what I am … even if my nature were like theirs, I should still have to fight them. (1976, p. 12)

Apart from the opportunities for guilt-free sexual liaisons, the 'rebellion' against the will of the mother was important for Isherwood to be able to believe in himself as a writer. This is from *Lions and shadows* (his first autobiography, published in 1938 by the Woolfs' Hogarth Press):

> Did I really want to sham my way through life, impressing other people, perhaps, but knowing myself for a coward at heart? Of course I didn't. Besides, what was going to happen to my work? As long as I remained a sham, my writing would be a sham too. (p. 312)

Rose Kamel notes that his coming of age had been too late for Isherwood to 'prove his manhood under fire' (1982, p. 163). Instead, in what she identifies as the 'reconstructive autobiographical drive', Isherwood turns to 'the weapon of language', to articulate his 'personal myth'. The 'apprentice', Christopher, was in the process of becoming Isherwood, 'the god-like creator of a written artifact—his autobiography' (p. 163). Kamel makes further, perceptive use of *Lions and shadows* when she cites this passage:

> Isherwood the artist was an austere ascetic, cut off from the outside world, in voluntary exile, a recluse. Even his best friends did not understand … he was subjected daily, hourly, to a 'test' of his own: the self-imposed Test of his integrity as a writer. (*Lions and shadows*, p. 97)

Kamel notes the self-mockery here but also acknowledges that Isherwood was serious about his 'calling', and compares him to James Joyce,

> who also regarded his Daedalus with some measure of ironic detachment but who nevertheless was prepared to use 'silence, exile, cunning' so that he might experience the divine power of creating the world and himself anew in his novels. (Kamel, p. 164)

Dis-locating himself from Britain and re-locating to Germany allowed Isherwood to consciously put some distance between himself and 'the upper middle class institutions he had come to despise' (Kamel, p. 164) and to rehearse different possibilities of self-hood. Learning a new language was an extension of that purpose. Here I could invoke postmodern theories on the role of language in constructing identity, but the linguists Edward Sapir and Benjamin Lee Whorf, who were Isherwood's contemporaries, approached the topic from a cross-cultural perspective that is particularly apt here. They pointed out that:

> No two languages are ever sufficiently similar to be considered as representing the same social reality. The worlds in which different societies live are distinct worlds, not merely the same world with different labels attached. (qtd in Daniel Chandler, 1994)

The Sapir/Whorff hypothesis suggests that the structure of one's language influences the manner in which one perceives and understands the world and, therefore, that speakers of different languages will perceive the world differently. Isherwood, the expatriate, enlists the learning of the new language (German) in the project of rehearsing new subject positions. Later, when he moves to California, he will 'metaphorically' absorb 'the language and customs of his adopted country' (Parker, p. 477) too. Furthermore, after almost half a lifetime of using British spelling, this person who wrote every single day and whose job consisted of putting down words on a page, had switched to American orthography (p. 477).

Everyone I have met who knew Isherwood has commented on Isherwood's taking up the American idiom. Yet, listening to his voice from various audio recordings, he didn't lose his British accent (Aldous Huxley, even less so). On the other hand, his long-term life companion, Don Bachardy, born and raised in California, took on Isherwood's own hybrid accent and manner of speaking. For someone working in the Hollywood studios and publishing with American houses, perhaps this is not as surprising as Parker finds it, but the eagerness to rehearse new identities is well taken.

The re-construction of identity through language was to figure in Isherwood's approach to religion, drawn from what he called the 'Indianness' of Vedanta, which was reinforced by the close textual work required for translation from the Sanskrit of the key Vedanta texts he worked on with Swami Prabhavananda.

Isherwood first visited Berlin briefly in March 1929, when he was 24, after dropping out of medicine and following the publication of his first novel, *All the conspirators*. He soon returned (November), and would remain based there until 1933. After brief liaisons with several 'rent' boys, he settled into a semi-permanent relationship with a young man named Heinz Neddermeyer. With an allowance from his gay uncle Henry, Isherwood wrote (mostly book reviews) and taught English conversation to supplement his income (and he was usually broke). This proved a fertile time for the fiction for which he was to become famous, documenting the period that saw the rise to power of Hitler.

War was stalking Europe and young men in Germany were being drafted for military service. By May 1933, he and Heinz were uprooted, moving from one European country to another so that Heinz could escape conscription. This period of desperate avoidance included an attempt by Isherwood (with his mother's assistance) to get his lover into Britain (otherwise Isherwood was loath to return there). But Heinz was rebuffed at the border, unable to maintain the fiction of coming into Britain at Kathleen's invitation to work as 'household help'. (The rebuff was revealed later to have been based on 'moral' grounds.) Despite their restless peregrinations, the attempts to avoid the inevitable were eventually frustrated in 1938, when Heinz was arrested and imprisoned as he crossed the border back into Germany, trying to renew a visa. After serving time in jail, Heinz was conscripted into the German army.

The enforced restlessness and series of disappointments placed Isherwood under intense stress. His disaffection from England, and his sense of the suffocating values that country represented to him, deepened, and Europe offered no safe haven. The diaries from this time—1938 in particular—provide a telling portrait of a self in crisis. After describing his body in less than flattering terms, this is how he addressed his 'character':

> I once read the title of a German novel (I forget the author's name) Der Mann ohne Eigens[c]haft. [Man without qualities/character/attributes]. For the more I think about myself, the more persuaded I am that, *as a person*, I really don't exist. That is one of the reasons why—as much as I'm tempted to try—I can't believe in any orthodox religion. I cannot believe in my own soul. No, I am a chemical compound, conditioned by environment and education. *My 'character' is simply a repertoire of acquired tricks,* my conversation a repertoire of adaptations and echoes, my 'feelings' are dictated by purely physical, external stimuli ... Der Mann ohne Eigens[c]haft is never to be trusted. (Diary 20 Aug 1938, qtd in Parker p. 391; emphasis added. The novel was by the Austrian author, Robert Musil.)

As his fame was increasing, so was his self-doubt. This passage and the sequences brought together by Parker (p. 390ff) show that Isherwood was better at seeing himself, faults and all, than many give him credit for.

If Isherwood was a man in search of a self, he was always prepared to re-locate, moving out of situations that he felt were suppressing his need to explore new and various possibilities of being and becoming, and his own life experience was constantly re-visited for its re-working into literary 'myth'. Much later, when he was lecturing on writing at the University of California, he said: 'I observe my life to find out its meaning. Maybe I write a novel to give it meaning' (Huntington CI 1070; qtd in Parker, p. 508).

Whether his writings were nominally fictive, or autobiographical (he often said he couldn't tell the difference), Isherwood was constantly probing, reflecting, and re-inventing versions of selfhood. Even the ostensibly fictional books would be recounted by a 'namesake' narrator. Critics unsympathetic to his quest sometimes take this self-referentialism as a form of egotism and a superficial reading of the autobiographical approach often conflates this technique with 'narcissism'. On closer attention, however, these simplistic interpretations fall apart.

Following his famous dictum 'I am a camera', the Isherwood namesake serves as an observer, a *point de repère* for the central characters. (The narrator-as-camera trope, which he was later to regret using, is famously attributed to Isherwood, but was first used by Katherine Mansfield.) It's interesting to hear Isherwood's own take on this issue, when he was interviewed after the much later publication of the autobiography *Christopher and his kind* (1967):

> I feel very strongly that the 'I' of the 1930s was quite different … not absolutely different, of course, but considerably different. This thing of being interested in myself was actually not nearly so true of that period because in the books I wrote about Berlin I was far more interested in describing other people. That way I reduced myself down to almost a kind of scanning device; an observer, a recorder, a camera—to coin an unfortunate phrase which became much too widely used about me. Because I really was never a non-mixer at all; quite the reverse! I didn't sit there watching all these people, I was up to the neck in their affairs and doings and often gravely compromised by them but you know, it all sounds like

> you sat kind of aloof watching the thing. That wasn't me at all. Nevertheless in this book it is, because I wasn't talking about myself then. But now I am; that's the only difference. (BBC Radio 2, 1979)

It is hard to sustain the charge that merely by having a narrator figure identified as Isherwood, or Christopher, or some combination of his names, amounts to narcissism, then. But as we will see, that is precisely what many commentators have done. Here he asserts that his focus was on *other* people.

In his review of the last of the autobiographies (*My Guru*) for *The New York Review of Books* in 1980, Stephen Spender noted that Isherwood has 'often been accused of egotism in his work':

> Yet in the sense in which the word is usually employed this seems to me to miss the point. The self-solidification of the true egotist acts as a wall between him and people. The strident ego sings only its own tune, blocks out the sounds of the others. The Isherwood ego is not of this kind. ('Issyvoo's conversion', p. 18)

Spender reads it, then, in the manner suggested by Isherwood himself:

> … it is an acute self-consciousness that makes even his most disinterested actions seem mockery to him. His ego is also an instrument of sensibility through which the people the novelist observes become transformed into characters in his fiction. (p. 18)

By the late 1930s, Isherwood was in fact increasingly disgusted with his ego self and its 'repertoire of acquired tricks'. Recalling his feelings on his departure to America with Auden, he wrote in his diary:

> Why were we going to America? I suppose, for myself, the chief reason was that I couldn't stop travelling … I was also running away from myself: that was why I never stayed anywhere long. I could remain in Portugal, for example, as long as I could believe in an objective Portugal. But sooner or later Portugal would dissolve and reveal itself as the all-too-familiar,

subjective 'Isherwood Portugal.' Then I fled in disgust. (13 Jan, 1939. *Diaries volume one*, p. 4)

Not everyone reads him as sympathetically as Spender. DS Savage, for example, wrote in 1979 (when most of the oeuvre had been published): 'his writing can now be seen to spring from a self-preoccupation of all but narcissistic intensity'. The misapprehension endured.

There are critical issues in play here that I believe need to be closely reviewed. If the rhetorical construction of the homosexual as a religious pariah by the churches has faded from public discourse (which I would dispute), in any case the marginalisation was enthusiastically taken up by psychology, and the pathological model has carried the baton of stigmatisation forward in a so-called 'secular' age. Savage's critique was published in the journal *Literature and Psychology*. His credentials appear to lean more toward the literary than the psychoanalytic, but the attempt to thoroughly psychoanalyse writers through their texts was fashionable at the time. By refusing to grant Isherwood's sincere spiritual practice any validity, in his representation of Isherwood Savage ignores the effects of that practice. If spirituality is as I have defined it—an inquiry into the nature of being—what is really going on in all of Isherwood's self-probings will be overlooked or misinterpreted by such narrowly-framed analyses. This characterisation of Isherwood is still extant even today, as became obvious in tracking the reviews of the Parker biography in 2004.

Narcissism and performance

'Narcissism' is a term used rather loosely by literary commentators, but seldom in the strictly clinical sense, even when they approach literature psychoanalytically.

In chapter two, I touched briefly on how the discourse of psychiatric medicine laid the groundwork for a pathologising of queer desire, and has been in its own way as insidiously homophobic as the rhetoric of the mainstream churches. To grapple with these negative constructions is part of the struggle undertaken by any queer man trying to recover an authentic selfhood. Isherwood could be viewed as a precursor in this and other areas, but many critics continue to characterise this search for self as narcissistic (somewhat crudely represented as self-obsession). To illustrate my point: reviewing the Parker biography for *The Irish Times* in 2004, Robert O'Byrne opined that Isherwood 'was vainglorious to a ludicrous degree' ('A fraudulent rebel', p. 13), claiming that 'like all self-centred people', Isherwood understood himself very poorly. 'Nobody fascinated Christopher Isherwood as much as Christopher Isherwood', O'Byrne continues, arguing that Isherwood's 'crystalline prose style managed to conceal that character flaw from readers' (p. 13). He depicts Isherwood as a 'fraudulent rebel ... without much honour or respect' (p. 13).

While acknowledging that some critics today still hold to that construction, it is my position that the confusion about identity and the 'interest in exploring himself' which O'Byrne finds so lamentable, was the spur for an interrogation of selfhood that drove Isherwood's writing, and his personal journey into Vedanta philosophy and practice, too. It is that very research which has revived interest in Isherwood today, not only from a queer readership, but also from an audience for whom the problematised self is a critical post-modern issue.

Isherwood was later to make great literary use of the trope of the 'performing' self, rehearsing different possibilities for identity. But at this stage, actually seeing through himself in this way was the beginning of a stripping away of illusions which can (and in his case, did) prepare him for either a psychological breakdown, or a spiritual breakthrough (or both) and, clearly, by the time he was preparing to leave Europe it was having a destabilising effect.

Isherwood asks himself what his faults are (whether he is a coward, a liar, selfish, vain, and so on) but, in an interesting foreshadowing of his later shift in metaphysics, he sees this as 'the interest which Der Mann ohne Eigens[c]haft is bound to feel in his *outward* personality just because he knows himself to have no inner life at all' (Parker, p. 392; emphasis added). Isherwood had begun to see himself simply as a 'character' who performed in public—at lectures and readings, when meeting strangers—just as much as he performed on the page (diary entry 1938; qtd in Parker, p. 393). Isherwood identifies the same hollowness in his relationship with his mother. '[T]ogether we admiringly regard Christopher Isherwood—our ventriloquist's dummy, our joint creation' (qtd in Parker, p. 393). He realises that to all his friends (save Auden, perhaps) he is a façade, and that he is in danger of being locked into that false front as a public persona to his readers. In the prefatory note to *Goodbye to Berlin* (1939), he writes:

> Because I have given my own name to the 'I' of this narrative, readers are certainly not entitled to assume that its pages are purely autobiographical or that its characters are libellously exact portraits of living persons. 'Christopher Isherwood' is a convenient ventriloquist's dummy, nothing more. (p. 9)

Within all this is an unflinching and devastating self-examination, and it was occurring at the height of his fame. Parker claims that Isherwood didn't *want* others to see behind the façade (Auden was the only exception) and he judges the disclaimer as 'already too late' (Parker, p. 395). But behind the performativity, the feeling of not knowing himself, with no reliable basis around which to form an integrated subjectivity, was acute and deeply felt. Were he content to bluff his way forward, regardless, perhaps Isherwood would deserve the kind of treatment he has often received for this confessionalism, but a more insightful view from someone like Lionel Trilling might recognise here the sincerity which he regarded as the *sine qua non* for 'authenticity' (Trilling 1972; see below). Without sincerity there would be no crisis of conscience.

A more sympathetic and expert reading of 'narcissism' can be drawn from the psychoanalyst DW Winnicott, of the British object relations school. Winnicott argues that when the environment does not support the developing personality, and requires the person to sacrifice his or her own spontaneous needs to adapt to environmental demands:

> there is not even a resting-place for individual experience and the result is a failure in the primary narcissistic state to evolve an individual. The 'individual' then develops as an extension of the shell rather than that of the core, and as an extension of the impinging environment. (*Through paediatrics to psycho-analysis* p. 212; qtd in Gunn, 2000, p. 111.)

Winnicott provides a reading of narcissism that makes it easier to understand Isherwood's increasing sense of unreality during the early decades, and his self-confessed inability to shake off the 'performing' self—an issue to which I will return shortly. Winnicott's use of 'resting-place' recalls Francisco Varela's treatment, noted in the previous chapter, where he discusses the wisdom traditions' concept of the virtuality of self: 'It is no ground whatsoever; it cannot be grasped as ground, reference point, or nest for a sense of ego' (Varela, p. 68). Winnicott continues:

> What there is left of a core is hidden away and is difficult to find even in the most far-reaching analysis. The individual then exists by not being found. The true self is hidden, and what we have to deal with clinically is the complex false self whose function is to keep this true self hidden. (qtd in Gunn, p. 111.)

It is clear from the reference to Robert Musil's 'man without qualities' that Isherwood was deeply dissatisfied with the 'complex false self' diagnosed by Winnicott and he would go on to make extensive literary use of the play of false selves (Faraone 2008, see below). It is interesting to contrast his representations of the confusion and disorientation of the 'complex false self' with the more assured handling of the trope in his later writings. In the later works, the result of his deep inquiry into the nature of what Winnicott calls the 'core' is quite discernible, but this only came about through his prolonged study and practice of Vedanta, as we will see in the next two chapters.

At this point in his life, however, Isherwood was dissatisfied with his own lack of what I would call 'authenticity'. This is a troubled term, I know, but its meaning—in the context of Isherwood's struggle to find a reliable basis for selfhood—will become clear. I use it partly with an existentialist connotation, but I am influenced by Lionel Trilling's *Sincerity and authenticity* (1972). 'Now and then,' begins Trilling, 'it is possible to observe the moral life in process of revising itself' (p. 1). Trilling was concerned to trace the shift whereby the process through which the arduous enterprise of sincerity (of being true to one's self), and the elevation of 'authenticity' as an ethical principle, came to occupy a place of supreme importance in the moral life.

This modern ideal of authenticity is read in a positive light by a cultural historian, then, as a sincere and rigorous quest, and characteristic of the times.

The confessional honesty of Isherwood's self-disclosure has sometimes led commentators to question his personal ethics. Perhaps DS Savage's fault was not so much his failure to acknowledge Isherwood's progress beyond this state—his critique was published late in Isherwood's life, after all—but that his lack of comprehension of Isherwood's years of Vedanta study and practice prevented the critic from allowing his subject to make any progress, and so he failed to recognise its influence and give it its due. Others, more charitably, have admired how Isherwood turned his obsessions into his art.

I am interested in the shifting subject positionality, its dis-location and re-location, and how radically altered this is by Isherwood's mid-life encounter with Vedanta. I have noted already that Isherwood himself becomes a character in many of the texts. Even where he re-works events and characters from his life into fiction, there's a 'Christopher' or a 'Christopher Isherwood', sometimes referred to in the third person, sometimes written as 'I'. In *Prater Violet* (1945), for example, the director Berthold Viertel (with whom Isherwood worked on a film in London) is affectionately transformed into the character Friedrich Bergmann, while Christopher Isherwood plays himself, or a version of himself carrying his own name, 'Christopher Isherwood'. In the earlier *Mr Norris changes trains* (1935; the US edition was titled *The last of Mr Norris*) in which the shady real-life figure of Gerald Hamilton becomes Mr Norris, 'William Bradshaw' (Isherwood's middle names) is the narrator. In the *Berlin stories* (US edition 1945), where his friend Jean Ross is transformed into Sally Bowles, he is, in the nomenclature of his landlady, 'Herr Issyvoo'.

There is more at stake here than narcissism and the simple plundering of Isherwood's own life experience as material for his fiction. If at first Isherwood found he couldn't really make a book work without placing himself, or a version thereof, into the story, as the kind of *point de repère* to which Spender alludes, this process led to some problems in the writing, as in the life. Isherwood explained the technique in an interview in 1972:

> The whole endeavour of the Christopher Isherwood persona in the novels is to be in the background as much as he can because what he is trying to

> do is tell a story. He is not telling *his* story, or only incidentally, and only just to explain why he was there with those people. (Geherin, p. 145)

Isherwood contrasts this point of view with his early novel *Lions and shadows*, which *is* about himself. He agrees that the persona as character creates problems in various texts, and finds it works best in *Prater Violet*. But the device started to wear thin early, as Spender was all too ready to point out to his friend:

> I can't help protesting against the little comic-cuts Charlie Chaplin figure into which you are so adept at turning yourself, especially as you are now called Isherwood in these stories. The self-portrait could scarcely—even in *Lions and shadows*—be more evasive. By sneering at the more self-pitying and even tragic aspects of yourself, you are really showing a typically English brand of dishonesty, which consists in admitting the real and then making it seem unimportant by the exercise of humour. (Letter to Auden and Isherwood, May 1938, qtd in Parker, p. 387)

(This critique came much earlier than the kinder, retrospective appraisal from Spender in 1980 that I quoted above.) The point is that at the time—he was still on the run in Europe—Isherwood shared this dissatisfaction. He responded to Spender that the 'Isherwood character' was 'an evasion and altogether too harmless and too knowing—"the sexless nitwit", as somebody called him', and he promised Spender that he would drop 'Isherwood' altogether in future.

Not simply a technical problem in the writing, then, this uneasiness was deeply felt, reaching into the very heart of his sense of self. But if he was dissatisfied with the method in the early writing, he hardly ever abandoned it, even as his sense of self stabilised. In fact, some commentators would say that most of the novels in which the Isherwood character bowed out of the picture—such as *A meeting by the river* (1967), or *The world in the evening* (1984)—were weaker for it, although this is not the case with *A single man* (1964). Even in the third autobiography, *Christopher and his kind*, published 1976, when he had a good three decades of Vedanta under his belt, he writes about 'Christopher' in the third person, which is an interesting choice to make in an autobiography. Whereas in the early years it can be read partly as the marker for a personal identity crisis, by this time the influence of Vedanta had matured both the man and the technique. (In the biography of his parents, *Kathleen and Frank*, which comes late in the oeuvre, he still refers to himself as 'Christopher', in the third person. The effect there, simply, is to keep the attention on the main protagonists.)

As the Vedanta practice and study deepened over decades, the spiritual work played into this examination and re-examination of versions of the self. Those interested in Eastern approaches to meditation, even in their hybrid forms, might recognise this other meaning track running here. By 1980, Spender was aware of the importance Isherwood's spirituality had had, so he was also not unaware of the parallels between the ironic literary positioning of the ego self and the detachment of the observing 'I', in its relation with the ego mind, that comes about through meditation practice. Although I will examine this more closely in the next two chapters, let me look at this issue briefly.

Detachment and the 'witness self'

Isherwood would have been cognisant of this trope of the 'witnessing self' that observes from a point of detachment the business of the everyday mind in the foreground of awareness. I have checked this with dedicated practitioners within the Ramakrishna Vedanta tradition—people who knew Isherwood and observed his practice. One of them, Pravrajika Vrajaprana, tells me:

> Swami Prabhavananda's instruction to him was to remember at all times that he was the Atman. If you really make a point of thinking of that and giving yourself that identity instead of all the other slippery ones, then you've got a core of stability deep within. There's nothing narcissistic about that. I think this made many people insecure, since they are made so differently. (Personal correspondence, October 2008)

I believe it was the growing awareness of this shift in point of view that provided a basis for the interrogation of the self that Rose Kamel and others have noticed at work in his writing. Commentary that merely psychologises the literary devices in play and fails to acknowledge the

Advaitist dimension to Isherwood's thinking neglects the psycho-spiritual dynamic processes that provide better insight into the work of this truly independent and original writer. As his meditation practice was sustained over many decades, this would have become more and more obvious to Isherwood, feeding the dissatisfaction and impatience with the petty personal self that mark his closely monitored journaling. Vrajaprana makes the point that:

> Chris's real *sadhana* [spiritual practice] was his practice of truthfulness, which began with unwavering truthfulness to himself … he didn't allow himself to get away with much. He was a harsh critic of himself as well as others. Nothing slides away. (Personal correspondence 2008)

In light of this assessment, the charges of narcissism begin to look facile. In fact, as this intriguing fragment turned up by Peter Parker would suggest, the insistence on focusing on the personal reveals a more challenging process at work:

> When I write a novel in the third person, I write a sentence and then I put the pen down. I am so bored by it. The knife is no longer in the wound, just suspended over it. (Letter to Jeremy Kingston, 1961; qtd in Parker 2004b, p. 583)

If the 'wound' is narcissistic, there is something more rigorous going on here than suggested by Savage's infantile characterisation.

Self-scrutiny and its reception

In the reception of Isherwood's work and reputation that was to follow, the exercise of 'honesty' (which could be characterised as self-scrutiny, rather than the mere 'self-absorption' of the egotist) becomes a mirror that, as often as not, reflects the values and biases of the reader. Reviewing Peter Parker's biography for *The Guardian* ('Wrestling with destiny'), Alan Hollinghurst doesn't flinch at the 'negative' traits in his subject. After noting the difficulties ('mutual exasperation and mistrust') experienced by Isherwood's friends—John Lehman (who was his editor), Stephen Spender, and the writer Dodie Smith—Hollinghurst recognises:

> I suspect he was funnier, and more fun to be with than quite comes through the biographical record, where the evidence against him is cumulatively crushing: he was vain, cowardly, malicious, misogynistic, despotic. (p. 9)

(Hollinghurst, however, is unable to see beyond Parker's construction of Isherwood's Vedanta study, which he characterises as an 'extended dim comedy of misapplied energy' [p. 9].)

Fellow writers tend to show more appreciation for Isherwood than do literary critics, but Hollinghurst's next, prescient point is one that those who accuse Isherwood of 'fraudulence', or dishonesty, need to factor into their appraisals:

> The huge mitigating factor is that all these judgments were endorsed a hundred times over by Isherwood himself. His diaries record recurrent struggles to understand the enigma of his own personality, his spiritual emptiness and addictiveness. (p. 9)

Thom Gunn gives an astute reading of Isherwood's writing technique in a 1990 article for *PN Review*. 'It seems artless,' Gunn writes, 'but Isherwood was never artless. Rather, he became a master of self-concealing artfulness' (p. 40). Gunn shows insight not only into the technical skill; he is aware of the religious element, too, even where it is subtly concealed in the text, and he is one of the very few commentators who recognises that, for Isherwood, 'a ceaseless self-exposure is a religious as well as a stylistic necessity' (p. 40). This is crucial to understanding the point of his quasi-*confessional* practice.

Many of Isherwood's papers, manuscripts and correspondence are collected at the Huntington Library in San Marino, California. Reviewing an exhibition staged at the Huntington to celebrate the hundredth anniversary of Isherwood's birth, Bernard Weinraub wrote:

> The exhibition tries to place Isherwood in a literary landscape where critics often ignored him, though writers lavished praise on him. Graham Greene said one novel, *The last of Mr. Norris* [published in the UK as *Mr. Norris changes trains*] was 'a permanent landmark in the literature of our time.' Gore Vidal called him 'the best prose writer in English'. (Weinraub 2004, D5)

Weinraub also quotes James Berg, co-editor of the collection *The Isherwood century*:

> British critics and the New York literary establishment marginalized Isherwood, usually discussing his being one of the first significant gay writers but never his literary contributions. (D5)

Weinraub also quotes Chris Freeman saying that 'British critics consistently asserted that Isherwood's only good writing took place in the 1930's in Europe, before he moved to the United States, where he became a pacifist and a naturalized citizen and took up Eastern religion' (D5). Unlike the British critics, Freeman asserts that Isherwood's 'best work' took place in the 1960s in California, citing titles such as *Down there on a visit* and *A single man* (D5).

Researching the critical reception of the Parker biography in the literary press during 2004, I found that the alleged British ignorance of the writing of the later period was almost universally evident. Even in a sympathetic treatment by Alan Taylor (in *The Sunday Herald*), who notes that Isherwood's books 'were ignored in his homeland, a revenge, it has been suggested, for Isherwood's betrayal', Taylor unwittingly *contributes* to the oversight:

> The literature of the 20th Century would be the poorer without *Goodbye to Berlin*, *Mr Norris changes trains* and *Lions and shadows*. But in comparison to some contemporaries—Graham Greene, Anthony Powell and Evelyn Waugh—his promise was never fully realised. (p. 11)

Typically, Taylor considers no titles from the American period. Again, the exceptions to this gross oversight come from fellow writers, such as Alan Hollinghurst, who finds:

> The one fierce success of these years is *A single man* (1964), the short account of a day in the life of an ageing gay university professor in southern California. Rightly, Parker thinks it 'Isherwood's most profound and most skillfully written book'. (p. 9)

This is the same title that Dennis Altman, in his review of the Parker biography for the Melbourne *Age*, finds 'slight', (p. 4), yet elsewhere, novelist Edmund White calls *A single man* the 'founding text of gay fiction' (p. 3). White also acknowledges that the diaries and other posthumous publications have revised Isherwood's reputation 'downwards', showing him to be 'alcoholic, bitchy, vain and ill-tempered, like many writers, perhaps, but with this difference: he is exceptionally self-aware and unusually eager to reform' (p. 3). White finds Parker's 'a fairly sour picture of a man who was famous for his charm' and, almost alone among reviewers, recognises a jeering tone behind the biographer's studied neutrality:

> Sometimes while reading this biography I felt that Isherwood was being treated by the author as an impostor, a not terribly talented or disciplined writer. Although the conclusion to this very long book is even-handed, in countless parenthetical remarks scattered throughout, there is a jeering, mocking tone. (p. 4)

Alone among the reviewers in acknowledging Isherwood's Vedanta-related works, the pamphlets, the biography of Ramakrishna, and the translations that he worked on with his Swami, White is also the only one to recognise how the Parker biography manages to 'cast doubt on Isherwood's religious sincerity' (p. 4), which is a significant choice for a biographer to make. White goes on:

> Since the source of these aspersions is Isherwood's own diary and letters, it is rather as if a biographer of Chekhov were to read his constant complaints about his house full of guests and his inability to write a novel, and comment, 'Poor Chekhov was so relentlessly sociable that he never managed to write anything important'. (p. 4)

White praises Parker's mammoth biography, but concludes:

> I'm not sure that he is entirely in sympathy with Isherwood, however. The novelist seems in this version a bit too narcissistic, flashy, triumphant for Parker's taste; he appears to be more in tune with Isherwood's starchy mother and extravagant loser of a brother. (p. 4)

But White is the exception. Again and again, as reviewer after reviewer across the world re-iterates the habituated readings, one struggles to recognise Isherwood behind the straw man they make of him, but the mistake is re-inforced in scholarly literary analyses, too. DS Savage epitomised this occlusion in the vigour with which he maintained his line on Isherwood's sexuality as regressive. He refused to allow his subject any conscientious ethical or moral courage (and pointedly ignores evidence to the contrary). Savage would have it that:

> a price had to be paid for the homosexual regression which affected Isherwood's entire career. He remained, in the JM Barrie-Peter Pan tradition, the little boy who refused to grow up. (p. 77)

Savage reads Isherwood's choice to drop out of Cambridge as evidence of this infantilism:

> The capricious spoiling of his examination papers which led to his resignation from college, and the abandonment of his medical studies in London, were acts of self-sabotage altogether in line with his reversion to schoolboy rebelliousness. (p. 77)

Were he to have applied some of the psychologising he was so fond of, perhaps Savage could have recognised the need—especially strong for a homosexual youth—to separate his own developing subjectivity from the overwhelming influence of his mother, and construed this instead as a healthy, rather than merely petulant, or rebellious, urge. Peter Parker's much-praised portrayal of Isherwood's younger brother Richard, who was also 'homosexual' but failed miserably to eke out an existence independent from his mother (when she finally died, they were sharing a bed, to keep warm in the crumbling family mansion), is a sad if salutary counter-point; but of course this information was not available to Savage in 1979. (Isherwood dedicated the volume *Exhumations* to Richard, and allowed the family estate to flow to his brother following the death of their uncle.)

In his intention to reduce all of the young man's choices to regressive tendencies, rather than important choices in his very personal individuation process, Savage presses his point home:

> Thus was the way cleared for him to leave England and respectability for a bohemian life in Berlin, where he was to encounter Sally Bowles and the other retarded adults in whom he was to take such unaffected delight. The burning of boats which preceded his departure for Germany, and his wide-eyed captivation by thrilling tales of the sexual perversities available in Berlin, are of a piece with the avoidance of an adult vocation, and with the relapse into self-acceptance as a homosexual. (p. 77)

Terms such as 'retarded', 'perversities' and notably, 'relapse', clearly indicate Savage's standpoint. If Berlin represented an unparalleled opportunity for Isherwood (then in his twenties) to explore his sexuality, Savage's alliterative description of the city as 'the pullulating centre of European profligacy', is laughably lurid. Looking back, Isherwood noted ruefully: 'seldom have wild oats been sowed so prudently' (*Christopher and his kind*, p. 28). Isherwood addressed the attraction of the city in a radio interview around the same time that Savage was writing his skewed characterisation:

> One of the great attractions was the 'boy life' which was supposed to be going on there; the gay life was supposed to be very very permissive and easy to follow. That now feels very strange to me. I realise that it was not nearly as permissive and accessible according to modern standards as people believe and as I believed at the time. But really you know the great thing was simply getting away from England to some other place. Getting away, shedding to some extent the whole British persona and … learning to speak, at least to some degree, German, so that I could be a different person with a different language. That gave me a great feeling of security. (BBC radio 2, 1979)

The desire to get away from England and all that it stood for, is somewhat understated in this interview. John Lehman's 1987 memoir notes how strongly Isherwood actually felt about the Mother Country. Lehman reports that Isherwood was 'suspicious of him as being in league with the "enemy", a phrase which covered everything he had, with a pure hatred, cut himself off from in English life' (qtd Vidal, p. 13). Isherwood was amused by the description, and writes in *Christopher and his kind* that 'C' *was* 'suspicious of and on his guard against' this seeming 'incarnation of authority—benevolent authority, but authority, none the less.' (He sees the poet in him as Lehman's saving grace ...)

So was it 'authority'—the representation of the entire British system of power—that rankled with him? Was it just that Berlin gave him the freedom to pursue his sexual desires, or a deeper yearning to explore who he was, including the sexuality? It is clear that he didn't feel he could do that in England (family bequests notwithstanding). There is a school of thought, contrary to that of Savage, which would say that to embrace your sexuality is a choice made more from courage than a mere refusal to 'grow up'. Typically, Isherwood was able to present that possibility humorously:

> Christopher was delighted with his way of life and with himself for living it—so much so that he became bumptious, and actually wrote to a woman he knew in England, telling her: "I am doing what Henry James would have done, if he had had the guts." (*Christopher and his kind*, p. 31)

Isherwood's desire to write was his other strong drive, as John Lehman tells it. Perhaps he felt freer to do that beyond Britain as well. He recognises in the interview that it was 'a very serious step and ... a prudent step' even if, at the time 'it seemed to be plunging into the abyss of vice and general depravity ... at a rather late age,' he adds, '... an alarmingly late age; I was already 25!' (BBC radio 2, 1979).

Savage is content to ignore all these indicators of ironic self-awareness, pressing his thesis further through his reading of the 1938 novel *Mr Norris changes trains* (which he calls 'a minor masterpiece'). He does get the central issue right: viz., 'Bradshaw's search for personal identity through association with the innocently naughty Arthur Norris' (p. 72), and the struggle to maintain a personal ethical position under the influence of a more powerful personality. But Savage charges that the writer's interest in his characters reveals a preoccupation with the immature, and 'implies some identification with these qualities in the writer himself' (p. 72).

It is clear that Isherwood had struggled to find a personal ethical position against the impact of powerful social forces (as many young men do) as his sense of self evolved and these texts provide a clear example of Isherwood turning his obsessions into his art. Savage fails to recognise not only the comedy in these portrayals but also the ironic distancing that his use of a namesake narrator ('William Bradshaw') allows Isherwood. Savage calls these eponymous narrators 'mouthpieces', which they seldom are, complaining that Isherwood's detachment 'conceals an actual intense complicity with his empty-headed, puerile subjects' (p. 73). By doggedly and reductively collapsing the reflections, Savage misses what in later, more sophisticated uses of the technique becomes a source of great insight, in Isherwood's interrogation of the contingencies of identity. Even while acknowledging that other sections of *Down there on a visit* were 'written with the directness of Isherwood at his near best' and 'not lacking a certain pathos', show 'as little capacity as ever on the writer's part for rising above and evaluating the situation he depicts.' (p. 83). Earlier he complains about the author's unreadiness, for all his self-concern, to 'grasp, evaluate and comprehend experience so as to grow inwardly to maturity' (p. 72), the Savage diagnosis of immaturity is decidedly premature. He completely accepts the neo-Freudian proposal that the 'homosexual perversion (for as such Freud certainly regarded it)' (p. 79) was 'generally inseparable from all such psychological regressions to an earlier stage of development' (p. 80) and offers the diagnosis that 'it is not homosexuality as such, but the regression to infantilism upon which it hangs, which is the heart of the matter' (p. 85). On the one hand he criticises what he calls 'the relapse into self-acceptance as a homosexual' (p. 77), but on the other, quoting the 'Mr Lancaster section from *Down there on a visit*, where Isherwood is ruminating over the adolescent self, Christopher, he ignores the fact that Isherwood diagnoses his own state of mind, without idealising his subject. Reading through a psychoanalytic lens he has this to say about the 'relapse':

> it is a protest against one's being in the world and a refusal to accept responsibility for culture and history, at the core of which lies an essential refusal to be one's self, or more accurately, to *become* that which one *is*. And it is almost certainly related, in some arcane way, to an original reluctance, or half-refusal, to accept the conditions of physical life and birth. (p. 85)

Mario Faraone traces the literary trope of the mirror and the study of images as a thread running through Isherwood's oeuvre. Mirrors produce images as versions of the real and, as a literary device, are frequently deployed as a vehicle to raise questions about the difference between appearance and reality—a very fitting device for a writer preoccupied with examining versions of the self. While Faraone attributes the fascination originally to Isherwood's fondness for the cinema, he notes that the way the writer uses the motif changes, through what he identifies as two different stages in the writer's development:

> In Isherwood's so-called 'first narrative stage', that stretches from *All the conspirators* (1928) to *Lions and shadows* (1938) and *Journey to a war* (1939), the presence of the mirror assumes modalities which are distinct from those belonging to the conversion period to Vedanta, the Hindu-oriented philosophy and religion, when a shift in his deployment of the image reflects the shift in his ontology. (Faraone 2010)

Faraone discusses an early use of a mirror reflection in the novel *Mr Norris*: 'At this stage of growth, William-Isherwood is the Lacanian child who scarcely recognizes himself in the image held by the mirror' but the mirror 'soon takes on the characteristics of investigator and becomes a vehicle to study the author's changes of character and personality' (2010).

The Narrative 'I'

At this point I want to examine briefly how this struggle to locate a reliable 'self' can be read in the textual narrativisations. Rose Kamel draws a distinction between the 'historic self' (in Alfred Kazin's terms, the narrator's 'felt relation to the life data themselves') and the 'fictive self' (Kamel 1982, p. 162). She invokes Northrop Frye, and other recent theorists of autobiography,

> who observe that 'selfhood' evolves from a confluence of literary conventions … onto which the writer's imaginative reordering of memory imposes a character, theme, point of view and style, thus making of selfhood an artifice and of autobiography a fictive pattern. (p. 162)

Kamel notes Isherwood's characteristic use of himself, or a version of himself, as a character, and how his plots 'roughly correspond' to events in his life and how this all re-worked into 'building a personal myth' (p. 162). Others have remarked on the 'fertile ambiguities' (Rosenthal 1994, p. 760) provided by having a character with the same name as the writer, whereby that narrator and the character 'Christopher', or 'Isherwood', are not perfectly aligned with Isherwood, the author. But Kamel recognises another issue underlying this practice: that for Isherwood 'the centrality of his selfhood' had become problematical. The myth is consistently 'unravelled' by the very fictive strategies that 'distance him from us and distance his multifaceted 'selves' from one another' (p. 162), she writes, but she also recognises the artifice at play in the texts:

> His autobiographies suggest that we read him as a fictional character described by a somewhat unreliable narrator in turn created by an implied omniscient author who can erase and cancel out his narrator at will. (p. 163)

While Kamel's analysis of the style is purely literary, Gore Vidal recognises the cinematic influence in the technique: 'This particular *auteur du cinéma* seldom shoots a scene without placing somewhere on the set a mirror that will record the *auteur* in the act of filming' (1976, p. 14). Isherwood was an avid moviegoer and worked on films in London even before his departure for Los Angeles.

We see this device at work on multiple levels in 'Mr Lancaster', from *Down there on a visit* (1962b) in which he juggles with points of view of himself as narrator and protagonist at different points in time. The narrative draws on experiences Isherwood had decades previously (he dates it as 1928, when he was twenty-three years old) when he had holidayed with an older bachelor with distant ties to his family (a cousin of his mother), who invited young Christopher to visit him in 'a North German Harbour city'. Writing about himself in retrospect produces a distance that allows for ironic detachment from his former, callow self and the creative licence to re-work events and the characters. However, it also acknowledges a journey from one subject position to another. Again, the effect is cinematic.

'Now at last, I'm ready to write about Mr. Lancaster,' writes Isherwood, with the wisdom of hindsight dating a completely new chapter in his life (1962b, p. 89). But he pauses:

> [B]efore I slip back into the convention of calling this young man 'I', let me consider him a separate being, a stranger almost, setting out on this adventure … For of course he is almost a stranger to me. (p. 91)

At first he seems to be only giving himself the licence to re-invent:

> I have revised his opinions, changed his accent and his mannerisms, unlearned or exaggerated his prejudices and his habits. We still share the same skeleton, but its outer covering has altered so much that I doubt if he would recognise me on the street. (p. 91)

But in the next three sentences, Isherwood makes an almost imperceptible segue into metaphysics:

> We have in common the label of our name, and a continuity of consciousness; there has been no break in the sequence of daily statements that I am I. But *what* I am has refashioned itself through out the days and years, and until now almost all that remains constant is the mere awareness of being conscious. And that consciousness belongs to everybody; it isn't a particular person. (p. 91, emphasis in original)

That is a subtle introduction of a far-reaching philosophy, which hints that the 'I' looking back has made a very long journey indeed. The distance is not only in time, and the shift is not only due to the inability of an unreliable memory to reconstruct the world of an earlier self. It hints at an awareness of a depersonalised consciousness that transcends the individual, which he will explore, later, in *A single man*, a novel published in 1964, when he had engaged with Vedanta study and practice for more than twenty years.

But Isherwood does not overplay his hand. He moves back to a more conventional apologia: 'The Christopher who sat in that taxi is, practically speaking, dead; he only remains reflected in the fading memories of us who knew him' (p. 92). (Perhaps not so conventional, after all: 'of *us* who knew him'?) He is writing about himself at a younger age, but the point of view has shifted in a way that allows the adult Isherwood as narrator to exist alongside his former self, both contemporaneously with the youthful Christopher *and* as the mature narrator. So, even while he continues with the conventional commentary, a double-lensed irony is at play:

> I can only reconstruct him from his remembered acts and words and from the writings he has left us. He embarrasses me often, and so I'm tempted to sneer at him; but I will try not to. I'll try not to apologise for him either. After all, I owe him some respect. In a sense he is my father, and in another sense my son. (p. 92)

Having given himself the room, he deftly places the young man's naïve attitudes:

> His life has been lived, so far, within narrow limits and he is quite naïve about most kinds of experience; he fears it and yet he is wildly eager for it. To re-assure himself, he converts it into epic myth as fast as it happens. He is forever play-acting. (p. 92)

The younger character tells himself a story as a kind of protection from the unpredictable opinions of the world. While he keeps the news of the publication of his first book a secret, still he fantasises that they might read about it in a newspaper review. But he pushes such hope aside, as:

> All literary critics are corrupt and in the pay of the enemy … And why … put your trust in treacherous hopes of this kind, when the world of the epic myth offers unfailing comfort and safety? (p. 93)

Isherwood pushes the grandiosity to the limit, in a charming characterisation of the shifting uncertainties of callow self-absorption. The youngster imagines looking back from a point ten years in the future, when the publication of *All the conspirators* will have 'marked the beginning of the modern novel as we know it' (p. 93). But Isherwood, the mature narrator, soon pulls back:

> No, I will never sneer at him. I will never apologise for him. I am proud to be his father and his son. I think about him and I marvel. But I must beware of romanticising him … I keep forgetting that he is as blind to his future as the dullest of the animals. As blind as I am to mine. (p. 93)

In her memoir *Tiger's eye*, Inga Clendinnen invokes this same passage from 'Mr Lancaster' as she probes the reality of the self, viewed at different ages:

> Am I that person? Is my consciousness really continuous? To put it more elaborately; it may not only be a question of whether I state my memories truthfully (sometimes), or whether I remember accurately (I do and I don't), but whether the 'I' is sufficiently continuous to claim possession of those early memories at all. (p. 238)

Having opened up the point of view and exploited the possibilities for humour, Isherwood zooms out: 'Now, as the taxi ride comes to an end, I shut down my own foresight and try to look out through his eyes' (p. 93). After this delicious placement of the relationship between self as narrator and former self as *ingénu*, Isherwood takes his junior self on his first overseas adventure.

Later in the same piece, he uses a mirror as a device to turn the sense of self around for appraisal. Young Christopher has been abandoned, without explanation, outside a banquet, when his host is involved in a mysterious annual meeting:

> Very very occasionally in the course of your life—goodness knows how or why—a mirror will seem to catch your image and hold it like a camera. Years later, you have only to think of that mirror in order to see yourself just as you appeared in it then. You can even recall the feelings you had as you were looking into it. (p. 105)

He goes further back in time to gather another example:

> For example, at the age of nine, I shot a wildly lucky goal in a school football game. When I got back from the field, I looked into a mirror in the changing room, feeling that this improbable athletic success must somehow have altered my appearance. It hadn't; but I still know exactly how I looked and felt. (p. 105)

This viewing and reviewing the self at different points in time works as comic play at one level, and at another as the kind of arc of character development typical of a *Bildungsroman*; but it also lays the groundwork for a new and different philosophical standpoint. Thus, while Rosenthal may note Isherwood's fascination with the 'shifting, elusive selves that exist in a single person's lifetime' (1994, p. 762), I suggest that in the mature period there is a significant shift, philosophically, in addition to the technical interest Rosenthal proposes when he points to 'the challenges those different selves pose to the writer in both trying to understand and then to represent them in works of fiction and autobiography' (p. 762). The mastery of the multi-focal point of view works on the reader, too. Gore Vidal comments on the 'alarming effect' achieved by the 'sly use' of shifting pronouns: 'You never know quite where you stand in relation to an Isherwood work' (1976, p. 10).

Rosenthal, Vidal, Clendinnen and Kamel, already cited, note how the play of versions of the self becomes the very form and subject of the writing, but I am turning the screw another notch by drawing attention to this additional layer of awareness operating here. Written well after his encounter with Vedanta, this text, 'Mr Lancaster', shows that Isherwood is by now able to play confidently with the questioning of what is 'real' about the versions of the self. So, we should be able to recognise this as a distinct progression from the 'comic cuts' performativity that Spender (and Isherwood himself) criticised in the earlier phase, which reflected his own psychological insecurities. By this point—writing 'Mr Lancaster'—he had not only been meditating regularly, he was editing the Vedanta Society magazine, and engaged in close study, with his guru, of key texts of the Advaita Vedanta tradition, as they prepared new English translations for publication. (He was also, by now, in a relatively stable relationship.)

But I am getting ahead of my own narrative. Let me backtrack to that earlier period when Isherwood was in search of a self and rehearsing new possibilities of selfhood in Berlin. Jamie Carr is struck, in reading the correspondence from the 1930s between Isherwood and his mother, by 'the increasing insecurity and sense of urgency the letters convey as the decade unfolds' (2007, p. 171). We have already noted the specific causes of the anxiety Isherwood was experiencing during that period, and the destabilising effects of that anxiety. We might read the textual rendering of the self as a literary analogue that reflects both the personal and the wider social and political uncertainties of what has been called the 'Age of Anxiety', turned into literary aesthetic form that effectively underscores 'the relation between the historical and the personal' that Carr notes. (While the phrase was born to typify the period between the two World Wars, WH Auden's Pulitzer-prize winning poem of the same name, composed as 'A Baroque Eclogue', first published in 1947, is set in a war-time bar in New York. It was turned into a ballet, with choreography by Jerome Robbins and set to Leonard Bernstein's 2nd Symphony, which was based on Auden's poem.)

If, in telling the stories of their lives, queer folk are 'not just reporting the past but also shaping the future, forging an identity as much as revealing it', as Edmund White says (p. ix), Isherwood's personal myth was still a work in progress. Initially, on arriving in California, his output was sporadic. In 1939 he wrote to his friend and editor John Lehman that he was tired of 'strumming on that old harp, the ego, darling Me' (qtd in Parker p. 436). The hollowness he felt had been assuaged somewhat by a brief interest in the progressive ideas of the British anthropologist John Layard who had so impressed WH Auden, and whose ideas Auden had introduced, in turn, to Isherwood. Auden was deeply interested in psychoanalysis and brought Freud and others to the attention of his friend (Osborne 1980). Isherwood acknowledges his 'phase of Freudian myth-making' in *Kathleen and Frank* (p. 133).

Layard had taken up the ideas of an American psychologist named Homer Lane who had pushed the 'Doctrine of original virtue'. Lane proposed that 'human nature is innately good; the unconscious processes are in no way immoral' (qtd in Parker 2004, p. 163). As an antidote to the religious notion of Original Sin, Lane held that 'the only sin was that of disobedience to the inner law of our own nature' (p. 163) and Isherwood cites this passage from Layard-Lane early in *Christopher and his kind*, as 'Life-shaking words!' (p. 2).

These were influential ideas at the time, and must have prepared the ground for Isherwood's acceptance of the concept of a personal 'dharma'. The idea that repression led to neurosis, which was to become commonplace in future decades, as psychological discourse increasingly entered popular parlance, was accompanied by the corollary belief that this repression could manifest itself in criminal activity or disease. If, as Parker summarises the theory, 'psychological and physical health could only be achieved by being true to yourself' (p. 163), Isherwood—as a prime example of the de-centred psyche—was still having trouble locating that elusive self. Yet, as we have seen, the social requirement for hypocrisy (Wilde, Symonds etc.) did not sit comfortably with this new thinking. As we have seen, if there were models for hypocrisy available in Edwardian times, Isherwood refused the invitation to respectability as a mask in the performative play of socially sanctioned hypocrisy. He was engaged in a struggle that would later render him a role model for a generation of men seeking the authenticity of a life 'outside the closet'. So, I would have to place the influence of Layard and Homer Lane solidly within the context of Trilling's 'sincerity' and 'authenticity'.

Isherwood had taken the opportunity to gain some illumination about the 'meaning' of his sexuality, psychologically constructed, through his association with the notorious research institute founded by Magnus Hirschfeld in Berlin (quite possibly the only city in Europe where such an establishment could flourish, albeit briefly). Sympathetic as Hirschfeld undoubtedly was—and he was soon to be hounded out of the country by the Nazis, who later destroyed the Institute and ceremoniously burned the contents of its unique research library—he contributed, perhaps unwittingly, to a developing discourse which would increasingly tend to pathologise 'deviant' sexualities. His diagnosis of

Isherwood's personal sexuality as 'infantile' would scarcely have helped the young analysand go forward.

DS Savage relied heavily on this pathologising construction to read Isherwood's quest for an authentic sexuality unsympathetically, but Lionel Trilling's analysis of the times provides a more constructive contextualisation. In *Sincerity and authenticity* Trilling makes a distinction between two notions of selfhood. He proposes that 'sincerity', or being true to yourself, with an eye to being true to others, had been 'the dominant concern of Renaissance and early modern thought and literature, from Shakespeare through to Rousseau'. But he identifies 'another conception that gained momentum throughout the 19th century, beginning with Wordsworth, and emerging with full force in the 20th, that presented a new, more morally demanding ideal of being what or who one is, apart from all external conditions' (p. 1).

What is important at this point is to recognise, simply, that Savage's charges of an immature obsession with the self as all that is going on here are myopic. For, in this reading of texts composed in the writer's early years, Savage completely misses the irony, the comedy and the youthful, experimental nature of this phase of Isherwood and his characters' lives. By relocating to Berlin in the early 1930s, Isherwood was taking on the task of coming into his own conscientiously held positions. He came to recognise, for example, that the Marxism of his friend Edward Upward, that he went along with for a few years, was not his own:

> From the very beginning, I now realize, I have made a mess of my leftism. Laziness, dilettantism and cowardice have prevented me from doing the only possible thing: becoming a humble rank-and-file worker, as you did. Then this stupid little phase of notoriety as a writer pitchforked me into the limelight as Wystan's [Auden's] second fiddle … I don't belong in any movement; and I cannot really take sides in any struggle. My only integrity can be to see the members of both sides as people, only as people, and to deplore their sufferings and crimes as personal sufferings and personal crimes. ('Letter to Edward Upward', 6 Aug, 1939, qtd in Parker, pp. 445, 446)

Apart from the important shift—'to see the members of both sides as people'—that would become the turning point in his move towards pacifism, I want to flag the rigorous tone of Isherwood's principled self-scrutiny here. As we have seen, Edward Upward had established himself very early on in Isherwood's life—at the time of his refusal to take confirmation in the Anglican faith—as a kind of ethical touchstone. Few of the critics who find him so wretchedly lacking in 'commitment' to causes admit that they are prone to take their cue from Isherwood's own critical self-revelation, without giving due weight to the conscientiousness exposed by that scrutiny. If at times Isherwood's self-portrayal might be construed as 'performative'—self-abnegation as part of the charming persona he was noted for—the ability to see himself in a less than flattering light and expose himself this way, even in the public texts (as opposed to the diaries), was a quality that Isherwood's guru would later recognise as essential to the writer's spirituality. That is to say, this self-scrutiny ('the knife in the wound'), which was part and parcel of his approach to writing and which was deepened by his spiritual practice, would become a strength, a possibility that Savage—by refusing to take into account Isherwood's spiritual praxis and allow for any maturation to occur—was simply unwilling to recognise.

Goodbye to Berlin

By 1937 Heinz was in jail, and Isherwood had to go back to England, which no longer felt like home. He had been with Heinz for five years. He was 33 years old. He had already published *All the conspirators, The memorial*, and *Mr Norris changes trains*, and written two plays with Auden. Despite the 'infantile' diagnosis he received from German sex researcher Magnus Hirschfeld (and later, from Savage), Isherwood had really worked at sustaining the relationship against great odds and, in the process, he had discovered a new quality in himself, finding that he wanted 'to be strong—to give protection, like a tree' (diary, 19 Nov 1937; qtd in Parker, p. 362). The reference could be construed as a hint of maturation in Isherwood's relationships. Even while continuing to seek out the companionship of a younger male, the extended duration of the friendship had allowed him to discover something about the nature of this protective, quasi-paternal potential in himself. He understood that this wasn't mere conceit; 'it is part of my deepest nature', he wrote (p. 363). Later, when he settled into a long-term partnership with the artist Don Bachardy, this would be expressed even more thoroughly, as he mentored the younger man's continuing cultural education and career path.

This possibility doesn't figure in the strictly psychopathological reading by Savage. For a scholar to present this reductive reading in 1979, ignoring decades of published work from Isherwood himself, shows not only how far a critic might be prepared to go in ignoring evidence that doesn't fit his thesis, but how deeply entrenched these fixed representations are.

I discussed the mentoring aspects of the relationship of the older man with a younger man in ancient Greece (the model of the *erastes/eromenos* pairing) with Bachardy in California, in January 2005. In the Greek model, the relationship was not solely one of desire; the older man was required to help the younger; there was supposed to be an educational benefit, an ethical training, a responsibility for the younger man's care. Bachardy said to me:

> Everything that I've learned in my life that means most to me all came directly from Chris. He absolutely transformed my life. And I tested him far more severely even than he tested Prabhavananda and I never got a false note out of that man. (See Marsh, 'Portrait of an artist as a Zen monk', p. 16)

(Isherwood's mentorship of his younger partner—which flowered in the development of Bachardy's remarkable talent as a portraitist—is confirmed by the testimony in the recent documentary film: *Chris and Don: A love story*, 2007.)

But all that is yet to come. Uprooted from Germany, with his first really sustained relationship shattered by the Nazis and at a loss for what to do next, Isherwood took up the opportunity to travel to China with Auden, as a war correspondent. Isherwood was acutely aware of the incongruity of their amateur role, and presents their project with some rueful humour, contrasting himself and Auden with the 'real' war correspondents:

> This wasn't a dream, or a boy's game of Indians. We were adult, if amateur, war-correspondents entering upon the scene of our duties. But, for the

> moment, I could experience only an irresponsible, schoolboyish feeling of excitement. We scanned the river banks eagerly, half-expecting to see them bristle with enemy bayonets. (*Journey to a war*, 1939, pp. 28–9.)

Back in England, the *Daily Worker* was less indulgent, criticising the pair for their 'bourgeois subjectivity', as being 'too preoccupied with their own psychological plight to be anything but helplessly lost in the struggle of modern China' and ridiculing them mercilessly: 'playing at being war correspondents, at being Englishmen, and being poets' (*Daily Worker*, 29 March 1939; qtd in Parker, p. 409). Isherwood said as much about himself in his letter to Upward:

> We went to China, and I produced this travel-diary which so annoyed the Left, because it was messy, personal, sentimental, and confused, like myself. (Letter to Edward Upward, 6 Aug 1939, qtd Parker, pp. 445–6)

Apart from undermining his politics, the episode only further increased Isherwood's deepening sense of personal inauthenticity.

Isherwood's politics

Isherwood had followed Edward Upward, his schoolboy model of conscience, into an enthusiasm for left-wing politics. They had all embraced Socialism and discussed ways to arrest the rise of Fascism. Even Auden had gone off to Spain to drive ambulances. A plan for them to go to Spain with a delegation of writers and artists to 'declare the solidarity of left-wing artists and intellectuals with the Spanish government' (*Christopher and his kind*, p. 217), was de-railed by the trip to China. But while Upward's sympathies were unequivocally Marxist, these were borrowed sentiments for Isherwood, and it wouldn't take much to separate the writer from his second-hand politics. Nonetheless, it would be a mistake to take Isherwood's self-deprecation as the whole story. There is an alternative account of the principled concerns underpinning these forays given in his *Approach to Vedanta* (1963), where he plays with a straight bat, giving us more insight than his 'comic cuts' characterisations, as Spender called them, often do.

Among other things, China re-instated for him the human cost of war: 'The visit to China brought me back from a world of political principles to a world of human values' (*Approach*, p. 8). This gave a broader-based orientation to his pacifism after the loss of Heinz to the 'other' side. What some commentators read as a lack of political commitment on Isherwood's part could be seen, then, as a conscientious, if nascent, ethic that—given the loss of his father and his love for Heinz—could never be comfortable with the lies promulgated by jingoistic patriotism to rationalise the pursuit of war. Christopher Lane highlights a similar conflict in the life of war poet Siegfried Sassoon, viz., the conflict between remaining loyal to his country during World War I and remaining loyal to his desire for his 'brother', even if that 'brother' is the enemy (see Lane 1995, chapter 8). Lane describes the pressures put upon Sassoon and his writing by these contrary demands and Isherwood would have been extraordinarily sensitised to the parallels with his own situation, which was a primary motivation in his pacifism. Looking back over the period that led to his move to America, Isherwood notes the influence of the war poets:

> I learnt—from my history master, from Noel Coward, from Wilfred Owen and Siegfried Sassoon—to loathe the old men who had made the war. (*Diaries volume one*, January 1939, p. 5)

I feel we have to recognise the emotional charge that this issue carried for Isherwood, intensified by the loss of his father and, in another sense, the loss of his lover too, in order to get a sense of the Zeitgeist. Reading Isherwood's letters to his mother around this time, Lisa Colletta remarks that 'they are one of the few records we have of Isherwood's life at this time that isn't filtered through the lens of time and memory' (2005, p. x) and for Jamie Carr they remind us of 'the grave uncertainties that plagued Isherwood and so many others in that politically volatile period' (2007, p. 170). Carr sees Isherwood struggling to retain some semblance of security when, as he puts it, 'the powers of hell are in the ascendant' (p. 57). Isherwood was not to know that Heinz would survive the war, as would Kathleen and his brother Richard, nor that Hitler and Mussolini would be defeated—such outcomes, as Carr notes

(p. 171), were far from certain at the time of writing, a time of mounting anxiety close to despair.

Isherwood was also disappointed by the increasingly repressive attitudes towards homosexuality he noted in both Fascism and Communism, and he was particularly alert to signs of it in later post-revolutionary regimes. For example:

> The tremendous stumbling block to me personally was the homosexual question: the treatment of homosexuals in Russia—which was absolutely in contravention to their original declarations, that the private life was no concern … The Russians started to equate homosexuality with fascism. And this in itself was such a loathsome piece of hypocrisy that, while I hardly admitted it to myself at the time, I see now that a government that can lie like that about one thing is really profoundly rotten all the way through, and just like any other government in fact—and not at all the Kingdom of Heaven! ('A very individualistic old liberal'; Webster 1971, p. 65)

Gore Vidal reads this as 'the voice of humanism in a bad time' (1976, p. 18). Many years after the War, lecturing at the University of California at Santa Barbara, Isherwood said of one of the plays he co-wrote with Auden (*On the frontier*) that it was 'dutifully leftist, but the only really sympathetic character is Valerian, the tycoon' (Huntington CI 1177). While Parker captures the indecision and personal insecurity in Isherwood's psyche at the time, he misses some of the true grit in Isherwood's positions.

Jamie Carr identifies the nexus of suspicions that feed into the standard if facile view that Isherwood's pacifism signified a retreat from the realities of life, a view compounded by the prevailing model of homosexuality as a failed stage in psychosexual development. His interest in Vedanta was interpreted in the same light, contributing to the stereotyping as 'passive', as lacking in daring, when the drums of war were amplifying the masculinist rhetoric that had so thoroughly alienated the young Isherwood after his father's death. That Isherwood was aware of these attitudes is addressed in his novel *Down there on a visit*, where the character of Paul and the narrator Christopher become conscientious objectors when America enters the War. As Carr says:

> Since each of these practices—'homosexuality', Eastern spirituality, and pacifism—are subject to judgments by others, their unification in this text discloses Isherwood's critique of the intersecting homophobic, masculinist, ethnocentric, and imperialist perceptions that compose these judgments. (2006, p. 38)

Isherwood's turn to the East is also an affront to Western values of rationality. The character of Ronny voices the common critique of pacifism as 'hiding one's head in the sand' but there's another twist often missed in condescending appraisals of Isherwood's spirituality. Ronny declares that:

> 'This Oriental thing appeals to intellectuals precisely because it's an escape from the intellect—and that's what they all long for. They long to be back—'
>
> 'Into the womb? You know, Ronny, I feel as if I knew everything you're going to say before you say it'. (*Down there*, p. 268)

There are traces, too, of Freud's put-down of mystical experience—the 'oceanic feeling'—as a hankering for the infantile nirvana of the womb, a regression to primary narcissism.

Carr's analysis is the first to draw out how the writer's intelligent encounter with Vedanta enacts a critique of the 'political economies of oppression and persecution' (2006, p. 40) that is built into Christian rhetoric. Her close reading of Isherwood's remarkable essay on the *Bhagavad Gita and war* recognises the nuanced philosophical and moral rigour that underpins his position. Carr shows how, through all these issues, Isherwood was involved in 'a negotiation with the discourses that subjectified him'.

For all the head-scratching puzzlement and facile judgments that greet Isherwood, it is here that we can recognise why he continues to be of interest for readers of the twenty-first century. Beyond the knee-jerk reaction of day-to-day historical politics, Isherwood insists on a rigorous self-appraisal, searching for a notion of duty that involves 'a critical understanding of action and self, not submission to a transcendent moral imperative' (Carr, p. 45). Isherwood was not an ideologue and he didn't write political theory. He was interested in character.

Peter Parker writes astutely about Isherwood's departure from politics:

> He was in Berlin not as a political commentator but as someone observing the consequences of politics quite literally at street level. Although he had seen the rise of fascism at first hand in Germany and had every reason to oppose it, his opposition was personal rather than strictly political, and was chiefly motivated by Heinz. (2004, p. 418)

Even if it made his friend Stephen Spender queasy, this writer could not be an ideologue, and this was to hold true even in the later writing. Any time he tried to fit his characters into a *schema*, he ended up with lifeless stories, and this held true not only with politics; when he tried to build his characters around a religious principle, the work tended to fall flat. *A meeting by the river*, for example, is generally regarded as an interesting failure for this reason. Isherwood put this down to yielding to what he calls 'a fatal desire for plot: I have a certain knack for plotting and I enjoy it very much,' he says, but he rates the 'plotted books' inferior to the others, giving *The world in the evening* as his example, which he criticises as 'a miracle of plotting but not much else … you see the bones through the flesh' (BBC Radio Interview 1979). He felt that certain qualities in *A meeting by the river* 'came out much better' in the stage version, which he co-wrote with Don Bachardy as a 'religious comedy' (Geherin, p. 151). In fact, as Allan Hollinghurst writes in his 2004 review of the Parker biography:

> [I]t was really only with Gay Lib in the 1960s and 1970s, of which Isherwood became a kind of literary guru, that the political fused convincingly for him with the personal. (p. 9)

Interviewing several people in Los Angeles who were mentored by Isherwood, it is clear to me that he was engaged in this way with the movement, a fact that Dennis Altman underplays in his assessment of Isherwood's value ('One snap too many', p. 4). Altman seems to feel that Isherwood should have been outspoken during the McCarthy era and damns the gay activism with faint praise: '[A]s he grew older, gay issues seemed the only political cause for which Isherwood could show any enthusiasm' (p. 4). As is clear from David

Geherin's 1972 interview, Isherwood felt that pleading the cause of one's 'minority' was more effectively done in pamphleteering, articles and speeches; to his mind, fiction was 'not a very good vehicle for propaganda' (p. 152).

Heading on out west

On the return from China their ship made a brief visit to New York. For both men, America represented fresh horizons. Having embraced all the political causes of his generation, they agreed on dropping the 'amateur socialist agitator' role:

> One morning on deck, it seems to me, I turned to Auden and said: 'You know, I just don't believe in any of it any more—the united front, the party line, the antifascist struggle. I suppose they're okay, but something's wrong with me. I simply can't swallow another mouthful.' And Auden answered: 'Neither can I.' Those were not our words, but psychologically it was as simple as that. (*Diaries vol one*, p. 6)

Parker claims that it was not as simple as Isherwood makes it sound, in retrospect:

> It suited Isherwood's self-mythologizing to present his passage to America as a road to Damascus: in fact he was in no psychological state to make any rational decisions about his life … eventually he would be able to acknowledge that he got into a terrible muddle, both in his beliefs and in his personal relationships. (p. 418)

I agree with the diagnosis. Knowing what one can reject—as not meeting the test of one's personal integrity—doesn't lead inexorably to a definitive mapping of the parameters of true authenticity. As the performative masks dropped away, Isherwood's need to find better tools to explore what was real in him was becoming critical. With the prospect of being caught up in a war in which his lover was on the 'other side', Isherwood began to wonder if pacifism was a more honest choice, in keeping with his own values, as hard as they might be to determine. Disgusted with England, he began to plan for a return to the States and the chance to seek out a new way of being and becoming. Disappointed with New York (where Auden enthusiastically took up residence), on his return Isherwood moved to the West Coast, where the influential figures of Gerald Heard and Aldous Huxley were living, and he soon joined them to discuss the possibilities of a conscientious pacifism. 'Heard and Huxley were the only two articulate pacifists he could contact,' he wrote in *Christopher and his kind*. 'They might be able to restate pacifism for him in terms of reason, instead of emotion' (p. 337).

David Robb provides a useful summary of the influence and standing of the now obscure figure of Heard in a journal article, 'English expatriates and spiritual consciousness in modern America'. (Heard had been, among other things, a science and current affairs commentator for the BBC. I have to acknowledge that my discussion here will not be able to pay sufficient attention to do justice to this fascinating figure.) Robb places Isherwood and Heard in the company of Arthur Koestler and Aldous Huxley:

> Collectively they created a minor literary movement that brought to the attention of American readers a wide variety of religious subjects including spiritualism and psychic phenomena, mysticism, pacifism, oriental philosophy, self-help therapies and consciousness-altering drugs. In addition to their importance as noteworthy twentieth-century authors, they represent facets of a more generalized religious awakening in the West. As a group, they helped stimulate this religious awakening in America and shape its distinctive eclectic form. (1985, p. 46)

David Robb emphasises how these writers attempted to reconcile 'religious insights with scientific and psychological theories'. He also notes how these 'secularized spiritual orientations' have stressed their separation from 'normative religious traditions' by insisting that they are not religions at all, but 'alternative ways of knowing', 'new metaphysical systems for a nuclear age' (p. 47). 'Regardless of the form,' he continues, 'the last four decades have seen a notable growth in the West of divergent or *ad hoc* 'religions' that have appealed to a highly educated and secular audience' (p. 47). Although the other figures Robb mentions took different turns, and the religious practices taken up by

Isherwood could not be characterised as 'ad hoc', it holds true that Isherwood was indeed a precursor to many modern (and post-modern) trends.

While the choice to de-camp to California was to prove crucial for Isherwood's personal quest, it was disastrous for his reputation back in Britain, where his stocks plummeted. His relocation provoked questions in the British Parliament and stirred up a storm of resentment that Isherwood never quite succeeded in living down, at least on that side of the Atlantic. Benjamin Britten and Peter Pears also moved to the States but it took them less time to resurrect their careers, as they returned to Britain in 1942 and registered as conscientious objectors to the war (Teachout, p. 58). While the move to America was to open up new avenues of creativity and personal growth, for the next generation of British literary critics Isherwood would always be the bad boy of the Weimar Republic and nothing good could ever be expected henceforth from a figure whom they viewed as a virtual traitor. This is part of the reason why his later works were so readily overlooked from that side of the Atlantic, and the oversight continues in many quarters today, as the reviews of the Parker biography clearly demonstrate.

Isherwood's movement away from his secondhand politics towards pacifism was, among other things, an attempt to extricate himself from other people's meaning systems. Yet in trying to sort out his own conscientious positions, he found himself turning to Huxley and Heard (and corresponding with other prominent pacifists) for support in this process. It was only when he met his guru that he met the mirror that could really bring him into focus.

At the same time, he needed to re-think his future as a writer, for in his muddled state his inspiration had floundered, while Auden's was in full flight. Soon, he was to discover the concept of finding one's *dharma*, in the Vedantist terminology. The English word 'vocation' carries something of the same meaning as 'dharma', but there are other, ontological ramifications in the more complex Sanskrit meaning, which Isherwood was alert to. Later, he wrote that 'dharma' was equivalent to:

> the particular duties, the way of life, which a man's nature imposes on him … Great stress is laid upon the importance of following your own dharma and not trying to follow the dharma of another … like Christ's parable of the talents: one employs one's talents because one has them, not in

> obedience to some external Power but because of the obligation the talents impose.

This definition is from *Ramakrishna & his disciples* (p. 7), Isherwood's 'official' biography of his guru's guru's guru, the founder of the line. The writing took several years (almost a decade), as the text was submitted for commentary and changes, chapter by chapter, to the headquarters of the Society in Calcutta, and was finally published in 1965. (In what follows I will refer to it in abbreviated form as *Ramakrishna.*) Isherwood found the experience frustrating. For his later book, *My Guru and his disciple* (1980), which was about his years of training with his own guru, Prabhavananda, he was free to make of it what he would, with less of the hagiographic imperative in any 'authorised', official biography, let alone one about a much revered saint.

While some critics would regard any acceptance of non-normative sexuality a 'relapse', Isherwood had to struggle towards self-acceptance and take up the duty of his calling before his writing could move forward again. He realised that to fulfil his sense of personal authenticity it was more important for him to be a writer, rather than a soldier, during a world war. Even as some of his more politically engaged friends found him 'politically muddled and naïve', as Parker points out, Isherwood 'saw his function as a writer less to analyse politics than to observe their effect on human lives' (p. 247). Perhaps if they were less inclined to dismiss Isherwood's spirituality as a merely superficial interest, his critics might have been more inclined to recognise a conscience at work in the man, even if his ethical choices were different from their own.

With his deep disaffection from the values of his homeland, Isherwood went through the kind of disillusionment process that I described in chapter two as a first initiation into spirituality, as I defined it. That stripping-away process left him very little to believe in. In a state of crisis, and suffering profound doubt about the reality of his self-concept, he went to America with no substitute in mind save for a vague pacifist idealism. Later, I will discuss how Swami Prabhavananda recognised the sincerity behind Isherwood's rigorous self-scrutiny as not simply a form of honesty but as a 'spiritual' virtue. DS Savage might use psychology as a screen for a moralistic viewing of the life and work, but Isherwood was to take his cues from a counsellor who came out of a different moral and philosophical tradition, one not blind to the need for ethical behaviour, even while it permitted the character to find its own natural expression.

4

Re-locations: Isherwood comes 'home'

Tell the mind there is but One. He who divides the One wanders from death to death.

—Katha Upanishad.

Where will a man find rest when he is bored or disgusted with his own ego performance? Perhaps we might assume that he would turn to religion. But, disgusted with his Anglican upbringing, Isherwood had decided to quit religion as a young man. Like many others of his generation, Isherwood saw himself as an atheist and briefly embraced Socialism before taking up a conscientious position as a pacifist. He detested his mother's pious embrace of Anglicanism and was particularly repelled by her class-based snobbery towards Catholics. During his parents' courtship, his father had tried to get his young wife Kathleen interested in Theosophy (*Kathleen and Frank*, p. 167) and after the marriage resisted her attempts to get him more involved in 'public religion'. 'To Kathleen,' wrote Isherwood, 'Christianity meant traditional worship publicly shared and church-going was its essential expression' (p. 190). Frank, on the other hand, who had had too much public religion in the army ('to him, church-going was like church parade'), was 'temperamentally attracted to Hinduism and Buddhism', notes his son, 'because it taught a private religion of self-effort, self-knowledge, and solitary meditation' (p. 190).

Peter Parker is critical of what he sees as Isherwood's shabby treatment of his mother, perhaps with some justification, but after the juvenile rebellion there was considerable respect from both sides, and it must be allowed that, like his other relationships, this one matured. Lisa Colletta, in her edition of the correspondence between Isherwood and Kathleen, claims that 'the letters reveal a different, more affectionate relationship that complicates' even Isherwood's own idea of himself as the 'anti-son' and problematises the generally accepted—especially since Parker—antagonistic view (Colletta 2005, p. viii). Colletta's analysis of the correspondence shows it to have been a richer, more complex one than the early rebelliousness might convey if one read *Lions and shadows*, say, alone. His 'autobiography' of his parents (1971) and later references in *Christopher and his kind* (1976) belie the simplistic construction that even Parker is tempted to follow. Colletta shows this correspondence complicates both biographical and critical readings of the writer and reveal a great deal more respect in the relationship than many, who want to see him as the immature homosexual, a failure in psychological development, will acknowledge. Even while he firmly rejected many attitudes of the Edwardian era and class his mother represented, Isherwood came to regard his mother and himself as 'fellow travelers' (Colletta, p. 154) and valued what the struggle between their points of view brought out in him.

In any case, Isherwood's failure to connect to the sacred through Anglicanism was not entirely due to a poor relationship with his mother. Parker has retrieved something of Kathleen Isherwood as a person in her own right, rather than as seen only through the eyes of her older son, but even Parker's favourable characterisation of Kathleen suggests why the religion of the mother would not be embraced by the son:

> Her letters and journals show someone who was in many ways conventional: she was a devout Christian, had a proper respect for royalty, and believed that people should know and keep to their place in the social hierarchy. (Parker, p. 10)

Isherwood was not prepared to follow that path. (The portrait of his brother, as it emerges in the Parker biography, is of a son more confused than dutiful, who stayed on with Kathleen in the crumbling family mansion, all the while slipping into disheveled and extreme eccentricity. It is a tragic portrait, and could be read as an endorsement of Christopher's contrary life choices.)

Thomas Merton's characterisation of the Anglican Church provides an unexpected but useful second opinion in this regard. In his autobiography *Seven storey mountain*, Merton describes his encounter with Anglicanism during a sojourn at an English school—Ripley—where he boarded for two years following an earlier, formative period at a French *lycée.* Commenting on his exposure to what he saw as a rather mild kind of religious sentiment (compared to the rigour of his previous Catholic school in France), Merton suggests that the religious life might require somewhat more:

> If the impulse to worship God and to adore Him in truth by the goodness and order of our own lives is nothing more than a transitory and emotional thing, that is our own fault. It is only so because we make it so, and because we take what is substantially a deep and powerful and lasting moral impetus, supernatural in its origin and in its direction, and reduce it to the level of our own weak and unstable and futile fancies and desires. (1975, p. 65)

I realise that this is the mature Merton, writing as a committed monk in a Catholic order, re-appraising the faith of his childhood and finding it somewhat immature. But it is nonetheless telling. It is not hard to recognise, in its lack of supernatural vigour (as described by Merton), the inadequacy of conventional Anglicanism to satisfy Isherwood's need. Merton continues:

> Prayer is attractive enough when it is considered in a context of good food, and sunny joyous country churches, and the green English countryside. And, as a matter of fact, the Church of England means all this. It is a class religion, the cult of a special society and group, not even of a whole nation, but of the ruling minority in a nation. (p. 65)

Isherwood's diaries from 1948 record his reading the Merton autobiography with great interest (diary entry, Nov 1948; *Diaries volume one*, p. 407).

I should re-iterate here that I am not arguing against any form of Christianity, nor for the ultimate 'truth status' of one form of religion over another. I bring this up because, even as caricature, Merton's characterisation speaks to that complacency with the fundamental classist assumptions of one's social milieu against which Isherwood was reacting. In a very real sense, religion—as Merton constructs it here—is very much to do with belonging within the context of the network of associations which knit together the kind of social identification to which I referred earlier this book; that matrix formed by the shared mythic and ritual practices, as well as class values, which marginalised our subject.

For someone undergoing the kind of crisis Isherwood was facing, this form of religion lacked the mystical power that might have helped him re-connect with the 'home self' he was seeking. Merton goes on to decry the lack of a 'mystical bond between people' (p. 65). As he sees it:

> The thing that holds them together is the powerful attraction of their own *social* tradition, and the stubborn tenacity with which they cling to certain social standards and customs, more or less for their own sake. The Church of England depends, for its existence, almost entirely on the solidarity and conservatism of the English ruling class. Its strength lies not in anything supernatural, but in the strong social and racial instincts which bind the members of this caste together. (p. 65; emphasis added.)

Isherwood was a member of the 'ruling class' but he rebelled against its snobbery and, in his own words, 'inverted it'. In Isherwood's own telling, as a young man 'he threw lords, landed gentry and all the rest of the ruling class together into the lower depths and exalted the workers over them' (*Kathleen and Frank*, p. 188). But this arrangement was unsatisfactory 'because it left him nowhere'; the benefits of such a community were simply not available to him as an unrepentant homosexual. His initial solution was to declare a 'private aristocracy of the arts' in which he could create his own peerage' (p. 188). We are reviewing a period long before the days of 'gay liberation'.

In his novel *Maurice*, EM Forster describes the character of Clive struggling to overcome 'the worst crime in the calendar':

> He came from a family of lawyers and squires, good and able men for the most part, and he did not wish to depart from their tradition. He wished

> Christianity would compromise with him a little and searched the Scriptures for support. There was David and Jonathan; there was even the 'disciple that Jesus loved'. But the church's interpretation was against him; he could not find any rest for his soul in her without crippling it. (p. 70)

After rejecting the politics and morality of his mother, and his 'caste', and given his rather urgent need for an anchor in a time of great personal crisis, it was unlikely Isherwood would turn to something so pallid as this class-based Anglicanism for psychological, or ontological, re-orientation. Whatever it was that his friend Auden found there was missing for him: 'The strength Wystan showed in contrast to my weakness was based on the Christian values which he had learned from his mother, as a child, and which he had never entirely abandoned,' Isherwood writes (*My Guru*, p. 5), and he notes: 'He didn't discuss these with me at the time, knowing what a violent prejudice I had against the whole concept of religion as I then understood it' (p. 5).

The roots of 'self'

A writer who is often compared with Isherwood is Andrew Harvey. Among his many publications, Harvey has published translations of poems by the Persian mystical poet Rumi, one of which reads:

> *Once you have tied yourself to selflessness,*
> *you will be delivered from selfhood*
> *and released from the snares of a hundred ties …*

The refrain that tags each verse of the poem runs: ' … so come, return to the root of the root of your own self' (Harvey 1994, p. 51).

Implicit in the mystic's call is the teaching that the missing 'root' of connectedness won't be found outside the self; nor is it found *as* the self. Rumi is pointing even deeper than the self, then, suggesting that 'self' is rooted within the Divine, *sine qua non*; that the connection is the very root of being and must be known as a felt experience, by direct contact; not through doctrines, rituals and belief, but deep within the soul. And, as Merton writes of the Chinese sage with whom he found so much in common:

> Chuang Tzu is not concerned with words and formulas about reality, but with the direct existential grasp of reality in itself. Such a grasp is necessarily obscure and does not lend itself to abstract analysis. (*The Way of Chuang Tzu*, p. xvi)

We are in perilous territory here: mysticism, as the direct apprehension of 'reality', is often treated with suspicion by churchmen, who have invested so much energy in countering the assault of rationalism that their religious praxis in many cases eschews the cultivation of non-rational states of awareness, presuming them to be of the same status as *ir*-rational. (I will come back to this later, but meanwhile Ken Wilber writes well about the category confusion; see 'The Pre/Trans Fallacy' 1980.)

Clearly, Isherwood was unable to find a nest for his restless subjectivity within his own cultural setting. After a series of displacements, and an increasing dissatisfaction with the performative ego, he needed a radical revisioning of his identity positioning that would allow him to locate what he called the 'home self' (Rumi's 'the root of the root of your own self'). As he wrote later, 'the desire, the *homesickness*, for sanity is the one valid reason for subjecting oneself to any kind of religious discipline' (*My Guru*, p. 120; emphasis added).

In my second chapter I proposed that the great disillusionment that many queer men go through—alienation from the normative discourses of family, church and the law—often takes the form of a stripping away of illusions. For some this can serve as an initiation, precipitating a rigorous process of self-inquiry and profound doubt, which gives them no peace until they find a resting place—a kind of docking point for their tired and battered subjectivity to re-connect and re-formulate itself. We have seen how Isherwood felt 'hollowed out' (as 'Der Mann öhne Eigenschaft'). Disillusioned with his home country, separated from his lover, horrified to watch the whole of Europe collapsing into war, he had failed to develop a sense of self that could survive the crisis. Looking back forty years later, he writes:

> I was empty because I had lost my political faith—I couldn't repeat the left-wing slogans which I had been repeating throughout the last few years. It wasn't that I had lost all belief in what the slogans stood for, but I was no

> longer wholehearted. My leftism was confused by an increasingly aggressive awareness of myself as a homosexual and by a newly made discovery that I was a pacifist. (*My Guru*, p. 4)

At first, his search for answers took the form of looking for ways to substantiate his pacifism. This led him to look up a former acquaintance, the writer Gerald Heard, who had moved to Los Angeles at the same time as Aldous Huxley (who would soon publish the influential *The perennial philosophy*, in 1945). Heard and Huxley were both involved with a guru, a Swami from the Ramakrishna Order, who was teaching Vedanta practice and philosophy out of a centre in Hollywood. Isherwood was not a likely candidate for conversion to any form of religion, and both Heard and the guru himself were not about to try to convert him.

Vedanta teaches that the object of existence is not to transcend, but to realise what we really are, a realisation obtained not though logic but through the direct intuition modelled by the sages. In the *Advaita*, or non-dual form of the teachings, only Brahman, the supreme principle, has existence, and ignorance ('*a*vidya', as opposed to 'vidya') of this reality leads to the erroneous belief that phenomena can exist apart from the Absolute. The idea of the personal self as a 'separate' entity, then, is a delusion that produces unnecessary stress and anxiety. For the restless, deluded entity to be brought back into re-union with the One that contains the many, what will be required will be not only a shift in the focal length of awareness to recover the root of the root of the self, but also a revisioning of previously held notions of identity that formed in ignorance of the real state of affairs.

In Isherwood's case, we see that 'the confusion, hopes and fears' of an entire era (Colletta 2005, p. xi) in the life—the political uncertainties between two major world wars, compounded by a personal crisis of identity—is reflected in the texts. The Vedanta study and praxis would become one of three major contributors to resolving the psychological and ontological crises for Isherwood, providing him an unprecedented opportunity (and a challenge) as a student of a profoundly integrative system.

Isherwood was initially suspicious of 'all this Oriental stuff' (p. 7) and his depiction of his initial prejudices towards 'Yoga', in *An approach to Vedanta* (published in 1963), is humorously overdrawn. He writes that he and his friends pictured Heard and Huxley in turbans, levitating and 'floating out over the desert at a great altitude' (pp. 15–16). On the other hand, as a Christian apostate, his loathing of religion in the same portrait is quite nasty. Yet I get the impression that he is writing to people in a similar situation that he had himself been in, to show them the way back from rejecting belief in authoritarian dogmas: '[W]hat Gerald recommended was a practical mysticism, a do-it-yourself religion which was experimental and empirical' (p. 23). (Empirical yes, but 'do-it-yourself' only in the sense that to embrace the doctrines up front was not an *a priori* requirement.)

So, Heard understood that it was no use hitting Isherwood with a full-on doctrinal assault. Both he and Swami Prabhavananda respected Isherwood's initial scepticism, emphasising praxis and first-hand, empirical experience over theory, refusing to even define the nature of the experience encountered there. The techniques were quite specific:

> Gerald wasn't asking you to take anything on trust. It was essential to try 'this thing' for yourself. If, after a reasonable time, you had found nothing, then you were entitled to say it was all a lie. (p. 24)

'This thing' became a shorthand reference for what they declined to define. If he was slow to accept the theoretical basis, Isherwood quickly came to respect and admire the swami:

> I do not believe in his teachings with the whole of my mind, and I will not pretend that I do, but I have enough belief to make a start. My reason is not offended. My approach is strictly experimental. I will put myself in his hands, and trust him at least as far as I would trust my own doctor. I will try to live the kind of life he prescribes. If, at the end of three or four years, I can conscientiously say that I have done what was asked of me and had no results whatsoever, then I will give up the whole attempt as a bad job. ('Hypothesis and belief', in *Exhumations*, p. 122. The essay was originally published in the magazine *Vedanta and the West* and written much earlier than *An approach to Vedanta*.)

Theoretical study was not far behind. Apart from the empirical benefits of meditation practice, this form of Vedanta—and more importantly, the relationship with the guru himself—came to represent an unexpectedly complete solution to Isherwood's struggle to find an integrative subjectivity. With his fiction taking a back seat, Isherwood was soon engaged in service projects for his teacher, and in 1944 published a translation of *The Bhagavad Gita* (*The song of God)* with his guru; this was followed by other key texts from the Vedanta tradition (the Shankara in 1947, the Patanjali in 1953, the Ramakrishna biography in 1965). As he said later: 'By the time we had finished translating the book I realized that I had been studying it with an ideal teacher and in the most thorough manner imaginable' (*Essentials of Vedanta,* p. 98).

Just as he had embraced German, in the 1930s, as a way of rehearsing a new possibility for selfhood, in spite of his initial 'prejudice' Isherwood found the 'very Indianness' of Vedanta helpful during the 1940s. He was 'grateful to Vedanta for speaking Sanskrit', as he put it; he could learn a religion afresh, without the associations carried from the Anglicanism of his upbringing:

> I needed a brand-new vocabulary and here it was, with a set of philosophical terms which were exact in meaning, unemotive, untainted by disgusting old associations with clergymen's sermons, schoolmasters' pep talks, politicians' patriotic speeches. (*My Guru*, p. 49)

The Yoga of selfless service

'Seva', or 'selfless service', is an important aspect of practice in most spiritual traditions, and service to the guru is something a keen aspirant is glad to offer in exchange for the teaching. It is important to recognise this as an intrinsic element in the tradition, as this is the weakest point in Peter Parker's characterisation of Isherwood as someone who was being exploited by his spiritual guide. As a form of 'karma yoga', service supplements the introspective process of meditation and the devotional relationship with the guru and, as an exercise in selflessness, shifts the focus away from the obsession with ego gratification towards the subtle transformation of subjectivity that results from a re-alignment of the personal with a greater

'Self'. David Galin (2003) suggests how such practices force the personal 'I' into considering other entities, contributing to new experiences and a 'new integrated structure to emerge' in consciousness. (See also Deikman 1997, 'The spiritual heart of service'.)

Let me develop this notion a little further.

The Advaita tradition is concerned to construct a non-dualistic conception of reality. Even in using terms such as 'Brahman' for absolute reality, that part of the absolute that exists in every person—the Atman—is construed as not separate from Brahman itself. Given Isherwood's ontological crisis, and his search for an integrating 'personal myth' (Piazza), it is significant that he entered into the study of the key concepts of the philosophy quite thoroughly. To illustrate some of the principles, I will cite extracts from the introduction to their translation of one of the key texts of this tradition, *The crest–jewel of discrimination* (in Sanskrit, the *Viveka-Chudamani*), written by the great 7th century, South Indian reformer Shankara:

> Shankara only accepts as 'real' that which neither changes nor ceases to exist … No object, no kind of knowledge, can be absolutely real if its existence is only temporary. Absolute reality implies permanent existence. (*Crest–Jewel*, p. 7)

The emphasis is on what is 'real', in the sense of 'unchanging'. So the question arises:

> What, then, *is* the Reality behind all our experiences? There is only one thing that never leaves us—the deep consciousness. This alone is the constant feature of all experience. And this consciousness is the real, absolute Self. In dreamless sleep, also, the real Self is present as a witness, while the ego-sense which we call 'ourself', our individuality, has become temporarily merged in ignorance ('avidya') and disappeared. (pp. 7–8)

In this context, Isherwood's angst—the disorientation, the psychological restlessness, and the attendant metaphysical or ontological displacement—could be diagnosed as a spiritual crisis which would not be improved by what could only be a futile attempt to stabilise what is *inherently* unstable, fragile and temporary: namely, the ego-sense that we call our 'self'.

I refer back to my chapter two, and Peter Conradi's acknowledgement that post-modernism, too, posits the self as 'a flimsy construct, an illusion, a myth, a fiction' (p. 49). According to Conradi, through meditation the practitioner discovers the 'flimsy' nature of the self ('as experience, not theory'), coming to the realisation 'that life is a stream of becoming, a series of manifestations and extinctions', leading to an awareness that the notion of the individual ego is 'a popular delusion' (p. 49). Through all the ups and downs of the next four decades, Isherwood made more than a theoretical acquaintance with 'the one thing that never leaves us'—Shankara's representation of the 'real'.

The practice of meditation given to Isherwood by the Swami (known as doing, or making 'japam'—the repetition of a 'mantra', or sacred phrase, with the aid of rosary beads for counting the rotations) was an opportunity for him to dig deeper into the layers of being—into the 'deep consciousness' to which they refer in this section—to locate the eternal, unchanging aspect of self, known in this tradition as the 'Atman', which partakes of the very same nature as, and is not separate from, the absolute principle: 'Brahman'. In this model, 'Brahman' represents the formless source of all forms, which are expressions of its own nature, and this includes consciousness itself. To recognise the eternal 'Self' is the basis not only for achieving personal fulfilment, but also lays the foundation for the realisation of the matrix of unity underlying all forms: 'The Self is everywhere,' says the Isha Upanishad. 'Whoever sees all beings in the Self, and the Self in all beings, hates none. For one who sees oneness everywhere, how can there be delusion or grief?' This quotation is taken from the introductory screed 'What is Vedanta?' from the Vedanta Society of Southern California, which states: 'All fear and all misery arise from our sense of separation from the great cosmic unity, the web of being that enfolds us' citing the Upanishads:

> 'There is fear from the second,' says the Brihadaranyaka Upanishad. Duality, our sense of separation from the rest of creation, is always a misperception since it implies that something exists other than God. There can be no other.

And they cite the pioneer figure who first brought the Ramakrishna message to the United States:

> 'This grand preaching, the oneness of things, making us one with everything that exists, is the great lesson to learn,' said Swami Vivekananda a century ago … The Self is the essence of this universe, the essence of all souls … You are one with this universe. He who says he is different from others, even by a hair's breadth, immediately becomes miserable. Happiness belongs to him who knows this oneness, who knows he is one with this universe. (See http://www.vedanta.org/wiv/philosophy/)

This is the form in which Isherwood encountered the teachings. In fact, some of the texts used to translate these concepts for a Western readership were written by Isherwood himself.

Intimately present within each being, Atman is indispensable for consciousness, and is the 'real' source of peace and bliss, because its nature is unchanging. The personal self, which is acquired as the outward persona, formed in response to the external world—it might be called the predicate self—is subject to change, and an unreliable basis for stability, happiness and satisfaction. The goal of spiritual practice is not to destroy that relatively illusory, 'false' self—it is needed to function as the mediator with the changing world—but to shift one's centre from close and exclusive identification with it to recover the deepest roots of being within the zone of the unchanging—the eternal, underlying basis of all life and consciousness, the Param Brahman.

Coming from a different tradition, Ken Wilber makes a similar point, with an important proviso:

> Precisely because the ego, the soul, and the Self can all be present simultaneously, we can better understand the real meaning of 'egolessness', a notion that has caused an inordinate amount of confusion. But egolessness does not mean the absence of a functional self (that's a psychotic, not a sage); it means that one is no longer *exclusively* identified with that self. (*One taste*, p. 276)

To recall Francisco Varela's description using a characteristically Buddhist formulation: 'It is called Buddha nature, nomind, primordial mind, absolute 'bodhicitta', wisdom mind, All Goodness, Great Perfection, That which cannot be fabricated by mind, Naturalness' (1999, pp. 68–9).

People who worry about the surrender of the ego are naturally suspicious of elements of submission in the guru/disciple relationship, sometimes falling into the trap of duality (with shades of Platonic idealism), separating the 'Self' as real and the ego as 'unreal', in a crude version of the doctrine of *Maya*. Fears rise, too, among queer readers of Isherwood who suspect another reactionary attempt to undermine their hard-won self-respect and the gains made by the sexual liberation movement and its penetrating interrogation of gender politics. Why would you want to surrender this heavily defended 'queer self' to a guru who is not 'queer'—is this not repression in another guise? Some commentators have produced revisionist readings that would make Jesus 'gay' or 'queer'—not necessarily the same issue—(Rollan McCleary, say), or reconfigure Ramakrishna into a latent (Jeffrey Masson, in *The oceanic feeling*, 1980), or 'conflicted' homosexual (Jeffrey Kripal, in *Kali's child*, 1998) but I think these readings, for all their psychologising, fail to provide insight into the deeper dynamics of the guru/student relationship, too often relying on the epistemic violence that post-colonial theorists such as Gayatri Chakravorty Spivak identify as occurring when projecting a (white) European epistemology onto the rest of the world.

The relationship of the personal self to this deeper underlying stratum of being is too often misunderstood, and what is going on between the guru and the disciple is often caricatured and misrepresented; so it needs further elucidation. I will come back to this below.

The Idea of 'God'

The fact that Isherwood gained a sophisticated insight into some of the more subtle aspects of the philosophy is evident from his nuanced understanding of the use of these terms, and his reluctance to translate them roughly as 'God' (for Brahman) or 'soul' (for Atman), as he might have done if this had been merely the 'flirtation' which Dennis Altman describes it as ('One snap too many', p. 4). Others value it more highly. Mark Hawthorne writes: 'The

English version of the *Song of God: Bhagavad Gita* was Isherwood's crowning achievement. The book was almost unknown to readers in the US at the time …' (1999; online).

I think it is worth looking at this in some detail, for to track his engagement with the system is like watching a bridge under construction (from 'East' to 'West') and the subtle details should really give pause to anyone who would dismiss Isherwood's engagement with Vedanta too lightly. For this goes to the very heart of the possibility that an unrepentant homosexual might engage meaningfully with the religious life. I should re-iterate that some critics have described Isherwood's engagement with Vedanta as 'experimental'; as 'lacking in seriousness', and compared it to his 'toying with socialist ideas in his earlier years' (Savage, p. 83). More recently, in *The Spectator*, Philip Hensher writes that Isherwood 'was one of the first Westerners to start the *fad* for Eastern mysticism' (2004, p. 56; emphasis added.) Hensher is full of admiration for Parker's biography ('this stunning, unflagging, monumental chronicle' [p. 56]), not without reason, for there is much to admire; but he is dismissive of Isherwood's interest in mysticism, adopting Parker's legalistic language ('you could not make a case for the defence here' [p. 57]) and he also opines that it was meeting *Auden* that was the 'defining moment' of Isherwood's life (p. 56). This suggests to me that he simply has not paid enough attention to the second half of the life, even though he was writing this in 2004.

John Sutherland, writing in *The London Review of Books*, gets the facts wrong when he refers to a 'late-life conversion to transcendentalism' (p. 23). In July 1939, when he met Prabhavananda for the first time, Isherwood was thirty-four. In August, he took his first instruction in simple, preparatory meditation practice and was initiated, and he was given a mantra practice in November of the following year (he was then thirty-six.) As he lived until the age of eighty-one, I fail to see how this conversion can be described as 'late-life'. Once again, indications that a more complex Isherwood existed—in place of the 'straw man' figure that the standard view would have him be—are written off, even as late as 2004.

The worst misrepresentation occurs in the very place where one might assume there would be the most thoroughness—in Peter Parker's earnest and immensely detailed biography. In the criticism that follows I do not wish to slight the richly researched documentation that underpins Parker's impressive biography, but the issues I raise are valid, and need to be re-assessed. Because the weight of the biography has led most commentators to accept it as authoritative, it has prompted many to echo Parker's mistakes in this area. I hope my critique here would clarify some key points.

Parker's account closely follows Isherwood's own diaries and autobiography in its portrayal of Isherwood's introduction to Vedanta by Gerald Heard. But when he gets to the point where Heard carefully avoids the word 'God', Parker is cynical about Heard's strategy. Heard quite reasonably avoided the theistic representation, for reasons to do with Isherwood's left-wing atheist sympathies and rejection of Anglicanism. Here is how Parker describes the introduction:

> In order to achieve this spiritual re-birth it was necessary to practice yoga. Although to most people 'yoga' suggested some form of beneficial contortionism (of the sort once practised by Isherwood's Uncle Jack), Heard explained that it was a Sanskrit word for 'yoking' or 'joining'. Through meditation it was possible to achieve union with 'this thing', which was Heard's *slyly evasive* term for what other people would have termed 'God'. (p. 435; emphasis added)

(Here we have another tantalising reference to a family member engaging with an alternative spiritual tradition.) He continues:

> Heard was also careful to avoid the word 'soul', although Yoga taught that people had two selves, a notion which would *seem familiar to anyone brought up in the Judaeo-Christian belief of body and soul.* (p. 435; emphasis added)

On the surface, this doesn't seem unreasonable. But there was more—as anyone familiar with Vedanta philosophy knows—than what Isherwood himself refers to as Gerald's 'natural fastidiousness' that prevented him from using the terms 'God' and 'soul'.

Even were he a prime candidate for conversion to a set of beliefs and practices that would answer the deeply felt need for a 'home self', Isherwood had to overcome an aversion to religion as he understood it at the time. As noted earlier, he was especially resistant to the notion of 'God'. The High

Church Anglican form of the God of his childhood had been represented as ruling, from 'high in heaven, with grim justice over us, his sinful and brutish subjects, here below', Isherwood writes:

> He was good. We were bad. We were so bad that we crucified Jesus his son, whom he had sent down to live amongst us. For this crime, committed nearly two thousand years ago, each new generation had to beg forgiveness. If we begged hard enough and were sincerely sorry, we might be sent to purgatory and even eventually led into heaven, instead of being thrown into hell where we by rights belonged. (*Approach to Vedanta*, p. 13)

If this was the child's-eye point of view, Isherwood also carried another more cynical opinion:

> My interpretation of the word 'God' had been taken quite simple mindedly from left-wing anti-religious propaganda. God has no existence except as a symbol of the capitalist superboss. He has been deified by the capitalists so that he can rule from on high in the sky over the working-class masses, doping them with the opium of the people, which is religion, and thus making them content with their long working hours and starvation wages. (*My Guru*, p. 11)

Isherwood had been through the disillusionment process I have described, and was unlikely to meekly accept conventional notions about God on faith. There was more going on here than 'sly evasiveness' on the part of Heard.

Isherwood was extremely 'fastidious' himself, when he came to work on a translation of one of the classic texts with his guru, refusing to accept an equation of the terms 'God' and 'Brahman'. I find that Parker is unaware of his own tendency towards ethnocentricity and simply too ready to equate concepts from different systems of representation as if they are describing the same reality, as he does when he presumes that the notion of two selves would be 'familiar to anyone brought up in the Judaeo-Christian belief of body and soul' (p. 435). Furthermore, he ignores the Advaita insistence on non-duality. The two selves might be 'familiar' to Parker, and to anyone in the Judaeo-Christian tradition, but his equation of the 'two selves' of Yoga with the Christian belief in 'body and soul' is not at all the same thing. Isherwood and his Swami were in fact referring to the superimposition of the ego-idea upon the Atman. (See the essay by Swami Prabhavananda: 'What is evil?')

Alan Watts has given a clear exposition of how different cultural mindsets shape a differently perceived—and theorised—universe. See, for example, his description of how 'Tao' is differently represented from 'God' and, more particularly, (with a nod to Joseph Needham) the differences 'between Hebrew–Christian and Chinese views of natural law, the former deriving from the "word" of a lawgiver, God, and the latter from a relationship of spontaneous processes working in an organismic pattern' (*The way of Zen*, pp. 11–12, 17).

At the very least, Heard was giving Isherwood an opportunity to find his way into the system empirically. Rather than providing him with a familiar, or an alien set of ready-made concepts, he was showing Isherwood that it was possible to find his way back into an experiential contact with the source of his life—his being, his conscious awareness—without buying into the whole unwieldy system of representations that enter along with theistic notions of 'God' in any form. (From the point of view of a Zen Buddhist roshi, say, this would be a perfectly respectable approach, and a long way from Parker's 'sly evasiveness'.) 'We all know that we exist', he was to write later in the Shankara translation:

> We are all aware of our own consciousness. But what is the nature of this consciousness, of this existence? Discrimination will soon prove to us that the ego-idea is not the fundamental reality. There is something beyond it. We can call this something 'Brahman'—but Brahman is only another word. It does not reveal the nature of the thing we are looking for. (pp. 30–31)

Isherwood came to appreciate the insistence on the experiential in the Ramakrishna Vedanta tradition, with what he describes as its 'undogmatic, experimental approach to truth':

> Shankara does not tell us that we must accept the existence of Brahman as a dogma before we can enter upon the spiritual life. No—he invites us to

> find out for ourselves. Nothing—no teacher, no scripture—can do the work for us. Teachers and scriptures are merely encouragements to personal effort. (p. 29)

In fact, the practice demands an active engagement with the inquiry:

> Mere assent, as Shankara insists, is not enough. It is only a preliminary step towards active participation in the search. Direct personal experience is the only satisfactory proof of Brahman's existence, and each of us must have it …

Isherwood's theology was to become quite articulated, in fact. For example:

> Brahman is the Reality in its universal aspect, as opposed to the Atman, which is the Reality within ourselves. The Reality is always the Reality, one and undivided; these two words merely designate two viewpoints from which it can be considered. Look inward and you see the Atman, look outward and you see Brahman; but Atman and Brahman are really one. (*Approach to Vedanta,* p. 66)

Isherwood recognised parallels with Christian mysticism, even if he had rejected its mundane presentation in Anglicanism (he equates the notion of 'samadhi', for example, with the Christian 'Mystical Union'). His friend and mentor, EM Forster, who spent time in India, quotes St Catherine of Siena: 'God is in the soul and the soul is in God as the sea is in the fish and the fish is in the sea' (Forster 1927, p. 136). This is very similar to a famous verse of Kabirdas, the medieval weaver/sage of India: 'paanee me meen pyaasee'; 'A fish in the water is thirsty/Every time I hear this/it makes me laugh' (Kabir 2006). Isherwood unpacks the theory thus:

> There is a word in Sanskrit for God-with attributes; it is Ishwara. But Brahman is the reality without attributes, without will, without moods. It is Brahman seen within Maya, that appears as Ishwara. If you translate Brahman as 'The Reality' or 'The Absolute', you still have to explain what you mean; these overlooked words have become so imprecise. If you use

> 'The Godhead', as has been done in translations from Meister Eckhart, you seem nearer to a definition, since the dictionary says it means 'the essential being of God'. (p. 66)

This is not merely the quibble of a translator, seeking the proper word. Under the tutelage of his guru, Isherwood's insight into Vedanta philosophy is learned and particular:

> The Atman, it has been said, is the Reality within ourselves. But when one searches for a single English word to say this, it cannot be found, because Christianity does not quite accept this concept. 'Soul' is out of the question; the soul is not God. 'Spirit' is utterly vague. (p. 66)

Given my earlier distinction between small s 'self' with capital S 'Self', it is worth continuing with Isherwood's description:

> Many translators call the Atman 'The Self'; but this word has unfortunate associations with 'selfishness'. Moreover, there are certain passages in which the translator is then forced to speak of the Self with a big S meaning the Atman and the self with a small s meaning the personal ego; a distinction which is lost when the words are read aloud. And an occasionally unavoidable use of the possessive form produces the horrible combination 'his Self'. You can more or less adequately describe the Atman as 'God Immanent' and Brahman as 'God Transcendent', but these phrases are too awkward for frequent repetition and they have the dryness of Victorian theology. (pp. 66–67)

With Isherwood, Heard and Prabhavananda were involved in the critically sensitive process of preparing someone with highly educated intelligence and sensibility. In the Judaeo-Christian teachings, the faithful are enjoined to 'have no other Gods before Me', and not to 'worship graven images', to paraphrase the familiar injunctions. These can be read on more than one level, of course. The issue is also one of praxis. When a student is preparing for the long and arduous kind of mystical practice that will prepare him or her for direct experience of the 'divine', or of the 'absolute ground of being', it becomes crucial that ideas and concepts do not take the place of directly felt experience. These are different ways of knowing.

The normal operations of the mind—both the trivial tendency to wander aimlessly through a myriad thoughts, which is the bugbear of anyone who has attempted meditation, as well as the higher functions of abstract thought and theorising—are to be deliberately bypassed, in order to allow other, latent states of awareness to emerge from behind the thought-clogged thicket of everyday awareness. The aspirations of the conceptual function to theorise about high-minded concepts such as 'God', and all forms of capital M, Meaning, do not assist in the process. This is not to denigrate theology, nor the function of reason; the point is to train the mind to recover a deep-seated—some say 'primordial', I call it 'original'—state of awareness described as 'being-consciousness-bliss' ('satchitanand' in Sanskrit.) Thinking about 'God' is not the same process, then, as training the ratiocinative function to give way to a more inclusive field of consciousness that supports and includes it.

In this way, it could be said that the idea of 'God', and what that concept 'means', is the most deceptive facsimile of the real thing because it is a conceptual substitute. Heard and the Swami would have been trying gently to help Isherwood move away from getting stuck on definitions, so that the idea didn't become a substitute for direct perception. This might seem to be an elementary point, but it is a significant one and Parker seems to simply be unaware of it. Of course, as an ancient and multi-faceted tradition, Vedanta incorporates a form of yoga that can use this reasoning function of mind itself to shift into realisation. It is called 'jnani' yoga. But Isherwood was a 'bhakta' yogi, a *devotee* of a teacher who, in his own being, revealed the deeper presence of Atman for those who had the 'eyes to see'. Antony Copley will disagree with me on that point—he says 'Isherwood was more drawn to *jnana* than to *bhakta*' (2006, p. 264)—but while the intellectual study might have characterised the early years I feel he has not recognised the intensity of the bhakti aspect in Isherwood's relationship with Swami Prabhavananda, especially as it developed over the decades.

Relationship with the guru

This is not to say that Isherwood parked his mind at the door. The Swami really earned his devotion. In a 1965 interview he recalls the nature of his original attraction, after the introduction by Huxley/Heard:

> I got more and more interested in what Prabhavananda had to teach. But in a way far more than his teaching I was, as one would say nowadays, "existentially" interested in the fact that this man, who was obviously completely sane, very intelligent, and not in the least bit a crook, believed in the reality of mystical experience … I had never met anybody who so completely convinced me that he believed in this possibility, that he had known people who had gone very far along that path, and that he himself had progressed quite a distance along it. (Wickes 1965, p. 34)

Asked if he was still a Vedantist (after almost 30 years) he stated: 'Very much so'; adding that they had remained 'very close friends' and that he still saw Prabhavananda 'constantly' (p. 34).

I need to give some indication of the way 'religion' is taught in this tradition and something of the role of the guru in the instruction. If I can do this successfully, some of the cultural myopia behind the misrepresentation of Isherwood's sincere and extended application to his new religion might be corrected, and something of the importance of spirituality in his life and work reclaimed.

In this tradition, the guru exemplifies the state of being of one who has attained a fuller awareness of that deepest reality, and acts as a kind of focusing device for his or her students to help them to 'tune in', as it were, to that reality as the basis of their own being and conscious awareness. If the ego version of self is inherently unstable, unreliable as the basis for happiness, and illusory as a point of identification, then surrender—or obedience to the guru—is the rapid path to re-locating one's true centre and re-connecting with the real self, which is One in All; for the guru embodies that awareness. Isherwood saw that modelled in Prabhavananda's focus on his own guru (Brahmananda, one of the original disciples of Sri Ramakrishna). Hence the distinction drawn by Prabhavananda in describing his own guru's detached kind of loving: '[He] didn't love others in this person-to-person way. Having realized God, who is love, he had become love' (*My Guru*, p. 41).

Once trust is established in the teacher, the fretful little ego identity may relax its grip; the restless, tap-dancing entertainer can relinquish the need to perform; and the anxious, alienated self might relax into the embrace of the Absolute (of which it is already a part). 'The dewdrop slips into the shining sea', as Sir Edwin Arnold evokes it in the last line of his famous poem, 'The Light of Asia'. (John Blofeld gives a lovely gloss on this image during an encounter with a Taoist Master. See Blofeld 1979, p. 163.)

The degree of trust implied in this description, and the re-alignment it requires, do not usually come overnight. In fact, there may be a long and arduous struggle, typically, in which the lesser self refuses to surrender to the greater reality, or its representative, the guru. Isherwood describes his own resistance clearly in *My Guru*, where he identifies it as 'an active underground force of opposition' (p. 52), and it is in such realistic—rather than idealised—details of the process that one recognises the veracity of his account.

The spiritual teacher will usually give some kind of meditation practice, often combined with some task construed as 'service' (as described above). This combined practice is intended to de-centre the directing ego, making way for a perception and direct experience of the underlying reality that is usually masked by the ego self. For the habitual patterns of thought, action and desire that make up the 'illusory' self are, otherwise, continually re-iterated (like someone knitting) to hold a coherent sense of self through time. The spiritual practices recommended by the guru are intended to 'unravel the knitting', as it were, and release conscious awareness into a full realisation of a deeper awareness of being (in this tradition, the 'Atman'; in the Zen example, the 'face before you were born', perhaps; although a Zen roshi would probably scoff). Certain qualities of feeling are associated with the influx of energy emanating from this deeper stratum and are variously described as bliss, profound peace, and so on. The terminology is not unfamiliar to anyone who has read the classic works of mysticism, from any tradition, even if the story of the 'struggle' may be skimmed over in some accounts.

The encyclopedia of Eastern philosophy and religion defines the guru as a 'teacher, particularly a spiritual master' (p. 121). To explain the role they give this example:

> When you come to a strange city and want to find a particular street, there are two ways to do it: either you can try all the streets until you come to the one you are looking for, which, if you are unlucky, will be the last; or you can ask a native. (p. 122)

The guru is the 'native', a guide in 'every way familiar with the realm of spirituality', who can show 'the shortest way to the place you seek' (p. 122). The encyclopedia entry goes on to make an important point about the voluntary nature of the relationship:

> As far as obedience to the guru is concerned, it is senseless if it is practiced from a sense of obligation against one's will. If one has the right relationship to the guru and trusts him completely, one will obey him out of trust and love, even when one does not immediately grasp the sense of his instruction. (p. 122)

The issue of trust, then, and the potential for the abuse of that trust, can produce much doubt in the aspirant.

The renunciate path

The student, according to temperament, may or may not agree to undergo intense training within a celibate, monastic setting. After finding his feet on the work front, writing for the movie studios, Isherwood did try the renunciate life, for more than two years. He moved into the Center on North Ivar Avenue in February 1943, learned the rituals and participated in the daily life of Prabhavananda's gregarious monastery, while continuing to write, although he didn't take the preliminary brahmacharya vows. After leaving, in August 1945, realising it was not the natural path for him, he continued to visit the Center for ritual and other occasions, edited the Society newsletter, and continued with his japam practice. Most importantly, he maintained a strong and affectionate relationship with his guru for almost forty years. This is something many recent commentators overlook or dismiss, failing to recognise—or respect—what this bond represented to him and how it could continue to evolve with such a change in lifestyle. In July 1960 Isherwood wrote in his diary that his current state of happiness was 'terribly insecure':

> All of this points to one thing—hold on to the anchor. Make japam. Nothing else can be relied on, and all other activity is, in the last analysis, merely symbolic. Do I entirely believe this? Very, very nearly. Ninety-five percent. Do I act as if I did? Very, very, very seldom. I rely on Swami to do the work. (*Diaries volume one*, p. 885)

There is no doubt that Isherwood's stormy relationship with photographer Bill Caskey in the period immediately following his departure from monastic life was a wild ride, but people not familiar with the tradition too easily assume that in leaving the monastic setting, Isherwood quit his spiritual practice, in spite of clear evidence to the contrary. In January 2005 I interviewed the publisher of Vedanta Press in Hollywood, Bob Adjemian, and he confirmed that Isherwood participated in temple events over decades and had many personal interactions with the guru. Also, my interview with Isherwood's partner Don Bachardy made it clear that Isherwood continued the japam practice, and that his devotion to the guru continued to deepen, right up until Prabhavananda's death (and perhaps beyond). This is also clear from his own accounts in *My Guru and his disciple*, and the diaries. While Isherwood was not especially attracted to Indian culture, he visited the Center regularly over many years. The Swami made sure that service projects were always available to Isherwood, and Bachardy speaks warmly of times when each would be doing their japam practice in different parts of the house.

By way of contrast, Isherwood's long-time friend John Yale, who took the initiate name of Prem Chaitanya when he was first accepted as a student by the Swami, went on to complete the twelve-year period of training to become a Swami in the Order. This is called 'taking *sannyas*', or the full vows of renunciation as a monk; leaving aside worldly life altogether, forever. Yale was originally a publisher, and he was drawn to Vedanta directly as a result of reading Isherwood's writings. He worked with Isherwood on the preparation of the Ramakrishna biography and other projects and he helped edit the Society magazine, *Vedanta and the West*. Isherwood went to India for Yale's sannyas ceremony at which time Yale took on the name Swami

Vidyatmanananda. The figure of the monk in *A meeting by the river* is based at least partly on Yale, although in another sense, of course, the character represents one side of Isherwood himself. Yale's own description of a long and difficult relationship with Swami Prabhavananda lends some testimonial veracity to the theory of the role of the guru, and it is worth quoting at length:

> The trick is to bring this innate divinity up to consciousness—the most difficult task of one's life. This is what life is for. And what the guru is for, as Swamiji says, is to disperse the obstacles so that what is innate in the organism can become manifest … Since the principal obstacles are our ignorance and self-importance, which blind us, the guru works first and foremost to break down the ego (which we don't know we have). This is a delicate operation, for if he cuts too superficially there will be small success. If he cuts too profoundly he may, figuratively, kill the patient. In some senses, every human relation, no matter how trivial, is a guru-disciple relation. The problem with most human relationships is that because of the ignorance on both sides, not much enlightenment accrues to either participant. Wisdom in the mentor is needed (rare) and readiness in the learner (also rare). (Swami Vidyatmananda, *The making of a devotee;* chapter four: 'The devotee as disciple', n.d. online)

Isherwood was always inclined to relate to systems and ideologies through personal relationships, and, in spite of the initial caution coming from his atheism, and the 'underground force of opposition' already noted in himself, the personal relationship with a guru actually made it easier for him to gain entrée:

> The longer I remained in contact with Prabhavananda and the Vedanta Society, the more clearly I understood that religion—at any rate for a person of my temperament—must mean primarily a relationship: a relationship leading at long last to a direct union with the Atman; a relationship for the time being with some individual who can give you a dim glimpse of the Atman within him, simply by being what he is. (*Approach to Vedanta*, p. 71)

Significantly, Isherwood notes that 'such an individual doesn't have to be perfect'. He writes affectionately of Swamiji's 'bad habits', such as smoking cigarettes; something that people focusing solely in the externals might feel disqualified the guru from spiritual integrity. Isherwood, on the other hand, was quite prepared to give 'worldly pleasures' their due:

> This talk about the world's pleasures being wretched and tasteless is just silly, as far as I am concerned … You can wish them away and groan and say you never did like them, really. They have extraordinary beauty and significance, and woe to the wetleg who denies it. (*My Guru*, pp. 119–20)

Isherwood was fortunate to connect with a guru who was not afraid, in fact, of showing his human nature:

> But he must have no pretenses; he must be, at all times, himself. If there is this clarity in his character, then you can look into him as it were, and, very occasionally, get a glimpse of the something-else, the element which is not-he, not his personality, not his individual nature. And then you can begin to have faith in his faith. You can feel that he is holding you, like a rock-climber on a rope, just as he himself is being held by the rope that goes on up above him. This is what the disciple demands of the guru. It is a tremendous demand. (p. 71)

Literary psycho-sleuths are fond of interpreting the guru as a substitute 'father figure' for Isherwood, but this is not entirely satisfactory. In devotional songs, the guru is seen as mother, father, brother and friend, and several of these qualities are reflected in his own account of the guru-disciple relationship. 'God can be worshipped in all different ways,' he explained in an interview with Carolyn Heilbrun:

> You can look at him as a friend and as a lover—the whole Krishna thing came into that, you see. And you can also look at him as your father or your mother or your master. (1976, p. 142)

Later, he wrote that he was able to love his guru in a 'protective' way: 'as I loved little Annie Avis my childhood nanny' (*My Guru*, p. 39).

Tucked away at the end of that quotation is the reference to the master. If the guru is capable of embodying the relationship, then guru *puja*, or the worship of the guru by a *bhakta* (devotee), can focalise devotion and, as the relationship with Prabhavananda deepened over the decades, the Swami did, in fact, become the focus of puja for Isherwood, even while retaining those qualities appropriate as a very human friend to his student. Western psychotherapists now recognise in the guru relationship some elements of the kind of relationship their clients may form with their therapists—focusing on projection, and the dynamics of transference and counter-transference—although, in the light of the higher value they are inclined to place on Western forms of psychotherapy and analysis, they tend to be more comfortable writing about the psychological benefits of meditation practice, say, than to validate the guru/disciple relationship, which in Isherwood's case shifted from respect into a very deep form of love.

What Western, rationalist frameworks of understanding tend to miss is that the exercise of any, or a combination, of these possible approaches—as to a father, or a child, etc., even as God in person—opens up dormant pathways for experience which would remain only potentialities without the focus of devotional practice. Of course, as we will see later in the discussion of Jeffrey Kripal's appropriation of Sri Ramakrishna's legacy, the tendency to *pathologise* such forms of practice delimits the understanding of their powerful effects. This is partly a disciplinary problem—crude, psychologically reductive explanations transposed across mystical practice and experience—and partly the discursive limits of rationalism itself, with its dogged refusal to recognise other potentialities made possible in non-rational operations of mind. (I compare this to a situation where someone who has only ever listened to transmissions over AM radio frequencies refuses to consider the possibilities of FM broadcasts; but even that analogy is already outdated by recent technologies.)

I have discussed how unjustly neglected were Isherwood's later works in Britain, from this period on. *Prater Violet* (1945), for example, was virtually ignored (see Diary entry 10 June 1954, p. 702). There appears to have been residual resentment towards his pacifist stance, which had seldom been interpreted as conscientious, or principled. But that doesn't explain the kind of sneering references that slip into many of the treatments of Isherwood's sincerely practised religion, even today. Duncan Fallowell writes in the *Daily Express*, in 2004, that Isherwood 'disappears in extreme self-absorption like a black hole' ('Life was no Cabaret', p. 50). By now we're familiar with the charges: Fallowell is convinced that Isherwood's 'desertion of Europe' at its moment of crisis 'created a wound he never overcame' and opines that 'as a writer it also cut him off from his material' (p. 50). (This view was also espoused by the poet Philip Larkin *vis à vis* WH Auden; see Dennis 2009, p. 21). From this it would appear that Fallowell hasn't read beyond the Berlin period, yet he acknowledges that Isherwood 'wrote three or four more good books among a fair bit of dross'. (Apparently he wasn't so 'cut off' from material.) Despite the confidence of his opinions, it is hard to see what evidence Fallowell has for his claim that Isherwood became 'a ghostly figure' in 'his struggle to reincarnate himself in California' (p. 50), although he might have seemed that way for literary commentators who refused to acknowledge the work he was engaged with. Fallowell also reads Parker's biography rather myopically: 'Isherwood's bid to become real again did not succeed and the pull of this bloodhound biography is as *a study of conceit in decline*' (p. 50; emphasis added).

As for Eastern mysticism, Fallowell opines that it brought Isherwood 'no more happiness than a frozen pizza' (p. 50). This is a stunning assertion in the face of what is regarded by many as a spiritual classic: *My Guru and his disciple* (1980). Apart from claiming to have met Isherwood, Fallowell's qualifications to evaluate the writer's life or work are not evident. Here is Isherwood, the notorious homosexual, rehearsing unsanctioned subject positions by engaging in behaviour that does not fit the stereotype (homosexuality and religious practice are mutually exclusive). Therefore he could not possibly have succeeded in his religious devotions (for, if he did, the entire moral universe from which this canard is derived will be dangerously destabilised). The homosexual must remain the religious pariah.

There are several ways he can be criticised for not keeping his place in the moral order: the sincerity of his practice can be called into question; the 'success' of his practice can be mocked; and the provenance of his practice can be questioned—in this case, drawn from a system practised by a colonised people. One has to question whether any literary commentator would be prepared to do this with, say, Graham Greene's Catholicism.

American writers were less inclined to be as sceptical. Carolyn Heilbrun in 1970, Alan Wilde in 1971, Brian Finney in 1979, Claude J Summers in 1981; all published excellent books on the writer (without many of the resources available to Parker) and all treated the religious life with respect. So perhaps it was mainly among British literary critics that Isherwood became a 'ghost'.

Beyond monasticism

By publishing his diaries Isherwood opened himself to more than *self*-scrutiny. After his brief attempt to live the renunciate life, it does appear that he went on a bender. As the blurb for the second volume of the diaries (*Lost years: a memoir 1945–1951*) describes it: 'he careened into a life of frantic socializing, increasing dissipation, anxiety, and, eventually, despair'; so when he was preparing this manuscript for publication, thirty years after the fact, he was clearly not on the defensive. He includes explicit details of his romantic and sexual relationships of the 1940s, and many reviewers were disturbed by this frankness (e.g., Craft 2000, pp. 13–14). I suspect that it is this volume, *Lost years*—more than *Christopher and his kind*, say—which has led some critics to presume that the sex sprees and drunkenness must, perforce, have canceled out his spirituality ever after.

One has to acknowledge the double entendre of 'lost' in the title, of course. At the surface level, these were 'lost' years because Isherwood's usual diary-keeping went into abeyance and the text had to be reconstructed, but there is also the ironic sense that they were 'lost' in the sense that he had lost his way. But I wouldn't push this too far; it can be argued that this project was, in fact, in keeping with the overriding frankness that had more bearing on Isherwood's spirituality than monasticism. Craft, among others, seems to forget that the book is a re-construction of an earlier period, and assumes that what was a reaction to the restrictions of the monastic life carried forward for decades. The sub-heading for his review reads: 'The sex, spite and sourness of Isherwood's *last* years' (p. 13; emphasis added), yet clearly the period under review in *Lost years* is 1945–1951—the title makes it clear—and Isherwood didn't die until 1986. This is a common oversight. Even Antony Copley's

2006 study suffers from the similar unsubstantiated assumption, leading him to suppose that Swami Prabhavananda somehow 'failed' with Isherwood.

The second of the major factors contributing to resolving Isherwood's ontological and psychological insecurities was to be his long-standing partnership with Don Bachardy, the intimate relationship that began in 1953—after this wild, post-monastic period, and the breakdown of the affair with Bill Caskey. Bachardy was much younger than Isherwood and, as it survived the intrinsic stressors of a long-term commitment—especially one between two partners of such different ages—the partnership drew out qualities of patience, mentoring and a protectiveness in Isherwood that critics like Savage—who want him to remain forever the immature *puer aeternus* of the Berlin period—fail to recognise. The relationship was not monogamous and, as we have seen, Bachardy could be quite a challenge (in his own words: 'I tested him severely' he told me). The diaries document the rocky periods as well as the happy times.

Craft presents himself as a member of Isherwood's circle ('en famille' is his term) and while disapproving of Isherwood's affairs, happily goes into much of the gritty detail he professes to abhor. Katherine Bucknell and Don Bachardy confirm the connection: Isherwood was a great friend of Igor Stravinsky, and Craft was Stravinsky's adopted son, and colleague—he conducted for the composer and supervised recording sessions (see Bucknell 1996, p. 935). He was also Stravinsky's biographer. But it's not uncommon, even for someone who moved in the same social circles, to miss the point. Once again, Isherwood's candour provides ammunition for those who would put him down. Isherwood could have shaped the material in any way he wanted, so I must raise the question of why he didn't choose to show himself in a better light. I read this unrepentant sexuality as in keeping with the non-dualist form of spirituality he pursued. Accepting his sexuality was as much a part of accepting his 'dharma' as embracing his calling as a writer, the third major factor in resolving Isherwood's deepest anxieties. And the commitment to the sometimes difficult relationship with Bachardy became intrinsic to Isherwood's spirituality to the point where all three elements—Vedanta study and praxis, the 'householder' partnership, and the maturing of his gifts as a writer—were ultimately woven together into one richly satisfying life for Isherwood.

Katherine Bucknell says we have in the record of the Diaries 'the true account of how bad and how good a relationship can be'. She cites an entry from the (as yet unpublished) diaries, from 1967, where Isherwood discusses the opposition between sacred and profane love, asking how love could be profane if it were really love, and asserting that Bachardy had 'become his path to spiritual enlightenment' (*Don and Chris a love story*). This could be interpreted in two ways: either that the difficulties of the relationship—which went through very difficult periods—were a spiritual 'test' to be endured (his 'Cross' to bear, if you will); or that, to choose to love, through all the ups and downs, was the true maturity AND the true spirituality. Under the influence of Vedanta, especially given the 'Advaita' version taught by his guru, Isherwood came to integrate the various elements of his life into one fulfiling project.

A more insightful reading than that offered by Craft, Savage, and others comes from Adam Phillips, a psychotherapist from the British object-relations school. His review of *Lost years* for *The Guardian*, in 2000, recognises Isherwood's 'determination to track down even the most elusive and unappealing aspects of his past in order to understand and honestly portray himself, both as a writer and as a human being' ('Setting the Record Straight'). In contrast with the lingering charges of narcissism, Phillips interprets Isherwood's use of recollection not just as a way to construct the personal myth but as 'the best cure for egotism'. WH Auden said of Isherwood's use of autobiographical material, that he was

> that rarest of all creatures, the objective narcissist; he sees himself altogether plain and does not hesitate to record for us the lines that the face in the mirror has accumulated, the odd shadow that flaws the character. (qtd in Sutherland, p. C9)

Phillips observes, astutely, that 'we may look better if we rearrange the facts, but rearranging the facts is also moral propaganda' and he recognises that as a writer, Isherwood was aware of the need for an ongoing 'critique of the self-justifying voice' (Phillips 2000). This is the kind of self-reflection—reminiscent of the image of the 'knife in the wound' Isherwood used about writing in the first person—that proves useful practice in spiritual work as well and is, I suggest, a different kind of self-awareness than the familiar myopic stereotyping we have seen of Isherwood would allow.

We must also pay attention here to a significant factor underpinning the work: the Advaitist challenge to the 'curious and Western heresy which declares that the pretty and pleasant are more 'real' than the ugly and unpleasant', in Isherwood's words (*Ramakrishna*, p. 51). (The figure of Kali, which was the focus of Ramakrishna's devotions, symbolises this principle, integrating principles of dark and light.) There can be no traces of spirit/body dualism here: 'I feel, very strongly, that we must not despise the body,' writes Isherwood. 'The body is not a lump of corrupt filth, it is not evil. It is our faithful loyal servant, in sickness and in health' (*My Guru*, p. 120). No one could be more aware than Isherwood, however, that it might require some discipline: 'If you let it be the master, then it will display all its greed and stupidity and brutishness' (p. 120), he continues and, as he was not engaged in a hagiographic representation of his own history, the testimony of his own 'stupidity and brutishness' makes his unblinking self-portrait all the more convincing, for not being idealised. In spiritual work idealisation is a tendency—let me be clear on this—at least as dangerous as 'greed, stupidity and brutishness'.

Aware of the complexities of his very human nature, Isherwood was never comfortable in the role of the 'saint'. He entered fully into the life of the movie studios with a clear sense (at least in retrospect) of what he was up to:

> Should he have left the Center much sooner than he did? Looking back, I find that I can't say yes. It now seems to me that Christopher's embarrassment and guilt feelings were of little importance and his 'spiritual struggles' trivial. What mattered was that he was getting exposure to Swami, that his relations with Swami continued to be (fairly) frank, and that he never ceased to be aware of Swami's love. That he kept slipping away to see Bill Harris wasn't really so dreadful. (p. 7)

This is the version from the diaries, as given in *Lost years*. The guilt feelings he acknowledges here are considered of 'little importance', upon review, and stem from his discomfort with the expectation of celibacy that was part and parcel of life in the monastic setting, which he soon quit. The version in *My Guru* differs slightly, and includes this:

> [T]hat I had lost the respect of many outside observers was, on the whole, good—or at worst it was a thousand times better than if I had fooled anybody into thinking me holy. (p. 188)

In spite of the 'debauchery', then, Isherwood's relationship with the Swami continued to deepen, and so did his understanding of the nature of the path he was on. It doesn't take a very close reading of Isherwood's nigh on forty-year association with his guru to recognise that it became the most crucial of all the relationships—intellectual, creative and artistic friendships, sexual intimates, and so on—which Isherwood enjoyed. So, it is surprising, given the amount of documentation available, that this relationship is not given its due weight today. Altman's characterisation of it as a 'long flirtation', seems particularly ill-considered.

Owen Richardson laments the period in the 1950s when Isherwood's writing 'went to seed' (2004, p. 10). This is the conventional view, of course, but it ignores what Isherwood had been working on, namely, the translations with his guru of the major Vedanta texts, plus his own bridge-building articles on the tradition for Western readers (*An approach to Vedanta*, etc.). While literary critics may overlook this part of the oeuvre, it is important to any understanding of what was happening to Isherwood's subjectivity. While his admirers in Britain were lamenting the literary output, Isherwood was actually reaching out to a new readership, as a cultural translator. As he noted, ruefully, in an interview with Carolyn Heilbrun: 'People,' he said, 'get a wonderful view of my lack of production by blissfully ignoring two-thirds of my work. I *only* produced, I don't know, what was it—three, four books related to Vedanta in one way or another' (Heilbrun 1970, p. 27).

Apart from the translations he worked on with the Swami, he put out fascinating collections of essays by other leading figures of the time—Aldous Huxley was a major contributor to *Vedanta for the Western world* (1946, first US edn; 1948, British edn), and so was Gerald Heard. (Both editions went through several printings.) *Vedanta for modern man*, another collection of essays, also went through several printings.

However, in some cases it appears the omission borders on deliberate occlusion. Summing up Isherwood's memoirs, Owen Richardson omits *My Guru*, even though Isherwood regarded it as: 'the most worthwhile book I have written *and* probably one of the best modern books of its kind' (Diary, 17 Feb 1980; emphasis in original). So what is really going on here? Richardson inexplicably claims that 'the Hindu sect of Vedanta' had become 'fashionable in California in the 1930s', and finds that:

> Isherwood's obsession with Vedanta and his attempts to become holy, while wrestling with the temptation to have a fine old-worldly time with all that Hollywood had to offer—boys and stars—make wearing reading. (p. 10)

And what Altman has described as a 'flirtation', Richardson characterises here as an 'obsession'.

John Sutherland also suggests that the interest was somehow 'fashionable'. Comparing Isherwood's career with Auden's, he writes that 'Auden turned to the Western religion of his fathers, Isherwood to the Eastern mysticism of the tinseltown gurus' (p. 23). It's not hard to recognise a supercilious characterisation of all things Californian in this throw-away line, even if it was not as fashionable in the 1930s as this latter-day reference implies. Parker's biography has obviously flushed a discomfort out of hiding among these reviewers, one masked by the use of tendentious and sometimes erroneous terms, one that appears to be due to more than the lingering resentment at Isherwood's wartime defection.

Sutherland's is a perfect case in point of this persistence in reading Isherwood in a particular light. He spends 7.5 of his 8 review columns to reach only January 1939, yet Isherwood's life and literary output continued well into the 1980s. His reading of Isherwood seems to have stalled at this early stage, which is common among British commentators. Perhaps that is why he could mistakenly refer to Isherwood's 'late-life conversion to transcendentalism' that I have already noted. (It was neither late life, nor transcendentalist). Sutherland changed tack in his second attempt, in a column for *The Boston Globe*, January 2005, when he had had time to read the US reviews for both the British and US editions of the Parker biography. He cites David Kipen of the *San Francisco Chronicle*, who described Isherwood as 'a master stylist whose understandable importance to gay literature, California literature and the literature of pre-World War II Germany tends to obscure his contribution to literature, full stop' (p. C9). Sutherland makes my case for me:

> He may, with an odd admixture of fortune, become so well known for an early work, so intimately identified with same, that later work never quite gains its foothold. (2005, p. C9)

From these and many other examples, I suggest that, beyond the residual resentment towards Isherwood's wartime pacifism, what is embedded in this perverse refusal to take his religious life seriously is the unexamined master narrative that firstly creates a taxonomy of types, defining 'deviants' as Other, and then refuses to recognise clear instances when they don't behave according to the typology. Certainly Isherwood was stepping outside his inscribed cultural positioning, in the way Judith Butler describes—non-conformist sexuality and conformist religion are antagonists, according to this narrative—and myopic literary commentators, comfortably and even unconsciously ensconced with the cosy confines of the dominant meta-narratives, are sometimes unable to see what is before their eyes.

Hindu 'mumbo jumbo'

'With Isherwood, if you've got the boyfriends right, then pretty much everything else will fall into place.' This was the view of David Ehrenstein, reviewing the Parker biography for the magazine *The Advocate* in December 2004. If British literary commentators value only the pre-pacifist period, gay commentators are more inclined to read Isherwood strictly for the sexuality, buying into the rules of the game in exactly the manner Foucault describes:

> The notion of 'sex' made it possible to group together, in an artificial unity, anatomical elements, biological functions, conducts, sensations, and pleasures, and it enabled one to make use of this fictitious unity as a causal principle, an omnipresent meaning, a secret to be discovered everywhere. *(*1978, p. 154)

Who will recognise and acknowledge this other major bandwidth in the life and work? Joel Greenberg does acknowledge the importance of the Vedanta factor. In reviewing the Parker biography, he writes:

> What for some may have seemed like mere spiritual dilettantism became a central focal point of his existence. He even contemplated becoming a Hindu monk and for nearly two years lodged for that purpose in the Hollywood headquarters of the Vedanta movement on Ivar Avenue. (2004, p. R9)

However, Greenberg follows Peter Parker's own less than sympathetic reading of the guru figure: 'For all his saintliness, Prabhavananda cannily understood that in Isherwood he had bagged a celebrity convert and exploited him accordingly' (p. R9).

Isherwood raised this issue himself, quite frankly describing the period in a diary entry (8 July 1944), written at a time when he was discussing moving out of the Vedanta Center:

> Denny, that sourest of all critics, refuses to be impressed when I tell him about Swami's tolerance and open-mindedness. According to him, Swami is bound to accept me on any terms, because I'm so useful to the Vedanta Society as a translator and editor. I get very angry when he talks like this, and I think it's utterly unjust to Swami. (*Diaries volume one*, p. 353; and *My Guru*, pp. 163–4)

Denny Fouts was the basis for the character of Paul in the last section of *Down there on a visit*. He and Isherwood had set up a quasi-monastic living experiment before Isherwood actually moved in to Ivar Avenue. After a short-lived burst of enthusiasm for concentrated spiritual practice satirised in that text, Fouts's enthusiasm for Vedanta waned. The Swami also rebuffed Fouts, as Isherwood recounts in *My Guru*. In the diary entry, Isherwood again calls him 'the sourest of all critics':

> According to Denny Swami is bound to accept me on any terms, because I'm so useful to the Vedanta Society as an editor and translator ... But the

> fact remains that he *is* much more lenient towards me than he is towards the others. I don't think this proves anything either way, except that perhaps I'm much more tiresome and demanding. Maybe, also, the Swami realizes what a lot of karmas I dragged into Ivar Avenue out of the past. With Sarada, who's young and has a real vocation, he can afford to be strict; and, in many ways, I think he's fonder of her than of any of us. It's really no compliment to be let off lightly: it merely means that I am too weak to be disciplined. (p. 353)

As Isherwood used the entry almost unchanged in the 1980 publication (after decades more exposure to the guru's wiles), can we safely assume that Isherwood hadn't changed his own position, more than three decades later? Isherwood provides the evidence; the later readers provide their own interpretation, but fail to show little evidence from any *other* source to validate their opinion. Is that because it plays into their own prejudices? And are there factors contributing to such prejudice that have not been sufficiently closely examined?

Colonialist blinkers

To observers in literary society, Isherwood's relationship with an Indian guru, ascetic or not, was going beyond the pale. Already a persona non grata because of his perceived abandonment of Britain, this interest in an Indian religious tradition and the outright adoption of a guru, let alone an attempt to live a celibate life for a while in the Center, was not viewed sympathetically, let alone with insight. (I suspect that the stereotyping of meditation as an introspective practice contributed to the characterisation of Isherwood as a self-absorbed narcissist, and I think Jamie Carr would agree.) Auden, who returned to Anglicanism, regarded it as 'heathen mumbo jumbo' (*My Guru*, p. 204), although he did acknowledge that the Swami was probably a saint! There are elements of unreconstructed colonialism in play—not only in Auden—that continue today, and I want to examine this a little more closely.

Isherwood's mentor EM Forster's *A passage to India* had been controversial because it presented the British in India as crassly ethnocentric. I should point out, too, that it had only been four or five decades since Swami Vivekananda had established a beachhead for the Ramakrishna Society in the US. Isherwood notes with some amusement how the reception to Vivekananda was marked by American 'hucksterism' and suspicions of 'heathenism'. Vivekananda attended the landmark Parliament of Religions in Chicago, in 1893. (The Archbishop of Canterbury refused to attend, objecting that the very meeting of such a parliament implied the equality of all religions.) He also notes that the word 'Swami' was usually associated in the American mind with magicians and prestidigitators from travelling carnivals. In his introduction to John Yale's collection of Vivekananda's writings, Isherwood states:

> Even today, the name 'Swami' is associated with theatrical trickery, and most Americans are unaware that those who have the right to call themselves by it have taken formal monastic vows; that it is, in fact, a title just as worthy of respect as that of 'Father' in the Catholic Church'. (1962, p. xi)

That there was an ethnocentric condescension towards the value systems and practices of other cultures' spiritual traditions is underlined by Isherwood's owning such attitudes himself. In his personal account, *An approach to Vedanta* (1963), he looks back more than twenty years to examine some of the prejudices and suspicions he had faced when the subject came up among people in his own circle (and among his critics in Britain). Notwithstanding the fact that he had been an atheist, he writes:

> I think these objections were rooted in twofold prejudice. Whether I liked it or not, I had been brought up in the Christian tradition; anything outside that tradition repelled me as being unnecessarily alien. Also, as a member, whether I liked it or not, of the British upper class, I had somewhere deep inside me a built-in contempt for the culture of 'native', 'subject' races. If my subconscious had been allowed to speak that clearly, it would have said: 'I quite admit that you have the truth, but does it have to come to me wearing a turban? Can't I be an Anglo-Saxon Vedantist?' (*An approach to Vedanta*, pp. 34–5)

I am not alone in recognising the neo-colonial prejudice towards spiritual traditions from 'subject' races. David Robb picks up on the point in relation to the suspicion surrounding the reception of Aldous Huxley's turn towards spirituality and, specifically, Huxley's adoption of Gandhi's principles of nonviolence:

> Although Englishmen were well aware of Gandhi and his movement, the acceptance of his principles was effectively impeded by an ingrained British contempt for subject native races. (Robb 1985, p. 53)

In a footnote to his article, Robb cites this same reference in Isherwood, but doesn't note the irony of Isherwood's putting himself in the dock (p. 60).

What this amounts to is that we can't ignore the fact that Britain was a colonial power, India one of her prize possessions, and 'Hinduism' was the religion of a colonised and subjugated people. It seems to me that this is a major, unexamined source of the neglect evident in much of the coverage and analysis of Isherwood.

But one would not expect to find such an attitude in as detailed a biography of Isherwood as offered by Peter Parker in 2004. Parker shows himself to be a rather old-fashioned 'contemporary', and his style of literary biography quite traditional. Rarely does he declare his own positions, and at no point does he open up the process he went through personally in engaging with his subject—Isherwood's subjectivity. Where cultural biases are embedded and unacknowledged, they can produce a less than sympathetic portrayal of the subject being scrutinised. In an interview for *The Telegraph* in London, Parker gives only a nod in the general direction of such disclosure:

> I'm not a fan of the biographer popping up and waving his arms all over the place, unless you're writing a book like *The quest for Corvo*, a book about trying to write a biography. (2004, 'A writer's life', p. 12)

This is not Janet Malcolm writing about Chekhov, then, or Robert Dessaix writing himself into the life of Turgenev. What Parker's personal positions are—on Isherwood's sexuality, say, or on his religion—are unstated, and only come out indirectly. In the interview, he hedges:

> If you're writing a biography of a writer I think you are obliged to make literary judgments, but I do try to avoid wagging my finger over any of Isherwood's behaviour that perhaps personally I wouldn't approve of. (p. 12)

This is admirable in principle, and Parker does his best to maintain the stance of detachment. But if he manages to avoid wagging the finger in regard to Isherwood himself he does take the bait in relation to Swami Prabhavananda.

Parker characterises the guru as 'cunning', and 'exploitative' of Isherwood's talents, and as using his literary reputation to promote the movement (pp. 525, 818) and this is a point rather tamely taken up by most reviewers. I have to consider that this might have been true, but I also have to ask what evidence is given to support this opinion, which is offered as a straightforward judgment. Parker gets all the historical information about their meeting in place; he covers the translation work, the monastic period in the Center, the disastrous trip to India together. He even offers a relatively kind coda on the relationship much later in his book, without really showing that he has understood the nature of the work that has transpired between Isherwood and his teacher in the interim. Has Parker done Prabhavananda justice, or is he just parroting 'sour' Denny Fouts?

Crossing the divide

In the biography *Ramakrishna and his disciples* (1965), Isherwood, the former atheist, lucidly describes many of the key features of the Advaita position. He describes Hinduism as:

> a religion which recognises the male-female principle within the Godhead. The Hindu, believing that the Godhead must by definition embody all possible functions, is logically brought to think of it as being both male and female. (One of the greatest causes of misunderstanding of Hinduism by foreign scholars is perhaps a subconsciously respected tradition that God must be one sex only, or at least only one sex at a time.) (p. 48)

Given this fundamental position, the hetero/homosexual divide, then, would have even *less* traction in the guru's treatment of his disciple. Yet of all things to quibble about in relation to Prabhavananda, Parker wants to show that the guru's attitude to homosexuality is really quite different from what he showed to Isherwood, and that he is treating Isherwood with kid gloves because he doesn't want to lose his considerable cachet and literary skills. It is worthy of note that Parker tries to prove his case using language that he uses nowhere else in the lengthy biography:

> The most serious charge against *My Guru & his disciple* concerns the central question of Prabhavananda's attitude towards homosexuality. Isherwood recalls the occasion when he asked Prabhavananda whether it would be possible to lead a spiritual life while at the same time having a sexual relationship with another man, and the Swami answered somewhat equivocally: 'You must try to see him as the young Lord Krishna.' 'I wasn't at all discouraged by the Swami's reply,' Isherwood writes: 'indeed, it was far more permissive than I had expected. What reassured me—what convinced me that I could become his pupil—was that he hadn't shown the least shadow of distaste on hearing me admit to my homosexuality.' (*My Guru*, pp. 25–6; Parker, p. 817)

Parker employs language from the courtroom: he brings a serious 'charge against' Prabhavananda and chooses to read the guru's encouraging response as 'equivocal'. Yet for a man 'looking for a religion that would accept him as a homosexual' this was a critical issue. Intent as he is on the prosecution of Swami Prabhavananda, Parker fails to give his response its due, and mars the clarity of Isherwood's assessment that the guru had not shown 'the least shadow of distaste'. Clearly, this was a very important issue to Isherwood at the time; should I presume he was willing to fool himself on the matter? Here is what Isherwood has to say about it:

> Swami did not think in terms of sins, as most Christians do. Certainly he regarded my lust for Vernon as an obstacle to my spiritual progress—but no more and no less of an obstacle than lust for a woman, even for a lawfully wedded wife, would have been. (*My Guru*, p. 26)

And here he draws an important distinction:

> Christian sins are offences against God and each one has its fixed degree of magnitude. The obstacles which the Swami recognises are offences against yourself and their importance is relative to each individual's condition. In fact the Swami's attitude was much like that of a coach who tells his athletes that they must give up smoking, alcohol, and certain kinds of food, not because they are inherently evil, but because they may prevent the athlete from getting something he wants much more—an Olympic medal, for instance. (*My Guru*, p. 26)

Is this the guru 'equivocating', to keep the famous writer in his stable? Or as slight as it seems, does it mark a fundamental difference in the way the religion is practised? This is a very important distinction for someone with Isherwood's background. But determined to find the Swami at fault, Parker simply brushes it aside. Continuing with the courtroom rhetoric, he finds that:

> [t]his is less than candid. In attempting to persuade his readers—and perhaps himself—of Prabhavananda's winning combination of saintliness and worldliness, Isherwood is capable of withholding facts and fudging the evidence. (p. 817)

Pressing home his accusation, he brings up what he considers 'the most egregious example' of the Swami's alleged dishonesty, quoting from *My Guru and his disciple*:

> During November 1956, a young man whom Swami and I both knew was arrested and charged with sexual solicitation in a men's washroom. Swami's reaction was: 'Oh, Chris, if only he hadn't got caught! Why didn't he go to some bar?' This was one of the times when Swami's unworldly worldliness made me laugh out loud. (*My Guru*, pp. 221–22, qtd in Parker, p. 817)

Parker focuses his critique of Isherwood's Vedanta instructor around this differential treatment towards sexuality. His language is revealing here: 'serious charge'; 'withholding facts'; 'fudging the evidence'. So let me examine the 'evidence', as he presents it. Parker draws his facts entirely from Isherwood's account and offers no information from other sources to support his own interpretation. But there are contradictions in Parker's own account of this issue. He seems unaware that, as Isherwood refused to become a brahmachari, and didn't go on to 'take sannyas'—vows that require celibacy—he was not expected to renounce sex (this was years after he left the monastery). Gurus may continue to teach devotees whom they have accepted for instruction, including those outside the disciplines of the renunciate lifestyle. In fact, as he notes, '[I]nstruction varied from pupil to pupil, according to individual needs and temperaments' (*My Guru*, p. 19). Indeed, the young man in question continued his practice within the stricter confines of the Order's ashrams in India, presumably without coercion. Perhaps the problem here really has to do with Parker's ignorance of religious traditions other than his own, or perhaps he is unconsciously projecting the kind of Christianised moral value system from which Isherwood so articulately differentiates his practice? While Isherwood (and many of his readers) laugh at Prabhavananda's 'unworldliness', Parker cannot help express distaste.

There is an untested assumption operating in many ill-informed Western appraisals of others involved in the spiritual life, that their devotion isn't genuine unless it measures up to unquestioned assumptions about the need for chastity (as well as poverty). But to go on to say, as Parker does, that 'the *truth* is that Prabhavananda allowed Isherwood to 'get away with murder' for entirely pragmatic reasons' (emphasis added) is just an opinion. He argues that 'Isherwood was Vedanta's most distinguished Western convert' (p. 818), apparently forgetting Aldous Huxley, and Gerald Heard, both of whom were associating with Swami Prabhavananda before Isherwood came onto the scene, and both of whom published extensively.

In Parker's assessment, Isherwood appears as a kind of victim. What the movement needed, Parker claims:

> in order to secure its foothold in the Western world was someone famous, clever and articulate, someone who lived in that world rather than a cloister, and who could be persuaded to write books and articles, edit magazines and anthologies, provide lucid translations of and forewords to the works of others. (pp. 818–19)

I have already shown the integral role that service to the guru plays in this tradition. Prabhavananda did not have to manipulate Isherwood to gain his help.

Finally, Parker wriggles out of the mess he has stirred up with a lame disclaimer: 'None of this is to suggest that Isherwood had been duped in any way' (p. 819); leaving us to wonder why he brought the 'charges' in the first place, except perhaps to air his negative characterisation of Prabhavananda.

And before I leave this section I want to draw attention to the issue of 'sin'. There is a different set of principles at work in the Vedanta system that I think Parker fails to recognise, perhaps because of his unexamined culturally Christian assumptions. In the fifth chapter of the Isherwood/Prabhavananda translation of the Bhagavad Gita, this verse stands out: 'The Lord is everywhere and always perfect. What does he care for man's sin or the righteousness of man?' This is the nondualist basis of Advaita Vedanta in operation. It works from a different set of theoretical and psychodynamic principles that, as surprising as it is to those trained only in the Abrahamic models, does not rely on guilt, or judgement.

Katherine Bucknell has worked more closely with the original source materials than any other scholar, including the final years of the diaries (as yet unpublished). She writes:

> Swami did not regard Isherwood's homosexuality as a sin, and Hinduism, in contrast to Christianity, does not include the Judeo-Christian emphasis upon the problem of guilt. Swami simply regarded all forms of lust as obstacles to spiritual progress. (*Diaries volume one 1939–1960*, pp. xiii–xiv.)

Isherwood contrasts this modus operandi as quite distinct from the configuration of the 'Abrahamic God' who, as he sees it, becomes the Policeman God; the 'Vice Squad God' (one might add: the 'homophobic God').

There is no doubt that Isherwood's guru let him play on a very long rope, but if Parker wants to find cleverness and cunning at work in the wily Bengali, perhaps he should be drawing our attention to the skilful way that the Swami was able to continue to work with his student over decades. To force a student to adhere to a way of life that is not in accord with his/her dharma inevitably produces a reaction; a strong reaction that, in many cases, may fester into resentment, then rebellion, perhaps even leading the disciple into outright rejection of the entire system for the rest of this life. Is this cunning, then, or is it wisdom, on the guru's part? As someone with decades of experience observing the reactive nature of the mind, and guiding his students through rough patches, this is his field of expertise; but a literary commentator unfamiliar with the psychodynamics of such a relationship may fall back on clichéd, poorly thought through representations of the guru-as-exploiter, familiar from unchallenged media stereotypes.

Isherwood was not afflicted with self-loathing around the nature of his sexuality. As much as he might have rued the dissipative effects of his periodic binges, he was not struggling with the sense of transgression still common today among those whose internalised conscience remains indoctrinated by a culture of shame.

Jamake Highwater writes perceptively about the operation of guilt, and the sense of pervasive transgression, by drawing a comparison between two literary figures: Franz Kafka and Arthur Rimbaud. Highwater borrows Philip Rahv's analysis of Kafka as a man obsessed with a sinfulness that corresponded 'to nothing he had actually done or left undone,' but nevertheless remained 'lodged in the innermost recesses of his being' (Rahv, cited Highwater 2001, p. 36). In Highwater's reading, Kafka:

> returns again and again to face a judgment that never comes, a victim of his own willingness to succumb to self-doubt, self-contempt, and self-incrimination for a sin he did not commit. (p. 37)

He describes Kafka as a 'moral hypochondriac who could not be cured of the disease from which he suffered, because he didn't have the disease in the first place' (p. 38).

Even though it is still a common feature of the religiously-derived moral imagination today, I think we need to recognise in Isherwood someone who freed himself from this toxic, internalised sense of guilt, especially after quitting the short-lived experiment of monkhood. His earlier exposure to Socialism, and his atheism, worked as a kind of de-programming from Anglican religious conventions, and that process prepared him for thinking about the meaning of his life in a new way. It allowed him to review the nature of his sexuality freed up from religious intolerance. Once freed from that destructive paradigm, Isherwood could become what he was all along: a bhakta (a devotee)—not a monk. Even if they sometimes overlap, these disciplines—renunciation and devotion—operate along different axes, and the wise spiritual preceptor recognises and responds to the mode of engagement appropriate to the individual practitioner. Isherwood's engagement with 'the Divine' was principally mediated through and by his love for Swami Prabhavananda, so we might expect that a biographer would try a little harder to put his cultural blinkers aside to gain insight into the nature of the bond, and the real nature of the instruction that was operating here.

Devotion

With all the promiscuity (with its concomitant complications and dramas), the glamorous life of the studios, the company of celebrities and the colony of European expatriates, and so on, one has to ask what this other sphere provided for Isherwood that he should continue his association with Swami Prabhavananda, voluntarily, for the rest of his life. Isherwood would write, as late as 1980, that he would be grateful to Gerald Heard for the rest of his days for helping him approach the Swami and understand his teachings (*My Guru*, p. 29). Without connecting with the Swami and Vedanta, he almost certainly would have had a breakdown.

Yet devotion to the guru remains a mystery. Why? From my own observation, over thirty plus years, I would say: the guru evokes sincerity. The guru calls to the heart. To respond, the aspirant must turn away from the voice of scepticism and the delusional safety of irony, attending with humble simplicity to the response that rises from deeper layers of conscious awareness than those accessed through the familiar sophisticated posturings of a heavily defended ego. The guru functions as a tuning fork, sounding a note of rigorous honesty to—in a sense—purify the student. Rather than thickening the carapace of ego—formed out of lifelong interactions with the social world, reinforced with cynicism, strengthened by competition, assuaged with ego gratifications, clutched close in fear—the work carried out within this relationship grows an awareness of the innocent *core* of being, and works at developing this core. (In east Asia, I found they speak of spiritual practice as 'cultivation'.)

In this process, the ego is not reified; the work is carried out on another level. And it is not a passive relationship, on either side. The guru is coaxing the student to release him or her self from the tight, sphincter grip of ego to learn to trust and surrender into the embrace of the deeper field of conscious awareness that includes it. The guru holds the awareness of the deeper reality in focus for both of them. Service, devotion, growing trust, meditation practice to familiarise oneself with deeper zones of feeling and awareness—all assist in the gradual process of realising the continuity of being of the 'individual' self with all that is, and the interdependency of all things. Alan Watts provides a skilful re-working of this Vedantist vision of continuity in contemporary terms, in his *The book on the taboo against knowing who you are*:

> You cannot teach an ego to be anything but egotistic, even though egos have the subtlest ways of pretending to be reformed. The basic thing is therefore to dispel, by experiment and experience, the illusion of oneself as a separate ego. The consequences may not be behavior along the lines of conventional morality. It may well be as the squares said of Jesus, 'Look at him! A glutton and a drinker, a friend of tax-gatherers and sinners.' (p. 26)

(Existential Christian theologian Paul Tillich's notion of the 'Absolute Ground of Being', too, is remarkably similar to the ancient Vedantic vision.)

So, by holding to the awareness of the deepest stratum of being, beyond the personal self, the guru performs a mirroring function for his/her student. The guru models and reflects the reality of that level of being/awareness for the student, who is less practised at holding those deeper states in focus and much more familiar with the busy workings of those habituated personal aspects of mind/consciousness that grow in relation to the 'external' world. The mirror functioning may also show up these more superficial aspects of being, too, as Isherwood describes to great comic effect in his account of his first meeting with the Swami:

> I felt terribly awkward—like a rich, overdressed woman, in the plumes and bracelets of my vanity. Everything I said sounded artificial and false. I started acting a little scene, trying to appear sympathetic. (*My Guru*, p. 24)

The guru's expertise is to treat each student according to his temperament and potential, but he can only work with what the student gives him to work on. In spite of all the talk about the surrender of the ego, the guru should always respect the student's exercise of free will, for the association remains a voluntary one, as I noted above: 'As far as obedience to the guru is concerned, it is senseless if it is practised from a sense of obligation against one's will' (*The encyclopedia of Eastern philosophy and religion*, p. 121). Isherwood had a healthy, functioning ego and there was to be no full-on, frontal assault against it; he resisted the opportunity to take the brahmacharya vows, for example, partly because he would have had to surrender the name 'Isherwood' to take on an initiate name—as his friend, John Yale did. But through years of meditation practice he developed the habit of shifting the focal length of awareness, a process through which the ego or personal self reconnects with the ground of being. (The meaning of 'Yoga' can be defined as a 'yoke', or union; and the meaning of 'religion' unpacked from the Latin roots as *re-ligare*, being bound together again. Perhaps in their core practices they were never intended to be so far apart.)

'Bhakti', or devotion, binds the student in a loving relationship with the Master, where to try to overcome the resistance of the ego's will-to-power might only produce further resistance. The wider point that needs to be made here is that renunciation is not the *sine qua non* for such practice, but love and respect for the guide is. This path suited Isherwood's temperament. Gerald Heard, who preferred a more ascetic style, criticised Swami Prabhavananda's gregarious, noisy ashram, earning a rare rebuke from the Swami. Aldous Huxley's research into psychedelic drugs led to a disagreement with the Swami, too, although he continued to write articles for the Society's magazine, *Vedanta and the West*, until 1960 and served on its editorial board.

The job of the guru, once he or she has taken on a student, is to help him or her find ways to weave a busy life into the work directed towards the kind of realisation that they have asked for. If the student decides not to subject him or herself to the intensity of the training within the monastic setting, everyday life itself serves up plenty of confrontation to add grist to the work of transformation. Isherwood notes this, ruefully, in a seldom-cited diary entry. For all the carousing that ensued (with Bill Caskey) after quitting residence at N Ivar Avenue, he came to recognise that what he had begun would continue, willy-nilly:

> What I am really trying to run away from is myself.
>
> What I am trying to impose—under the disguise of reasonableness—is my own will.
>
> "Nothing burns in Hell except the self," [a reference to Meister Eckhart] and I am miserable because the self is burning. In the simplest, most terrible manner I am being taught that no other kind of life is possible for me. The monastery is *here*, is wherever I am. When Swami said: "Ramakrishna will hound you," he wasn't kidding. (*Diary*, 27 April 1951)

Katherine Bucknell, the perceptive editor of the *Diaries*, excerpted this section in her introduction (pp. xxvii–viii); however the fuller version is even more revealing. It begins:

> Thy will be done—how often must I say it. Every day, every hour, every moment. How happy my life would be, if I would just give it to him! I have my duty, my *dharma*, so clearly set before me. Write, work, meditate, offer everything to him.

Bucknell has expressed surprise (in private email correspondence) that readers would doubt Isherwood's continuing engagement with Vedanta, given the testimony of the final autobiography and the Diaries; yet, surveying reactions to the 2004 biography by Peter Parker, it is clear the prejudices continue to operate, perpetuating the occlusion that is at the heart of several dismissive treatments of Isherwood.

It is worth contrasting Isherwood's relationship with Prabhavananda with John Yale's experience. Yale (later known as Swami Vidyatmananda) was the American devotee who was originally attracted to Vedanta by reading Isherwood's apologia. He struggled with the yoga of bhakti, but found the wherewithal to persevere with the long novitiate that led to him taking the vows of the sannyasin and he spent his last years as an assistant in a Vedanta Centre at Gretz, in France. While Yale persevered with the renunciate path, his correspondence with Isherwood, archived in the Huntington collection, speaks poignantly of his admiration for Isherwood's path. This is not intended to denigrate Yale's own choices. The account of his own practice offers many insights into the Vedanta path as undertaken by a Westerner. In this early correspondence it is clear he looked up to Isherwood as something like an elder brother and he too published accounts of different stages in his own process. (His *A Yankee and the Swamis*, originally serialised in the magazine *Vedanta and the West*, and first published in 1961, is among the first of these. There are boxes of his papers, too, waiting to be mined by some enterprising scholar.)

When Isherwood settled into a long-term relationship with Don Bachardy, the Swami treated them as a 'householder couple' (a model that certain churches still find impossible to countenance, well into the twenty-first century). We need to recognise the thorough engagement between the student and the guru here. For example, there is a diary entry included in *My Guru*, where the guru is clearly concerned to see that Isherwood is firmly rooted in the practice:

> He said that when I go up to Montecito, he wants me to make a great deal of japam. 'When once you are established in that, you can go anywhere. It is all the same.'

This diary entry was used in *My Guru* (p. 170). Even allowing for a wild period with Bill Caskey—his lover after leaving the Center—there are myriad indications of Isherwood's continuing involvement with the guru, the practice, and with ongoing service projects, notwithstanding some grumbling. And *My Guru*, published in 1980 when he was nearly 76, is itself a testimony to the long history of the engagement. Also, the assumption that in leaving the monastery he quit the practices relies too heavily on the model of religion as the 'public practice' which Isherwood identified in his mother's Anglicanism, rather than the private kind of religion to which his father was drawn (see *Kathleen and Frank*, p. 190). There are first-hand accounts of Isherwood in his later years, chanting the 'Hymn to the Guru'—an act of personal devotion known as the 'guru stotra', with words taken from an ancient scripture, the Guru Gita—and weeping with joy, an image that doesn't square at all well with the facile mis-representations of his religious devotion that we have noted. Now, a Stotra—as a hymn of praise—can be directed towards representations of 'God' or aspects of the divine; that it can be directed towards the guru is a significant issue here.

It is clear that Isherwood and the Swami enjoyed real friendship, a feeling of camaraderie but, as is the nature of these complex relationships, another factor comes into play. I said earlier that in this tradition, the guru exemplifies the state of being of one who has attained a fuller awareness of that deepest reality, and acts as a kind of focusing device for his or her students to help them to 'tune in', as it were, to that reality as the basis of their own being and conscious awareness.

So, even while the status of human friendship holds, there is another track running that allows a sort of bifocal awareness which, at times, allows the personality of the guru to become more and more transparent, as it were, and the deeper identification with the Atman radiates another aspect of Being which the student recognises as a potential within his or her own awareness. (That is why it is considered a great boon to have the company of such a figure; and this is a significant factor in the first hand accounts of those first generation of disciples who testified of the effect of being with Sri Ramakrishna during his exalted samadhi states.) Given the scepticism that has become entrenched in Western approaches to such figures (and the tawdry versions provided by Jeffrey Kripal, et al.) and the exclusivist privileging of Reason as the highest application of mind, these aspects of the religious life have little currency, yet for those who have known them, these figures have opened up new horizons of experience and awareness. Isherwood was acutely aware of the difficulties in presenting this information to a sceptical readership, so his accounts are suitably modest. The Swami himself was cautious about mentioning the nature of his spiritual experiences to outsiders (see the incident described in *My Guru*, pp. 293–4, where a devotee expresses concern because Prabhavananda has mentioned during a television interview that 'he has had the lower form of samadhi'). So Isherwood makes sure that he anchors the other, more exalted track with full acknowledgment of the human 'failings' of his Swami:

> Such glimpses of his weaknesses and faults helped me to see him doubly—as Abanindra Nath Ghosh and as the receptacle of "This Thing," the Eternal … Abanindra, with his weaknesses *and* his virtues, is fading away, while "this thing", which has always been present within him, is becoming more and more evident. (*My Guru*, pp. 246–7)

The practice continues (or not!) and the role of service (the karma yoga, discussed earlier) becomes even more crucial, so that the life is still focused in the direction that the student has, after all, requested. The Swami kept the translation work up to Isherwood, and engaged him to compile the official biography of Sri Ramakrishna, who was the original inspiration for the Order which his first ring of disciples—Swami Vivekananda was among them, as was Prabhavananda's guru, Swami Brahmananda—founded in his memory. Isherwood was fortunate to have led a long life, and to have had the time to sort out these issues empirically, in real-time, rather than in idealised theory, so his accounts of the process are tempered by real experience, which is one of the factors that recommend this part of the writing as of continuing interest to other (flawed!) human beings today.

5

The rascal and the saint

Live in fragments no longer. Only connect, and the beast and the monk, robbed of the isolation that is life to either, will die.

—EM Forster, *Howards End*

Senior monks from the headquarters in Calcutta supervised the writing of the Ramakrishna biography. This made the task difficult for Isherwood and prolonged the writing for almost a decade. While he rankled at the sanctification project they required, nonetheless he toed the party line. In contrast, Isherwood's notorious honesty and his critical self-scrutiny are more evident in his own diaries, where 'every gripe, complaint, bad mood, drunken spree and sexual encounter' is recorded, with little attempt to make himself look good. Some commentators are shocked by Isherwood's self-disclosure and have come to regard him as a less than admirable figure (e.g., Altman, 2004), based on the self-portrait that emerges from such texts. How could he possibly be making any spiritual 'progress' while engaged with such un-spiritual pursuits as a love-affair? (and a stormy one at that!) Yet the Swami would laugh at Christopher's self-deprecation, and praise his honesty as a supremely 'spiritual' virtue.

This was most marked during a disastrous visit to India in 1963, when Isherwood was uncomfortable with the exaggerated respect he was being shown by the other devotees, as a famous literary figure. Isherwood made the trip on this occasion, not only for the celebration of the Centenary of Vivekananda's birth (and a 'Parliament of Religions' event), but also to witness the final vows of his friend John Yale, whom he knew from the early days in the Hollywood centre. (Celebrations had begun in January to mark Vivekananda's birthday and lasted through the year. The final event—the 'Parliament'—began in the last days of 1963 and into early January, 1964.) Isherwood went out of his way to counter what he saw as exaggerated and entirely inappropriate respect towards him by demonstrating respect in turn towards even the youngest Swamis, 'taking the dust of their feet'.

Asked to speak at a large gathering, fully aware of his weaknesses and feeling distinctly 'un-holy', Isherwood grumbled, feeling that he was back in the midst of the kind of religiosity he had always avoided. (If his own guru ran a relatively loose ship back in Los Angeles, the headquarters in Calcutta was more traditionally straitlaced. There is evidence that this became more the style of the Los Angeles Center, too, after Swami Prabhavananda's death.) Isherwood complains:

> 'I can't belong to any kind of institution. Because I'm not respectable.' Swami laughs: 'But Chris how can you say such things? You're almost too good. You are so frank, so good. You never tell any lie.' (Diary, 7 Jan 1964, qtd in Parker, p. 719)

Isherwood used the occasion to 'out' himself as a very wayward disciple, devoting the lecture to extolling the praises of one of Ramakrishna's early and most beloved devotees, Girish Ghosh. Ghosh was an actor and theatre manager who was inclined to turn up at his Master's ashram drunk, sometimes after visiting prostitutes. But his deep love and reverence for Ramakrishna was reciprocated: the saint would sometimes dance with glee in the presence of people who were inebriated, catching their mood, as it were, and spinning off into his own, rarefied state of intoxication. (As a good non-dualist, Ramakrishna was inclined to see God in everything!) Isherwood writes that Ghosh became something of a 'patron saint' for him and he felt closer to him than any other member of Ramakrishna's circle.

We might recall Isherwood's earlier admiration for his friend Edward Upward's refusal to be confirmed at boarding school, and his regret at his own compliance. (Confirmation is a ritual statement of adherence whereby the candidate affirms the vow of adherence made on his or her behalf when they were baptised as babes). With all the gratitude that had grown in relation to his guru, and the practices he had been doing for more than twenty years, Isherwood was unlikely to represent himself in a way he felt was hypocritical, for the sake of conformity in the more overtly religious setting of the Calcutta ashram:

> As long as I quite unashamedly get drunk, have sex and write books like *A Single Man*, I simply cannot appear before people as a sort of lay minister. The inevitable result must be that my ordinary life becomes divided and untruthful … For me, religion must be quite private as I'm publicly concerned. I can still write about it informatively, but I must not appear before people on a platform as a living witness and example. (Diary entry, 31 Dec 1963; qtd in Parker, p. 717)

Why would he take Girish Ghosh as his role model, from among the other worthies who were among the first rank of Ramakrishna's earliest disciples? Isherwood was (and is, today) a somewhat controversial figure within the Ramakrishna Vedanta Society. His relationship with Don Bachardy (thirty years his junior) certainly raised some eyebrows at the time (and caused difficulties with his great ally, the psychologist Evelyn Hooker), even if the Swami insisted on treating them as a householder couple during formal events at the Temple.

In an earlier talk he had given to the Vedanta Society of New York, Isherwood addressed both the discomfort he felt around the issue of the 'insider/outsider' phenomenon—of 'belonging' to a religious congregation—and the question of being seen as a 'role model' himself:

> Ideally, I know, that example should be spotless. Ideally it should inspire others to think: well, what he or she believes in has certainly transformed his or her life, and I think that it must be something that I could believe in too. ('Address to the Vedanta Society of NY', 26 March 1952. His notes for the talk are included in the papers collected at the Huntington.)

Typically, Isherwood confesses that he falls short of this ideal. So what he says next is revealing of the nature of his religious practice:

> I have always been very much sustained in my failures to present an adequate specimen of a Vedantist by other words which Swami Prabhavananda said to me. He said, 'Purity means telling the truth.' And I believe that the one absolutely essential thing if we are to communicate anything that we really have learned here or through our teachers to others, is that we are absolutely frank—absolutely frank about our own weaknesses, and absolutely frank about what we really believe, and absolutely without pretense about things which perhaps we would like to believe, like to be, but to which we haven't yet arrived. ('Address to the Vedanta Society of NY' Huntington CI 1014)

This is a crucial point, and not simply because he was reluctant to be read as a 'saintly' figure. Isherwood's religious practice was mediated through the one-on-one relationship with his guru, which was more important for him that 'belonging' to a religious congregation and earning the respect of the faithful.

Advaita Vedanta

The other factor, which most critics are unwilling to engage with, is the appeal, for Isherwood, of a system that did not revolve around dualities. In the passage quoted above, he shows concern that his 'ordinary life' might become 'divided'. He felt that in this form of Hinduism he had found a religion that allowed for an accommodation with his sexuality in a non-divisive way. (Diary entry, 26 Nov 1970). To recall his very first meeting with Prabhavananda, when Isherwood blurted out that he was in love with a young man, 'Vernon' (this was before he had met Bill Caskey, or Don Bachardy), and asked if that would be a problem, the Swami simply encouraged him to see the young Lord Krishna in the person of his lover. This is not because the Swami was a squishy moral relativist, desperate to recruit a prominent Western intellectual to the cause, as cynical or simply uninformed Western commentators have assumed. There is a profound metaphysical underpinning here from a religious philosophy that sees all individual variations as aspects of one Being, in the face of which the Western reification of the 'individual', particularly, falls short. Different narratives of the self have been elaborated within these traditions and must perforce influence how identity and subjectivity are conceived, represented and understood.

At the time of this first meeting, when Isherwood was still carrying the cluttered conceptual baggage of his pre-conceived notions of 'God', and unaware of the deeper layers of being that would become accessible through his future spiritual practices, he was relieved:

> What reassured me—what convinced me that I could become his pupil—was that he hadn't shown the least shadow of distaste on hearing me admit to my homosexuality. I had feared a blast of icy puritanism: "You must promise me never to see that boy again, or I cannot accept you." (*My Guru*, p. 26)

This had been the first indication for Isherwood that he was working within a tradition that operated from a different set of principles.

Let us look at how he came to understand the philosophy. I return to the point made earlier that the Swami did not come from a tradition that divided the world into good and bad. Of course Prabhavananda is concerned to encourage behaviours that support the practice, and discourage those that don't. John Yale's testimony is relevant in this regard:

> Why do people feel attracted to a rascal and run away from a saint? because a rascal is true and all saint is a myth; if he's held up as an all-saint by his friends and protectors, we know we're being humbugged … Swami ji didn't care a snap whether a person was good or bad but he hated hiding; covering sores with flowers [speaking of another Swami, Turiyananda] he used to turn up his nose at good people and Jesus said: why callest me good; no-one is God but my father who is in heaven … ('The making of a devotee'. Online)

The real issue is to get to the point of honesty, not just present the 'good' face and hide the 'bad'. Hence Isherwood's admiration for the unlikely figure of

Girish Ghosh. How remarkable then that he felt that he was unworthy to be Ghosh's disciple:

> I failed to go the whole hog, as he had, either in debauchery or devotion. Ghosh dared to reveal himself shamelessly to Ramakrishna, thereby making a sacrifice of his own self-esteem and self-will and submitting totally to Ramakrishna's guidance. That was his greatness. (*My Guru*, p. 196)

Thus, there is a rather different process underway than merely being on one's best behaviour! Isherwood notes, ruefully: 'I am sorry now that through my long relationship with Swami, I never once came into his presence drunk. Something wonderful might have happened' (p. 197).

The corollary might be: 'Beware of the guru who sees himself as a holy man.' Opportunities for self-aggrandisement are usefully curtailed in this system by the fact that the guru given so much respect by his own students is, in turn, in harness as a servant of his or her own Master. Aligned in hard-won humility within that chain of discipleship, his (her) own disciples might catch reflections of glory there, and gain inspiration to persevere in their own journey, but if the guru begins to think he (she) is the *source*, problems are likely to ensue; and the light dims for both parties.

I can illustrate this issue further by reference to Isherwood's description of a notable incident when Gerald Heard defected from the Swami's side. (I should say in advance that this particular incident should not be taken as representative of Heard, in entirety, but it was an important milestone in Isherwood's journey.) Heard was famous in his own right. He gave lectures and published extensively on spiritual matters and was renowned for meditating six hours a day. He maintained celibacy even during his friendship with Chris Wood. Distressed by the relaxed atmosphere at North Ivar Avenue, Heard yearned for a more austere lifestyle, so he built a monastery in Trabuco Canyon, south of Los Angeles, for a gathering of more serious practitioners. Described by Isherwood as a 'dyspeptic' 'life-hater' at this time, Heard tended to 'perform' the holy man. This was a strong contrast with the real thing: Swami Prabhavananda, the chain-smoking, gregarious Bengali. But the Swami explicitly rejected Heard's criticisms of his teaching style (*My Guru*, pp. 74–7). 'Mere outward austerity is a degenerate form of ritualism,' wrote the Swami in response to Heard's published criticisms:

> A Spiritual soul never makes any demonstration of his renunciation or of his communion with God. He even sometimes raises external barriers to shield himself from the eyes of the curious' ('Renunciation and Austerity'; qtd in Isherwood 1980, p. 75)

If that is a traditional Asian rationale for a kind of spiritual modesty, it's interesting to get a completely modern 'Western' take from transpersonal psychologist Ken Wilber's dissection of the issue, in which he interrogates the common expectations we tend to have for the 'sage' to manifest egolessness. 'We expect our sages to be an *absence* of all that drives us …' he writes:

> egolessness does not mean the absence of a functional self (that's a psychotic, not a sage); it means that one is no longer *exclusively* identified with that self. (2000, pp. 276–7)

Coupled with this expectation, conventional expectations look to religion,

> not for advice on how to live life with enthusiasm, but on how to avoid it, repress it, deny it, escape it … Anytime a sage displays humanness—in regard to money, food, sex, relationships—we are shocked, *shocked*, because we are planning to escape life altogether, not live it, and the sage who lives life offends us. We want out, we want to ascend, we want to escape, and the sage who engages life with gusto, lives it to the hilt, grasps each wave of life and surfs it to the end—this deeply profoundly disturbs us, frightens us, because it means that we, too, might have to engage life, with gusto, on all levels, and not merely escape it in a cloud of luminous ether. (p. 279)

This is a challenging point of view, especially in the context of contemporary suspicion of such figures. Wilber continues:

> We do not want our sages to have bodies, egos, drives, vitality, sex, money, relationships, or life, because those are what habitually torture us, and we

want out. We do not want to surf the waves of life, we want the waves to go away. We want vaporware spirituality. (p. 279)

Swami Prabhavananda was following the disciplines of the sannyasin, so perhaps to apply the Wilber framing would be overstating the case, but the point holds that—in his own model—the 'Spiritual soul never makes any demonstration of his renunciation or of his communion with God'. The guru is concerned to help the student to recognise the essential elements of the practice, whatever the lifestyle. Firmly established in the awareness of the Atman, and dedicated to returning the student's awareness to that deepest potential awareness, on his/her side the guru sees through the stratagems presented by the student's ego self. After much trial and error, and endless evasions, the student learns to stop hiding what he or she assumes to be the unacceptable parts of the self. 'Come as you are', might be the invitation, 'not as you think you *ought* to be. And don't bother showing me your holy face!' As I noted earlier, it was Isherwood's honesty that the guru valued and praised (and thereby reinforced), over many years of discipleship. (Isherwood noted that Swami would sometimes engage in a subtle and not too subtle campaign to get him to move back to the renunciate lifestyle, but he came to accept Don Bachardy as Isherwood's partner.)

Peter Parker wants to attribute this to the Swami's flattery of Isherwood's 'vanity', which seems to be the only construction he can imagine. We are not looking at *The lives of the saints* here—holy lives held up as exemplars for the faithful. This is the aspirant struggling on the spiritual path. For, far from providing an escape into a cosy retreat from the 'real world', as it is often characterised in sceptical accounts, regular meditation practice brings the real state of one's mind from day to day uncomfortably into focus. Even if practitioners are yearning for entry into the bliss fields, as they peer into the mirror of contemplation they will be confronted by the actual condition of their body/mind. After getting drunk, their heads will be befogged. After chasing a thousand and one desires, their attention won't return tamely when summoned, to apply itself to the inner work.

Those who would read Isherwood's critical self-disclosures as evidence of a lack of progress in the spiritual life, then, are reading the evidence in reverse. Apart from Adam Phillips's insightful review of *Lost years*, the only other commentator who seems to understand the struggle—and its resolution—with any insight, is Jeffery Paine, in *Father India.* See, especially, Paine's treatment of Isherwood's dream of being in bed with the Swami—in a male whorehouse!—described in *My Guru and his disciple* (p. 210). 'If, as Vedanta holds,' writes Paine, 'everything that lives is sacred, that sacredness had finally to include Isherwood, too' (p. 224).

Isherwood provides another example that further undermines the typically lop-sided evaluation of his spiritual life. Just after acknowledging that the Swami might be more lenient towards him than the young men in the ashram (who were living under different rules), Isherwood writes:

> Once, fishing for a compliment, I asked Swami why he so seldom scolded me. He answered, 'I don't scold for the big faults'. He gave no sign of awareness that this statement had crushing implications, I was so taken aback by it that I didn't question him further. (*My Guru*, p. 164)

Tolerant as he was, this guru was no push-over.

As for Heard, he reconciled with the Swami, and gave the Trabuco Canyon project over to the Vedanta Society for use as a men's ashram. He continued to write for Society publications (and joined Aldous Huxley in experiments at expanding consciousness using psychedelic drugs).

Isherwood notes a mellowing in Heard in later times—see *My Guru*, p. 210—and acknowledges the warmth of the friendship, and Heard's acceptance of the partnership with Bachardy.

Seva, the yoga of selfless service

Peter Parker's biographical analysis tends to suffer from a lack of understanding of other aspects of the 'bhakti' relationship. I have already pointed out how, in this tradition, service to the guru is standard practice—the student, or disciple, is glad to have skills that can be useful to the work. By providing a way for the two to interact, service also has the inestimable benefit of exposing the student to the guru's instruction (and correction). Arthur Deikman delineates the dynamic insightfully. He describes service as a 'way of knowing', of making 'deeper contact with the interconnectedness of reality we call "spiritual"' ('The spiritual heart of service', p. 30).

To make that contact, it is necessary, at one level, to learn to 'forget the self'. Through service, the 'survival self'—or ego—changes roles, to become the servant rather than the master (p. 34). The 'survival self' is still needed to function in the world, Deikman writes, but 'it must not dominate consciousness' if a 'different experience of reality is to be made possible' (p. 34). So, the goal in this relationship, in which the guru becomes the 'master' and the student the 'servant', is to bring the student into awareness of the deeper interconnectedness of all being, usually masked by identification with the ego, or personal self.

While suspicious minds will inevitably look for opportunities for exploitation here—and there are examples where unscrupulous teachers have exploited the intrinsic imbalance of power—the guru's function, directly or indirectly, is to facilitate this shift taking place within the student's own internal psychic development. The guru's expertise, then, is not to simply crush the student's ego functioning, in some kind of gross power play, but to open up new possibilities for inner growth. Deikman's insight into these aspects (later cited by David Galin 2003) is finely nuanced and clearly informed by his being himself a practitioner. Commentators unfamiliar with this part of the training are unable to grasp how Isherwood could live a 'double life'—enjoying all the trappings of the Hollywood lifestyle while engaging with any form of spirituality that they can take seriously. Without recognising this, they will never understand how Isherwood, who seemed so absorbed in strumming the harp of 'the darling ego me' (Isherwood's own, critical self-characterisation from an earlier period) could be engaged in any process of freeing himself from self-centred motivations.

In my view, this clearly contributes to Isherwood's ability to render the self so ironically, in ways reviewed in the preceding chapter. Meditation on the source of the Self beyond the self, coupled with selfless service—in the context of a student-teacher relationship—re-orientates one's identification with the workings of the ego mind, making way for the realisation of the roots of self in the Atman, and the true relationship of Atman and Brahman.

It is a pity that for someone outside the tradition and so clearly unsympathetic to it, the dynamics of the relationship are a mystery that can only be de-coded suspiciously. In general human terms, Parker seems insensitive to the warmth of the relationship between the guru and the disciple in this case; or he seems to lose sight of it temporarily while trying to prove some kind of opportunistic manipulation of Isherwood's reputation by the guru. Three of the people I interviewed in Los Angeles recalled the warmth of Isherwood's spirituality. Bob Adjemian, the publisher of Vedanta Press, described him as 'mellow, caring, sensitive' and at the same time noted an 'absolute honesty' and 'complete lack of hypocrisy'. Isherwood's self-disclosure in the diaries (including *Lost years*), notable for the same rigour, has led to the negative stereotype we have seen in the reviews, as 'spiteful, sour, bitchy', etc., but it would be a pity if the dynamics of his real praxis were clouded by this partial portrait.

Isherwood continued to live out his sexuality openly after leaving behind his short-lived attempt to be a renunciate. He was instinctively distrustful of the tendency towards transcending the life in the physical body that he felt to be too like the stuffy Anglican religiosity he had already rejected as life-denying. He had realised how easy it would be to lose his own integrity in conforming to expectations, instead of finding his own reason for doing things. He would never write hagiography; neither about himself, nor about his own guru. He was uncomfortable having to write the biography of Ramakrishna for this reason. The account of his personal story in *My Guru* is refreshingly free of it. He was also clear that writing about 'perfect' people could make for boring reading (see, for example, his essay: 'On the problem of the religious novel', which I will discuss below).

My Guru and His Disciple and its reception

> I still don't know what to think of *My Guru*. I can imagine some really savage attacks on it and yet in a way I think it is the most worthwhile book I have written *and* probably one of the best modern books of its kind. (Diary entry, 17 Feb 1980)

Parker's lack of regard for this late autobiography fulfils Isherwood's prophecy of its reception. He finds the book lacking in rage, and comedy, and dislikes it for a 'sweet reasonableness that simply cloys' (p. 815). Fellow writers have not judged it so poorly as Parker. Nor have they had such a negative judgement of the guru. Edmund White called *My Guru and his disciple* 'a sweetly modest and honest portrait of Isherwood's spiritual instructor, Swami Prabhavananda, the Hindu priest who guided Isherwood for some thirty years' (1980, p. 9) and he is clearly not put off by the 'often amusing and sometimes painful counterpoint between worldliness and holiness in Isherwood's own life' (p. 9). Alan Hollinghurst found the book 'a humbling tribute to someone who revealed to Isherwood inner grounds for spiritual awareness' (2004, p. 9). Isherwood's own awareness of potential opposition to the book becomes a need to silence what he called 'the mocking agnostics' amongst his readers. He was not looking for converts, but he wanted to convince a wide range of people 'from asses like [John] Lehman to intelligent bigots like Edward [Upward]' that Vedanta had real meaning for him and had made all the difference in his life. 'Everything I write is written with a consciousness of the opposition and in answer to its prejudices,' he reminded himself (Diary entry, 23 Oct 1977, qtd in Parker, p. 803).

John Yale, the former publisher, found the book a complete success:

> You have done in an interesting way what you set out to do—present Swami Prabhavananda in terms of your relationship with him, warts and all … More a case study than a hagiography, I would call it a lively biography of a mystic done in the modern way and bound to appeal to anyone interested in you and/or contemporary movements in religion. You have touched on subtleties in the guru-disciple relationship never so clearly stated (as far as I know) before. (Letter dated 20 Aug 1979; qtd in Parker, p. 810)

Reviews of *My Guru* in the UK, however, were perhaps predictably condemnatory. A reviewer in *The Economist* found 'very little to convince the reader that he, or even his guru, has become a significantly better or happier man for it' (12 Jul 1980, p. 97). The anonymous reviewer, who criticised the Swami for 'using the writer's vanity to gain his co-operation on translations of sacred Hindu texts,' attributed what he downplayed as Isherwood's half-hearted persistence in the religion to 'the guru's persuasive and flattering tongue'. *Punch* was ethnocentrically 'confronted by an outlandish religion filled with weird rites called by strange names'.

Writing religion

If most literary commentators are unfamiliar with the kind of psycho-spiritual work undertaken within that guru/student framework, perhaps there is a problem of genre operating here that ought to be considered, as well. As an example, Irina Tweedie's unvarnished account of her five-year period of intense work with her guru (in the Sufi tradition)—*Daughter of fire*—is full of accounts of her dark moods and her constant grumbling—the agonies as well as the ecstasies she endured. Apart from the cultural blinkers, then, perhaps the continuing misunderstanding could be diagnosed as a problem of genre, so it would be worth considering how Isherwood saw the issues involved.

As a writer Isherwood had given the issue a lot of thought. Somerset Maugham had consulted him for the novel *The razor's edge* and, in spite of Maugham's ignoring some specific advice in that project, he and Prabhavananda were approached again by the movie studio to advise on the film adaptation. Isherwood also wrote about the difficulties of presenting the life of a saint in his essay 'The Problem of the Religious Novel'. (The essay has appeared in several places; the page references I use here are from the collection *Exhumations*, 1966.) Although he was addressing the 'problem' in terms of writing fiction, the issue of characterisation is pertinent. Isherwood says that writers are eager to find characters who will 'exhibit the maximum variety of reactions to external events' (p. 136). The saint is 'the ideal character', because:

> his motives are not dictated by fear, vanity or desire—because his every action is a genuine act of free will—you can never predict what he will do next. He accepts life more fully, more creatively, than any of his neighbors. And therefore he is the most interesting to write about. (p. 136)

The danger in writing about saints is losing the 'average Joe's recognition factor'. The writer 'has to prove to his audience that the Messrs Smith and

Brown and Jones are all potentially saints'. Yet, this is not the conventional image:

> The public has its preconceived notion of a saint—a figure with a lean face and an air of weary patience, who alternates between moods of forbidding austerity and heartbroken sweetness—a creature set apart from this bad world, a living reproach to our human weakness, in whose presence we feel ill at ease, inferior, and embarrassed. In other words, the dreariest of bores. (pp. 136–7)

Isherwood grapples with how to write this area of human experience:

> How am I to prove that X isn't merely insane when he turns his back on the whole scheme of pleasures, rewards, and satisfactions which are accepted by the Joneses, the Smiths, and the Browns, and goes in search of superconscious, extraphenomenal experience? … the average men and women of the world are searching, however unconsciously, for that same fundamental reality of which X has already had a glimpse. Certainly, they look for it in the wrong places. Certainly, their methods are quite unpractical … the whisky bottle is the crude symbol of Jones's dissatisfaction with surface consciousness, his need to look more deeply into the meaning of life. (p. 138)

We won't be told the story of a perfected being held up as an exemplum, then, but one 'in search of …' He would rather bring 'the evolving saint' down from the mountain and much closer to the lives of his ordinary reader:

> [T]he evolving saint does not differ from his fellow humans in kind, but only in degree. That is why X can only be understood, artistically, when his story is related to that of the Joneses, the Smiths, and the Browns. (p. 139)

Instead, Isherwood would open up the difficulties of the process:

> The greater part of my novel would deal, of course, with X's struggles towards sainthood, toward complete spiritual realization. I think that most

> writers have erred in making this phase of their story too somber and depressing. True, the path of the spiritual aspirant is hard. The mortification of the ego is tedious and painful. But I see no reason for the author to sentimentalize his hero's sufferings or to allow him to indulge in self-pity. Sportswriters find no pathos in the hardships of a boxer's training. The would-be saint is the last person in the world we should feel sorry for. His sufferings are purely voluntary. If his will slackens, they automatically cease. (p. 139)

Not only would he present the protagonist as 'struggling', he would also find room for humour:

> Surely the mishaps and setbacks which beset the path of spiritual progress can be recounted with some of the humour which invests one's failures in cookery or falls in learning to ski? (p. 140)

This analysis provides a marvellous guide for reading his deceptively simple novella, *A single man*, in which the shambolic protagonist, George, is presented as a tragic-comic Everyman figure, and the subtle presentation of Vedanta principles is seamlessly integrated into the narrative. I'll come back to this novel shortly.

Isherwood was clearly aware of the generic problems in writing the spiritual life but he is also acknowledging—alongside the alcohol and the sex, all the distractions from the 'pure', 'spiritual' life—the struggle. If commentators are unfamiliar with this aspect of the life, they don't need to look far for parallels. John Yale writes of the difficulties of his own path as a fellow student of the same guru. Even though he lived the disciplined life of the renunciate, for years Yale had trouble in harnessing the power of bhakti, and admired the affectionate relationship he saw had developed between Isherwood and the Swami.

For an unsympathetic reviewer, Isherwood's life is so very exposed; the self-reflexive openness which Phillips calls his 'experiment in non-confessional honesty' (2000) and his lack of interest in presenting a respectable, 'cleaned-up' version of himself, provide ample ammunition for judgement. By detailing so much of it in his account, Parker has in his turn opened Isherwood up to the same kind of scrutiny. Unfortunately, by following Parker, Dennis Altman and others miss the irony built in to Isherwood's mocking self-stance. On the other hand, Alan Wilde (1971) describes Isherwood as 'an ironic moralist'.

David Geherin drew attention to this feature in a 1972 interview with Isherwood, during which Isherwood agreed:

> A: There is a kind of irony in my work. And my humour … has a sort of double-edged thing to it, very often.
> Q: Directed inwards and outwards, at the persona as well as others.
> A: A little bit. It sort of makes fun of the persona. (Geherin 1972, p. 85)

If we read the life and its extensive documentation in the ironic spirit of Isherwood's own contextualisation, as spelled out in 'The Problem of the Religious Novel', we may value the life more charitably. I have tried to step outside the judgmental paradigm and endeavoured, not so much to evaluate Isherwood's spiritual 'achievement', nor criticise his moral and ethical choices, as to show how the study and practice of Vedanta assisted him in re-negotiating a subjective positioning that allowed him more room to express and explore the opportunities for being and becoming as a non-conformist and independent thinker.

Beyond the lack of charity or sympathy for Isherwood's religious and life choices, there is yet another factor that colours critical responses to him that I believe no one has taken account of.

Spiritual 'tact'

On a visit to the Hollywood temple in 2005, I met a nun who remembered Isherwood well, and who was in a unique position to comment on this issue. The nun, Pr. Saradeshaprana, was born in India of British parents, spent part of her life in Melbourne, and moved to Los Angeles in the early 1970s to join the Order. She drew my attention to the mannered British understatement, typical of Isherwood's class, which would preclude one from drawing attention to certain things in oneself. While this might seem at odds with the self-revealing life-writing, it has a particular bearing on the tactful reporting of his spiritual life. In spite of his early work as a pamphleteer, editing the Vedanta

Society magazine, and so on, Isherwood maintained a social and professional network of acquaintances drawn from literary and movie circles, among whom it would have been bad form (for someone from his class) to thrust his religious ideas forward. Don Bachardy tells an amusing anecdote about Gore Vidal visiting them for a dinner party:

> [H]e had just read *My Guru* and [he] was telling me that he had never been so shocked in his life. It was like he had discovered that Chris was one of the pod people in *Invasion of the Body Snatchers*! That he was not only tainted, that he was lost, that he could talk such rubbish …' (Marsh 2006, p. 24)

Vidal had been a friend for quite some time. So, even while he was quite prepared to write about his personal experience of Vedanta, Isherwood was inclined to refrain from proselytising among his friends and professional colleagues and even a friend could be utterly unaware of this part of Isherwood's life.

What I am calling 'tact' here is underpinned by something more than social decorum. Interviewed by Mark Thompson about his spiritual practice, Isherwood responded this way:

> The Hindus have a marvellous thing they say: If you've had any real spiritual experience, hide it, as you would hide from other people the fact that your mother was a whore! Strong words! In other words, for God's sake, shut up about it! And I'm mindful of that unless, of course, I'm speaking with people who are seriously interested. (Thompson 1987a, p. 48)

The coarse analogy employed here provides a strong contrast to the type of pseudo-pious, performative spiritual practice that requires downcast eyes, a hushed voice and reverential tones; a fact that Gerald Heard discovered when he had his falling out with Swami Prabhavananda over the boisterous atmosphere of the guru's ashram.

I suggest that Isherwood's reserve (where you might expect evangelism) contributes to the misunderstanding among commentators who presume that his spiritual practice was eclipsed after leaving the monastery. While we have already seen that he persevered in the practices and the association with his teacher over decades, he would have avoided any opportunities to 'boast' of special insight, or mystical 'success', and this contributed to a reserve in discussing his spiritual life that has apparently misled some commentators into assuming that it had gone into abeyance. Apart from the testimony of people who knew him from the Vedanta Society, there are references sprinkled through the diaries of his continuing japam practice—such as at the time of the death of Bachardy's father—which reveal how much a part of his daily life it had become (diary entry, 20 Jan 1978).

In any case, Isherwood was more at home depicting the 'struggle' than the sanctity. In his assessment of the difficulties of the 'religious novel' that I noted above, a portrait of 'the perfected saint' would require a certain 'genius',

> for the mystical experience itself can never be described. It can only be written around, hinted at, dimly reflected in word and deed. ('The problem of the religious novel', p. 140)

Swami Prabhavananda also gave a clear indication of this important feature of spiritual practice, which should not be overlooked by those who want to evaluate Isherwood's spiritual 'progress'. To recall the Swami's dictum: 'A Spiritual soul never makes any demonstration of his renunciation or of his communion with God' (qtd in *My Guru*, p. 75).

Given Isherwood's reluctance to talk of his spiritual 'progress', only a superficial reading would take the self-portrait at face value. Modesty about 'spiritual achievement' is still a virtue, especially if the ego is not to become grossly puffed up. Brooke Allen, who calls Isherwood 'petty, selfish, and supremely egotistical', and 'one of literature's pre-eminent navel gazers' (2004, p. 20), and Dennis Altman, who finds him 'not as admirable a man or a writer as I had hoped' (p. 4), probably fail to give Isherwood his due, at least partly because they are insensitive to this contrary principle at work within the context of his usual practice of self-disclosure.

It is important to note, too, the position that Isherwood arrived at in relation to his sexuality. In the autobiography, *Christopher and his kind* (published in 1976), he looks back to his arrival in the States in 1939 and recalls the moment aboard ship when he and Auden decided that the political causes to which they had lent their weight were not the real issue for them:

> Christopher had taken longer than Wystan to become aware of his own change of attitude because he was embarrassed by its basic cause: his homosexuality. As a homosexual, he had been wavering between embarrassment and defiance … He became embarrassed when he felt that he was making a selfish demand for his individual rights at a time when only group action mattered. He became defiant when he made the treatment of the homosexual a test by which every political party and government must be judged. His challenge to each one of them was: 'All right, we've heard your liberty speech. Does that include us, or doesn't it?' (p. 335)

Dennis Altman may find Isherwood's political engagement tepid, but Altman was engaged with a later historical period in the struggle for gay liberation. While Isherwood related to the struggle differently, he was not unaware of how politics impinged on sexual freedom:

> The Soviet Union had passed this test with honours when it recognized the private sexual rights of the individual, in 1917. But, in 1934, Stalin's government had withdrawn this recognition and made all homosexual acts punishable by heavy prison sentences. It had agreed with the Nazis in denouncing homosexuality as a form of treason to the State.
>
> Christopher—like many of his friends, homosexual and heterosexual—had done his best to minimize the Soviet betrayal of its own principles. After all, he had said to himself, anti-homosexual laws exist in most capitalist countries, including England and the United States. (p. 335)

The ideologue *versus* the poet

This issue—the (in)compatibility of politics and poetics, if you will—is dramatised in Robert Bolt's screenplay for the film version of *Dr Zhivago*. When the revolutionary Strelnikov takes the doctor/poet Zhivago from the train for interrogation, Strelnikov criticises Zhivago's obsession with the 'personal' as being less rigorous than the Revolution requires. All the power in this scene is clearly in the hands of the interrogator, and the viewer is made to feel that Zhivago is in danger at the hands of an ideologue, who may or may not have lost something of his humanity; (eventually, in spite of the hard-line position, Strelnikov permits the Doctor to resume his journey to safety). In drawing this parallel I am suggesting that, like Strelnikov with the Doctor, Altman implies that the resistant political and social struggle for gay liberation was not well served by Isherwood, who was too concerned with the personal. This is the old charge of narcissism, but the fire is coming from the revolutionaries, rather than the psychiatrists.

Private communication with correspondents in Hollywood convinces me that Isherwood mentored many men in coming out, in dealing with oppression, some with their careers as writers, and he was more than a token political rallying point in his time. Isherwood supported the 1978 protests against the infamous Proposition 6, driven by a State Senator (John Briggs; thus the 'Briggs initiative'), which was an attempt to introduce legislation to ban homosexuals from teaching in schools in California, and part of a national campaign by the religious right, with the strident support of singer Anita Bryant. (The period is covered by an Academy Award winning documentary focusing on the political work by assassinated gay activist Harvey Milk—*The times of Harvey Milk*, made in 1984—and a feature film, *Milk*, starring Sean Penn, released in 2008.)

Having found a conscientious basis on which to defend his sexuality, Isherwood wasn't likely to give it away lightly:

> [H]e must never again give way to embarrassment, never deny the rights of his tribe, never apologize for its existence, never think of sacrificing himself masochistically on the altar of that false god of the totalitarians, the Greatest Good of the Greatest Number—whose priests are alone empowered to decide what 'good' is. (*Christopher*, p. 336)

Perhaps, too, Altman underestimates the political effect of simply being 'out' in one's social milieu. Chris Freeman notes, in the documentary *Chris & Don: a love story* (2008):

> Chris and Don were never apologetic about being a couple. And there were lots of reasons that they could have been. The age difference thing; the difference in status, at the beginning of their relationship, in particular; but they never were … They would go to Hollywood parties when closeted people were surrounding them, and they were a couple. Christopher never took a woman with him to a function so that it would appear that he was straight. And Don never did. They went as a couple, and there would be men that they had had sex with, in the room, with their wives.

I have already shown the acute discomfort Isherwood felt with regard to his tendency to 'perform' a self. Decades of meditation practice and the regular meetings with his guru did little to deaden that awareness, making dissimulation even more uncomfortable. Because of the Christian worldview, which opposes sex and spirituality (and treats *homo*sex as an 'abomination'), some commentators are simply incapable of recognising the possibility that even through sex, Isherwood might have been seeking the same answers to his search for 'home'. Is this unrepentant sexuality really so far from 'God' as most Christian churches—Catholic, Protestant and Evangelical—are still inclined to preach? Training in dualistic systems causes the conditioned mind to compartmentalise elements of the life. For Isherwood, on the other hand, it was all one integrative project.

When the Kinsey/Pomeroy/Martin reports on sexual behaviour—in the human male (1948), and female (1953)—detailed what was actually going on behind the curtains of American bedrooms, they revealed a deep divide between puritanical public rhetoric and the actual behaviour of Americans they interviewed. The preface to the first report draws attention to this issue:

> The history of medicine proves that in so far as man seeks to know himself and face his whole nature, he has become free from bewildered fear, despondent shame, or arrant hypocrisy. As long as sex is dealt with in the current confusion of ignorance and sophistication, denial and indulgence, suppression and stimulation, punishment and exploitation, secrecy and display, it will be associated with a duplicity and indecency that lead neither to intellectual honesty nor human dignity … (Alan Gregg, preface, p. v)

Insofar as western religious discourse continues a (some would say Platonic) divide, it works to deny knowledge of what Gregg calls the 'whole' nature. Working in a tradition that (at least since Shankara) strives to establish a non-dualistic understanding of human (and divine) nature, Isherwood, on the other hand, was empowered to work towards integration. In 1948, Kinsey et al. had this to say on the categorical division of males that continues, alas, even today:

> Males do not represent two discrete populations, heterosexual and homosexual. The world is not to be divided into sheep and goats. Not all things are black nor all things white. It is a fundamental of taxonomy that nature rarely deals with discrete categories. Only the human mind invents categories and tries to force facts into separated pigeon-holes. The living world is a continuum in each and every one of its aspects. The sooner we learn this concerning human sexual behavior, the sooner we shall reach a sound understanding of the realities of sex. (p. 639)

In this final section I want to expand a little further on the Advaita principles that I propose are clearly in accord with this point.

Darkness and light—the Kali factor

Isherwood had a thorough grounding in Vedanta principles and philosophy, as they were represented in the Ramakrishna tradition. After his biographical study of the life of the saint, in whose memory the Vedanta Society had been founded, Isherwood was in a very good position to appreciate the Advaita, or non-dualistic (literally, 'not two') thrust of its teachings, especially as they had developed under Swami Vivekananda. Minds trained in rationalist models of reality, produced in terms of polarised oppositions, might fail to recognise the topography here. Isherwood wrote of Hinduism as 'a religion which recognises the male-female principle within the Godhead', which must, by definition 'embody all possible functions', and therefore can be thought of as being both male and female. 'One of the greatest causes of misunderstanding of Hinduism by foreign scholars', he wrote, 'is perhaps a subconsciously respected tradition that God must be one sex only, or at least only one sex at a time' (*Ramakrishna*, p. 48). That's a clear indication, then, that we are situated within a different set of principles than we might be if we were working within unexamined Abrahamic assumptions (at least until they are interrogated by feminist readings—see Lucy Reid's *She changes everything*, for example).

Isherwood was also deeply impressed by the example of the life of the 'insane' saint, Ramakrishna, whose focus for devotion was the Goddess figure, Kali. While Antony Copley—relying on a superficially Freudian reading of Isherwood's relationship with his mother Kathleen—presumes that Isherwood was unresponsive to the strongly female iconography of Goddess worship in Vedanta (2006, pp. 264–5), in fact Isherwood was strongly aware of its importance for Ramakrishna. Kali represents the very acceptance of light and dark aspects that Isherwood found so important and so aptly reflected in the Advaita philosophy.

The temple in Hollywood has an image of Kali on the central altar, as well as photos of Ramakrishna himself, and others of the early disciples. The iconography usually shows the 'Divine Mother'—MahaKali—garlanded with human skulls; She is commonly associated with death and violence. How could Ramakrishna find her 'sweet'? Isherwood describes the power of this 'gruesome' image as a representation of a non-dualistic deity. Hence his reference to the 'Western heresy' that declares that 'the pretty and pleasant are more 'real' than the ugly and unpleasant'. The Shankara non-dualist tradition, on the other hand:

> declares that the unpleasant and the pleasant are equally real (or unreal) and that both these strands of experience are woven by the same power. Kali, as we have seen, is a Shakti; and Shakti is the Power of Brahman, which both creates and destroys. So Kali is shown as the Mother and Destroyer, giver of life and death, blessings and misfortunes, pleasures and pains. (*Ramakrishna*, p. 51)

As 'Mother' God She is the source of life, giving birth to both male and female forms, and She embodies the cyclical nature of birth/death. To her devotees, working towards spiritual insight into the nature of Being, Kali is the destroyer of human delusion. While people outside the tradition find the darkness included in the image shocking,

> [t]o her devotees, the fortunes and misfortunes of life are simply to be regarded as 'Mother's Play'. And, surely, any other view of the human situation is mere sentimentalism. So we must learn to love Kali, whether we want to or not … (p. 51)

This is a profoundly different representation of an Absolute principle from that with which Isherwood was familiar from the religion of his childhood. At the very point of acceptance, then, where Parker and others are simply unable to go, Isherwood realises: 'When we have done so, we shall be able to accept our experience in its entirety. And thus we shall have conquered fear and aversion as well as desire' (p. 51). Copley's portrait of Isherwood relies too heavily on Isherwood's difficult relationship with his mother, and his reading founders on a speculative Freudian interpretation, so he misses this clear indicator that Isherwood did in fact grasp the very insight Copley claims he could not (2006, p. 262).

Buddhism carries this principle forward, too, as it tries to lead its adherents towards the state of equanimity (*upekkha*, in Pali). But as important a principle as that is, there is more than 'equanimity' at stake here.

Another factor with regard to the nature of Kali worship can be illustrated with a story told by Ramakrishna, who was first and foremost a priest of a Kali shrine. He likened the fierce Goddess to a powerful tigress with her cub. The same jaws that can mercilessly crush her prey for food, when responding to the plaintive mewling of her helpless kitten, gently pick up the cub and carry it to safety without injuring it. The implication is that in order to adopt the appropriate attitude as supplicant towards the implacable and otherwise indifferent Great Source Of All, the Goddess requires and responds to the humblest call for help. In this regard, The Goddess Kali Ma is the supreme feminine manifestation of compassion, as she frees her devotee from the prison of ego identification. Like Shiva, she gives liberation by dissolving the illusion of the ego (seen as the delusional, self-centred view of reality):

> When the ego sees Mother Kali it trembles with fear because the ego sees in Her its own eventual demise. An individual who is attached to his/her ego will not be able to receive the vision of Mother Kali and She will appear in a fear invoking or 'wrathful' form. A mature soul who engages in

> spiritual practice to remove the illusion of the ego sees Mother Kali as very sweet, affectionate, and overflowing with incomprehensible love for Her children. (From the online site: http://www.goddess-kali-ma.com)

I have already suggested how Vedanta teachings deal with 'sin' rather differently from the approach taken in conventional Christianity. I should point out that this doesn't imply that all actions are equally useful in taking aspirants towards their goal. Monastic codes (the 'Vinaya' code, for example, for Buddhist renunciates) are strict. A Tibetan Buddhist lama advises:

> It is precisely because our present life is so inseparably linked with desire that we must make use of desire's tremendous energy if we wish to transform our life into something transcendental. (Lama Thubten Yeshe, *Introduction to Tantra*, p. 35)

Recognising the nature of desire and learning how to re-focus it requires an integrative approach, rather than denial, and the teachings leave little room for deluding oneself. But if 'the unpleasant and the pleasant are equally real (or unreal)' and 'both these strands of experience are woven by the same power' as Shankara asserted, 'It is no use inventing a Devil as an alibi for our weakness' as Isherwood and Prabhavananda wrote in their short essay, 'What is evil?' (1947b, p. 57).

Whether or not this position is necessarily exclusive to Eastern representations of 'God', the ontological combination of positive and negative qualities—encompassing binaries within the same figuration—certainly makes the image more potent as an archetype and, I believe, in Isherwood's case, provided a foundation for an unapologetic acknowledgment of the less conventionally 'worthy' traits of his character that Western writers may be simply too culture-bound to appreciate. Peter Conrad wrote in the *Observer*, for example:

> Isherwood lost more than a few years in California. He also, as this sad and rather shaming book makes clear, mislaid his gift. (2000, p. 13)

However, there are notable exceptions. Stephen Wade sees Isherwood as a writer who:

> attempted to make fiction a way of knowing the self in its modes of solipsism … and its attempts at understanding the nature of being in the world. (2001, p. 3)

Wade is one calling for Isherwood to be seen as a 'serious religious novelist'. The latter approach is very much in keeping with my own position that frames spirituality as a relentless inquiry into the nature of being, rather than the mere social acceptance into membership of privileged religious groups, or adherence to normative codes of moral behaviour.

The suspicion of mystical experience

The life of Ramakrishna offers its own controversies and its own insights. While I don't have the space here to go into great detail, the Bengali mystic was already of interest to Westerners before Isherwood's pamphleteering. Freud, for example, had focused on the saint's mysticism—for which he used the term 'oceanic awareness'—as a prime example of what he characterised as an infantile regression to the womb (see *Civilization and its discontents*, 1929). The French writer Romain Rolland, who suggested the term 'oceanic' after reading *The future of an illusion* (1927), was Freud's main informant for the development of his reductive view of the saint's 'samadhi'. (Rolland published biographies of Ramakrishna, in 1929, and Vivekananda in 1930.) While Freud confessed that '[t]o me mysticism is just as closed a book as music' (Letter to Rolland, 20 July 1929)—a statement worthy of serious analysis on its own—he proceeded, nonetheless, to 'read' the closed book, tin ear and all, and lay the groundwork for what would become the lasting tradition of the psychoanalytic caricature that he made out of mysticism.

Lesser figures than Freud jumped so eagerly on the bandwagon that Ramakrishna's reputation has only partially recovered from the reductive, psychological dismissal of his enlightenment process in the West. Jeffery Moussaieff Masson's 1980 treatment, *The oceanic feeling*, is a problematic case in point and, for all its earnestness, Jeffrey Kripal's clumsy transposition of

Western psychoanalytic notions, in *Kali's child: the mystical and the erotic in the life and teachings of Ramakrishna* (1st edn: 1998) stirred up a more acrimonious debate than Masson's representation.

Another scholar, Narasingha Sil, had already proposed that Ramakrishna's frequent *samadhi* states were symptomatic of a pathological escape mechanism, offering the diagnosis that Ramakrishna was subjected to abusive trauma in his early years. Following Sil (1991 and 1998), Kripal claimed to be able to demonstrate Ramakrishna's 'conflicted homoeroticism', and prove that the saint's 'famous ecstatic and visionary experiences were driven by mystico-erotic energies that he neither fully accepted nor understood' (1998, p. 4)—the presumption being that Kripal *does* understand what poor Ramakrishna could not. This interpretation was offered in what was touted as an account 'as sympathetic to the historical Ramakrishna as it is critical of his traditional portraits'.

Epistemic violence

Needless to say, a storm descended upon Kripal's 'psychoanalytically-inclined' head (he was not trained, as Masson was, as an analyst) and for all the self-justificatory disclaimers in his responses to his many critics, as far as I can see Kripal fails to meet head on the critical issue of the (in)appropriateness of transposing psychoanalytic discourse, transculturally. To my mind, this is a prime example of what post-colonial theorists such as Gayatri Spivak would call 'epistemic violence', projecting a (white) European epistemology onto the rest of the world. Spivak finds *Kali's child* to be 'so full of cultural and linguistic mis-translations that the general premise cannot be taken seriously' (2007, p. 343) and has offered no further commentary on Kripal's assertions.

J-F Lyotard writes about epistemic violence in relation to his concept of the 'differend'. A differend is a disagreement between two parties who do not share the same 'rules of cognition'. In this analysis, the 'violence' comes from a dominating power relation that works to constitute the legitimising ideology embedded in its discourse, when applied across cultures (see Lyotard 1989). While Kripal rejects any critique of his work as a 'colonialist' project, it certainly bears the hallmarks of a kind of intellectual colonialism, using Western paradigms and presuming them normative, holding up psychoanalytic concepts as universal human traits that somehow transcend culture.

In other words, post-Freudian interpretations of the status of Ramakrishna's psyche serve to reinforce and legitimate European (in this case, Freudian psychoanalytic) theories as superior to different processes that are at work within the religious culture from which Ramakrishna emerged. According to Lyotard, epistemic violence happens because there is 'no universal rule of judgment between heterogeneous genres of discourse' or, in other words, no standard against which to judge across genres (1989, p. xi). To resolve the dispute according to the theories of one of the two parties necessarily wrongs the other.

At work behind these reductive and I believe culturally inappropriate configurations, then, is an unchallenged presumption of the universality and epistemological superiority of a constellation of theories that are themselves the result of a particular set of historical circumstances (European, Viennese, etc.).

Kali's child was promptly denounced by staunch and loyal Hindus, not only for its irreverent reading of a revered saint, as racist and neo-colonialist, which might be expected. But Kripal was also called to account for serious errors in translations from the Bengali (Tyagananda 2004), for poor scholarship (Atmajnanda 1997), and wrong-headed, reductive and simplistic application of outdated Freudian theory (Roland 1998). Despite these withering critiques, which could have all but shredded his theorem, Kripal has received a lot of support from Western scholars—his book was awarded a major prize by the American Academy of Religion, for example—yet he has failed to respond adequately to his critics' specific critiques. He fobs off Swami Tyaganda's close textual reading of his mistranslations by making only minor changes in his second, revised edition, and claiming that the changes make no real difference to his overall thesis. Kripal presumes that his critics lack psychoanalytic insight, yet two of his interrogators—Alan Roland and Somnath Bhattacharyya—are psychiatrists, Bhattacharyya a psychoanalyst of thirty years' standing.

Even if one accepts that it might be appropriate to psychoanalyse a dead saint, and agrees with Kripal that his numerous mistranslations (he acknowledges but a few) don't affect his basic thesis (a real stretch, following the exhaustive critique by Tyagananda), it seems to me that other fundamental errors undermine his case, such as his presumption that he can trace Ramakrishna's supposedly 'conflicted' homo-erotic desires back to instances of childhood sexual abuse, yet failing to demonstrate anything more than conjecture as evidence for this fanciful narrative. He relies heavily on the speculations of Narasingha Sil (1991) here and, while acknowledging them as such (n.b. Sil's own choice of language in this regard: 'we must bear in mind that his traumatic childhood might have resulted in bisexual confusion' [p. 29]), agrees with same: 'Sil is right about very many things, and this no doubt is one of them' (p. 298). Trapnell (2000), who finds Sil's treatment of his controversial subject in a later book (*Ramakrishna revisited*, 1998) 'generally balanced', also finds that at times Sil's criticisms of Ramakrishna's motives and spirituality 'seem heavy-handed', and Trapnell points to this very issue as an example of 'strained interpretation' (p. 101). He also doubts the assertion that 'the mystic's frequent *samadhis* are symptomatic of a pathological escape mechanism, employed by a consummate actor', which is also Kripal's characterisation.

Sil wrote his psychological study, *Ramakrishna revisited*, to bring Ramakrishna's 'complex sexual dilemma' out from behind the 'monastic Vedantic interpretation of his career' and character. Describing him as 'basically a misogynist' (1991, p. 44) he opines that Ramakrishna 'exhibited unabashedly an almost pathological fear of active sexuality' and while acknowledging another writer's explanation that this attitude in part reflected Ramakrishna's high-caste (Brahmin) background—'in which the social separation of the sexes is the norm'—he finds that such explanations 'do not explain the matter fully' and prefers to speculate that Ramakrishna's 'distaste for the female sex might have been an outcome of his innate feeling of jealousy toward the "rivals" from the same sex—rivals who could attract his boys to them' (p. 44). Sil knows he is treading a fine line, for in a footnote he makes a careful distinction: 'Ramakrishna exhibited strong homosexual feelings although … his sexual orientation was not "homosexual", in the conventional sense' (p. 24). The distinction, if valid, seems lost on Kripal.

Although Kripal relies heavily on Sil, the latter has dissociated himself strongly from Kripal's reading, saying he has no time for Kripal's 'ludicrous' display of 'psychoanalytic mumbo jumbo' (1998, p. 99). Trapnell misses 'a sustained self-consciousness of the relativity of the psychological perspective' (Trapnell, p. 101) in Sil's own book.

Once again, following Sil (1993), Kripal adopts the proposition that the Advaita teaching of the Mission following Ramakrishna's death was the result of a myth-making propaganda campaign by Swami Vivekananda. As he is so intent on pushing his argument that Ramakrishna was really a 'Tantric', in spite of Ramakrishna's explicit distaste for its practitioners, Kripal must underplay the importance of the Advaita initiation provided by the (naked) guru, Totapuri, who was so important in Ramakrishna's enlightenment journey. Thus we find Kripal resorting to innuendo, suggesting that 'something more than "vedantic instruction" went on between Ramakrishna and the naked Tota Puri in the small hut tucked away in the trees' (1998, p. 299). An earlier reference is even more explicit:

> One can only imagine what it must have been like for Ramakrishna, a homosexually oriented man, to be shut away for days in a small hut with another, stark-naked man. Vedânta instruction or no, it was this man's nudity, and more specifically, his penis, that naturally caught Ramakrishna's attention. How could it not? (p. 160)

It's a strange methodology that allows such blatant speculation—'One can only imagine ...' —which is then treated as established fact. Psychiatrist Alan Roland has this to say about this tendency in *Kali's child*:

> Although facile decoding has been the bane of applied psychoanalysis, Kripal seems unaware of just how highly speculative and inconclusive such an approach is. Throughout the book, Kripal's speculative decoding quickly becomes strong assertions of fact, and these assertions soon become adamant conviction. (1998, p. 33)

Roland criticises Kripal for conflating Ramakrishna's *samadhi* states with 'unconscious dissociated states', and 'states of heightened consciousness' with 'unconscious conflicts'. He asks for a more analytically rigorous understanding of 'the unconscious' than offered by Kripal, and rejects what he sees as the spiritual 'becoming deconstructed to unconscious motivation of a defensive nature' (p. 39).

Kripal disclaims any reductionist tendency and Brian Hatcher (1999) for one, accepts Kripal's disclaimers, as does William Parsons (1999); but others do not accept Kripal's denials. Unconvinced by Kripal's (1998) defensive reply to a journal article, for example, Gerald Larson—rather than back away from his charge of 'monocausal reductionism' (1997, p. 658)—replied to Kripal's rejoinder by renewing and broadening the charge, in 1998.

In a dispute that quickly became rather brittle, with furious denunciations in the Indian press stirring up protests among people who had not even read his book, Kripal received significant academic backing. He has lately withdrawn from the debate (without addressing some of the key questions raised). Curiously, late in his book he states that he has not resorted to the psychoanalytic theory of sublimation (a process—usually not conscious—through which primitive libidinal impulses are re-directed into more socially acceptable channels) to describe Ramakrishna's 'conflicted' eroticism, as it was transposed into states of spiritual ecstasy:

> I make no apologies here. I have not attempted a study of the problem of sublimation. I have, however, offered an "ontological critique" of the traditional model and its answers, insisting that such answers are woefully inadequate as long as they assume a materialistic understanding of sexual energies that in effect reduces the mystical, in the words of Jacques Lacan, "to questions of fucking." (p. 326)

Nonetheless, Kripal does go on to question whether the saint was 'sublimating' sexual energies 'into his admittedly powerful but nevertheless perfectly natural states', or, on the other hand, 'realising the erotic divinity in his own cosmic body' (p. 326). He raises the question posed by Jacques Lacan in a description of Saint Teresa's *jouissance*, depicted in the famous statue by Bernini—is it all about fucking?—only to finally 'insist', after a book-length exegesis based on anything but, that Ramakrishna's spiritual realisation 'be understood on its own terms, as a genuine religious experience' (pp. 326–7).

Kripal likes to have it both ways: he is *not* reducing mysticism to the physical, yet he refers to the first three *cakras* of the *kundalini* system as 'the

Anus, the Phallus and the navel' (p. 20), and he capitalises them, as if that somehow solves the problem. It seems to me that if he had pursued the sublimation theory, his psychoanalytically-inspired reading might have made more sense of what occurred in this celibate saint's psyche as he pursued his difficult mystical path.

After a protracted battle, Kripal has abandoned the field and posted a summary of his responses on a website. Two apologists for the Vedanta Society, unable to find a publisher in the United States, are preparing a rebuttal—*Interpreting Ramakrishna: Kali's child revisited*—to be published by Motilal, in India.

As interesting as this controversy is, for what it reveals about the pitfalls of cross-cultural readings of history, I have to leave the issues in abeyance to show what bearing the debate has on the Isherwood material. Kripal follows Sil (1997) in arguing that Swami Vivekananda steered the progress of the movement after Ramakrishna's death away from Tantra into an alignment with Advaita philosophy. And this is where the issues have a direct bearing on my own discussion. Isherwood came into the tradition many years later; the theory taught by his own guru was certainly inflected by the Advaita positions, which were fundamental to Isherwood's theoretical philosophical training, especially following the translation work he did with Prabhavananda on the Shankara text.

Kripal, who wants to see Ramakrishna as a Tantrika, rather than an Advaitist, downplays the importance of that initiation by Totapuri to an almost ludicrous degree, as we have seen. Spivak is just one who questions Kripal's privileging Tantra over bhakta in Ramakrishna's spirituality (Sil is another). But regardless of the merits or otherwise of Kripal's history, this Advaita presentation is the form in which Isherwood encountered the teachings.

Kripal likes to cite Isherwood as a likely supporter of his reading. So we should compare what Isherwood specifically wrote about Ramakrishna: 'I couldn't honestly claim him as a homosexual, even a sublimated one, much as I would have liked to be able to do so' (*My Guru and his disciple*, p. 249). Kripal bends the statement to read: 'for Isherwood, *there was not quite enough evidence* "to honestly claim his as a homosexual, even a sublimated one"' (1998, pp. xiii–xiv; emphasis added)—which is hardly equivalent.

Having informed them that he was doing his PhD on Ramakrishna and wanted to learn Bengali, Kripal received the hospitality of the Ramakrishna Mission Institute of Culture in Kolkatta. Many in the Order feel that they were 'burned' and question whether all academics use Kripalesque methodologies. I was concerned that, having circled the wagons in response to these 'attacks' on their beloved founder, the senior monks of the Order today might be more wary of Isherwood's own association with them—because of his sexuality—than Prabhavananda was in his time. While attitudes vary, Pravrajika Vrajaprana assures me that this is not the case:

> I don't think so. I don't think their attitudes have changed at all. I think most swamis are quite proud of the Isherwood stamp on Ramakrishna, though privately they'll say, "He was so devoted. He was so good. Why did he march for gay rights?" For them it was like, if you've found God, why bother with sexuality? Or if you want to bother with sexuality, then keep it to yourself. It's a private matter. At least that has been my experience with the swamis who've discussed it with me. Of course there are any number of swamis (or Indians, or people) who find homosexuality and/or homosexuals distasteful. But I don't see any different in that with swamis because of *Kali's Child* or Chris Isherwood. (Private correspondence, Feb. 2009)

What has come out of this, unfortunately, is a real distrust of academics and, for all their backing of Kripal during the controversy, it will probably take some time for Western academic approaches to the study of religion in India to differentiate themselves and demonstrate a fresh inquiry, independent of this particular psychoanalytic tack.

But there is another issue entangled here that has a bearing on Isherwood. Let me return the focus to Mother Kali, who was the focus for so much of Ramakrishna's devotion.

In her article 'Is there anything transcendent about transcendence?' Kelley Ann Raab gives a good basic description of Kali worship and meaning. She allows rather too much credence to Masson's poorly defended assertions on Ramakrishna's 'latent homosexuality' but otherwise presents a well-rounded picture to explain the boons of Kali cultic devotion. She also draws on interesting psychoanalytic material from Hans Loewald (1978), who, she writes:

> does not reduce religion to a form of pathological regression or repression of instincts … [H]e viewed religion as expressive of wholesome recognition of archaic levels of psychic life, in particular primary process or the unconscious drives. For Loewald, in religion the experience of unity with primary process is restored. Primary process in pure form is extant in the experience of eternity, a state which has been described by mystics such as Ramakrishna. (1995, pp. 335–6)

Unlike the construction by Masson and Kripal of Ramakrishna as a 'latent' or 'conflicted' homosexual (surely a difficult construction to sustain, especially given how 'homosexuality' itself has been problematised in postmodern scholarship), and mysticism as pathologically regressive, some find value in the integration of two different cultural interpretations, then:

> In primary process there is neither ego nor objects. This state constitutes the earliest grasp of reality and is that of the pre-oedipal infant living within the mother-child unit. During this period there is no opposition between inner and outer reality [she is quoting Sokolowski] … It is the deepest developmental process and has its origins in the mother-child matrix. (Raab, p. 6)

Raab also cites Sudhir Kakar (1991), who has tried to recoup Ramakrishna's standing after the onslaught of the Freudians, and acknowledges that Kakar has set the stage for a renewed psychological appraisal of mysticism, one that is not purely reductive (p. 338).

'Cross-dressing' and devotion

Kali was the long-term focus of Ramakrishna's devotions (his ardent bhakti sadhana rather undermining Kripal's dogged insistence that the saint was a Tantrika, not a bhakti!) and his devotional practices included a significant 'gender-bending' practice that Isherwood felt freer to discuss in his own late autobiography than in the official biography of Ramakrishna he wrote for the Belur Math. Ramakrishna 'expressed the desire to experience every sort of religious mood, including the mood of a female devotee to Krishna' (*My Guru*, p. 249). Isherwood writes that Ramakrishna

> regarded the distinction between the sexes as part of *maya*, the cosmic illusion; therefore he can't have thought of himself as being exclusively masculine or feminine. In daily life, he didn't appear effeminate, and when he dressed as a woman he changed so completely that his friends often couldn't recognize him. (*My Guru*, p. 249)

(He revisited the issue in the interview with Mark Thompson already cited: 'Double reflections'.) Isherwood explains the various attitudes that a devotee may assume in his/her worship of the Personal God, with the options of relating as a child to parent, or as a servant to master; as God's friend—even as God's parent—and also in the devotional practice called the *madhura bhava*—to God as *lover*, familiar in the iconography of Radha with Krishna:

> It is taught that every one of our human relationships can be sublimated to a non-physical, non-possessive plane, on which it is directed towards God and becomes a mode of worship. Thus, God may be regarded as a father, a Mother, a Child, a Lover, a Friend, or a Master. The approach to God as a lover or a bridegroom is, of course, well known to the Christian tradition. Every Catholic nun is regarded as a bride of Christ. (*Ramakrishna*, p. 52)

In this practice, Ramakrishna would dress as a woman to adopt the passive, receptive attitude towards God as lover: 'When Ramakrishna practised the *madhura bhava*, identifying himself with Radha in her devotion for Krishna, he actually wore women's dress and imitated feminine behaviour (p. 112). Isherwood is uniquely placed to un-pack the significance here, explaining that, as with the idea of 'man' and 'woman':

> [T]he distinction is not absolute … The world of physical forms is nothing but an expression of ideas which have taken root in the subtle mind. The idea of ego—which is the root of all illusion: I am I, and therefore other

> than Brahman—is physically expressed as I have a body. And from the body idea spring two further ideas, mutually exclusive: either I am a man or I am a woman. (p. 112)

Once again, this provides a very strong indication that Isherwood was working within the context of a very differently ordered worldview. The gender binary is a secondary division that does not hold in the realm of the Absolute. Moreover, through such a practice, the aspirant tries to move beyond the philosophical understanding of this principle into direct experiential awareness, slipping free of the socialised, conditioned sense of self, including identification with his/her gender. Rather than reading this, obtusely, as 'conflicted homoeroticism', we could understand this process—as Kripal protests he does, too—'in its own terms, as a genuine religious experience' (Kripal, pp. 326–7).

The notion of a male disciple adopting an approach towards the Ideal that strategically inverts his gender can be found in other traditions, too. Margaret Malamud analyses the psycho-spiritual dynamics of relationships of male students and their masters in Sufism in her article 'Gender and spiritual self fashioning: the master-disciple relationship in classical Sufism' (1996) and there is a large body of ethnographic literature to do with cross-dressing as an aid to accessing altered states of consciousness among shamans in various parts of the world that I will touch on briefly in the next, concluding chapter.

Raab explains that cross-dressing in a devotional context can be used to go beyond 'gender' (as we would construct it in the West) and describes how the Kali figure could be used as a tool for such deconstruction. Raab comes to the conclusion that Ramakrishna was both saint and 'insane', yet,

> to use Ramakrishna's own insight, to be both is also to transcend the categories of holiness and lunacy. We are left with the alternative that perhaps he embodied a third category yet to be defined—the man/woman goddess at play. (pp. 338–9)

While the central ashram of the Ramakrishna Mission in India is understandably uncomfortable with those Western analysts who read this as evidence for 'latent homosexuality' in Ramakrishna, they certainly do acknowledge that his level of consciousness and his behaviour were not that of the ordinary man. Isherwood tells the familiar story of Ramakrishna:

> Since childhood, Ramakrishna had shown from time to time an inclination to assume the character of a woman. Sometimes he did this simply in fun … Sometimes, he was expressing a devotional mood—as when he used to imagine, as a boy, that he was a child-widow devoted to the service of Krishna. There was a sweetness and gentleness in his temperament which many observers described as feminine. But the truth is that extraordinary being had such a wide range of characteristics that he seemed to be a quite different person at different times; now predominantly masculine, now feminine. It was perhaps because of the sense of sex-identity was so faint in him that he was easily able to assume the character of either sex. (*Ramakrishna*, pp. 112–13)

Ramakrishna took on the 'madhura bhavana' as a 'sadhana', or spiritual practice:

> As soon as he was dressed as a woman, Ramakrishna's mind became more and more deeply merged in the mood of womanhood. Those who saw him were amazed at the physical transformation which seemed to take place; walk, speech, gestures, even the smallest actions were perfectly in character. (p. 113)

Those who would jump at every opportunity to psychoanalyse Ramakrishna, reductively re-framing his behaviours according to highly speculative applications of Freudian analytic theories, seize on this practice as further evidence of his allegedly suppressed homoerotic desires but Indian psychiatrist Somnath Bhattacharya makes the point that 'cross-dressing' was a technique common to several of the saint's spiritual practices:

> It is easy to talk loosely with Masson about Ramakrishna's "transvestite activities", but dressing up in a feminine dress as a part of a legitimate and culturally accepted sadhana for a short period of time does not amount to transvestism. Ramakrishna after all also dressed like a Shakta and a

> Vaishnava during his Shakti and Vaishnava sadhana days and like a Muslim during his Islam sadhana—and these were male attires—only to try and make his identification with these cults complete. ('*Kali's child*: psychological and hermeneutical problems', n.d., online)

Kripal seems to want to equate transvestism with homosexuality, but Bhattacharya points out that, according to psychiatry's Diagnostic and Statistical Manual (IVth edition), most transvestites are *hetero*sexual. In spite of his disclaimers, Kripal appears to be pathologising a spiritual practice.

Rather than trying to read the practice simplistically as 'conflicted' homoeroticism, then, it seems to me more useful simply to recognise the elements of a fluidity of gender at play. For, in this tradition, Atman is said to be non-gendered. The spiritual practitioner is learning to loosen the bonds of the ego's identification with what are seen as the temporary aspects of being—all the elements of the predicate self—to re-align subjective identity with the deepest reality of his/her divine nature, which exists prior to the 'descent', or split, into duality. Intent on holding Ramakrishna up as a Tantric, Kripal has great difficulty accepting the Advaitist reading. If you are intent on psychoanalytic readings of this as psychologically 'regressive', so be it; however, it can be read, spiritually, as moving forward in *pro*gressive engagement with an integrative, holistic and fully developed sense of being.

What does this all mean for Isherwood?

Isherwood portrays Ramakrishna as 'an authentic spiritual phenomenon':

> by turns godlike and childlike, sublime and absurd, now expounding the highest philosophy, now telling funny animal stories as parables, now singing and dancing, now staggering in ecstasy like a drunkard, now admonishing his devotees with the mature wisdom of a father, now dropping his wearing-cloth and walking naked like a baby. (p. 278)

My purpose here is not to attempt to evaluate either Sri Ramakrishna's or Isherwood's own spiritual practice, nor to unpack the epistemological subtleties of the Advaita traditions, but I am interested in how Isherwood saw

Ramakrishna as a potential exemplum, and how the rich iconography of this inspirational figure, plus the broad, all-embracing invitation of an ancient religion, and its acceptance of his totality as a 'flawed' human being, resonated for him.

If they had understood something of this context, Peter Parker and others might have a better feeling for how this tradition was seen as more welcoming by Isherwood than the religion of his upbringing, and why what some have characterised as a 'fad' could have been such a successful and enduring avenue for him to safely explore new ways of being and becoming. If we were to ask, 'what was the key that unlocked this heart?' we need search no further than this:

> In India, the religious ideal has always been to obtain knowledge of the Atman, the divine nature within man, through direct experience; revelation has never been the property of a Church, as in the West. It is not towards any religious body but towards the individual seer, the knower of the Atman, that the community looks for an example to sustain it in its own struggles to gain enlightenment. (*My Guru*, p. 47)

Hence the focus on the guru, as well as Isherwood's paradoxical distinction between 'public' and 'private' religion that I noted earlier. There *were* group ritual practices and large gatherings at the Temple on N Ivar Avenue, especially on important anniversaries of the founders' significant dates, yet for Isherwood, the relationship with his teacher was a one-on-one phenomenon and the guiding light through the undergrowth of transplanted Indian cultural rituals.

Isherwood didn't need to idealise his own guru as a God-figure: 'Instead of claiming the greatness of a spiritual teacher, he was showing us an example of a great disciple—which was what we most needed, being disciples ourselves' (p. 47).

These factors are in strong contrast with the approach of Gerald Heard, whose style was more ascetic than that of the Swami. As we noted above, Heard split from the Swami for a while, disparaging the 'low standards of austerity' at Ivar Avenue, and the guru's smoking habit, as not serious enough for him. The Swami responded to Heard's letter in an article for the Society's magazine ('Renunciation and austerity') and Isherwood saw fit to cite it in full in the last autobiography:

> You would identify the life of renunciation with a life of poverty and discomfort and you would say that if a spiritual teacher lives in comfort and in a plentiful household he is evidently not living the consecrated life. Your view is too simple. A man of true renunciation concerns himself neither with poverty nor with riches. If the poor man hugs his few trivial possessions, he is as much attached and as much a worldly man as the rich man. Only the poor man is worse off—because of his envy … Mere outward austerity is a degenerate form of ritualism. A spiritual soul never makes any demonstration of his renunciation or of his communion with God. He even sometimes raises external barriers to shield himself from the eyes of the curious. (*My Guru*, p. 75)

Perhaps this suggests something of the quality of real, rather than idealised spirituality that Isherwood had encountered on his very first meeting with the man who became his guru:

> I felt terribly awkward—like a rich, overdressed woman, in the plumes and bracelets of my own vanity. Everything I said sounded artificial and false. I started acting a little scene, trying to appear sympathetic. (*My Guru*, p. 24)

Rather than looking to Prabhavananda for the conventional markers of piety, as Heard wanted to do, Isherwood developed a more nuanced understanding. Describing a situation in which a woman devotee was bullying the Swami to take charge of a difficult political situation in one of the other Centers, Isherwood comments:

> This was one of the rare occasions on which Swami appeared to me to be intimidated and temporarily helpless. Yet I didn't feel disturbed. Such glimpses of his weaknesses and faults helped me to see him doubly—as Abanindra Nath Ghosh and as the receptacle of "This Thing," the Eternal. If I had felt that it was Abanindra who was getting more and more spiritual, I should have been shocked by his accompanying weaknesses …

> That isn't what's happening, at all. Abanindra, with his weaknesses *and* his virtues, is fading away, while "this thing", which has always been present within him, is becoming more and more evident. (*My Guru*, pp. 246–7)

Within this context, then, we can better understand how Isherwood was able to function free of the 'anti-body' split he had rejected in the Christianity he knew, and we should look at other ways to interpret Isherwood's continued, otherwise naughty, sexuality. Perhaps it goes a long way to explaining how a life-long renunciate such as the Swami could be accepting of Isherwood's continuing sexual adventurousness, and how 'honesty' could be privileged over celibacy as a virtue, even telling him he had the makings of a saint. In an article on spiritual renewal and autobiographical narrative, Mario Faraone writes:

> The separation between body and spirit, thought and sense, one of the main bases for modern man's tragedy, is in Isherwood's view another example of *maya* [delusion]. Body and spirit, sense and thought, are divine gifts which must coexist in man without gaps of any sort. (2000, p. 258)

Vedanta teachings and practice had re-aligned Isherwood's consciousness and laid the foundation for a spirituality of everyday life, if you will, in which the practitioner realises a self re-contextualised within a continuity of existence with all that is—One without a second. Perhaps more wisely than Parker's cynicism would allow, Swami Prabhavananda had allowed Isherwood to pursue a path towards liberation perfectly tailored to his individual temperament.

Finally, let me take a brief look at the presence of the Advaita principles in Isherwood's writing.

Integration and *A single man*

There is textual evidence that Isherwood had more than a theoretical grasp of the fundamental Advaita ontology, and in his mature phase, he integrated Vedanta concepts seamlessly into his writing. In 1972, Harvard scholar S Nagarajan published a perceptive study of the most successful of Isherwood's later novels, *A single man* (1964), highlighting the Vedantic elements in the text. The protagonist, George, is far from an idealised, saintly figure. In this short novel, Isherwood solved 'the problem of the religious novel', as he himself had identified it. The difficulty of depicting the 'good man' is replaced, humorously, by the confused figure of a middle-aged college professor (the 'single man' of the title) whose lover has died. Clearly, we are not dealing with hagiography.

What was a little too schematic in *A meeting by the river*—the opposition of the spiritual and the worldly life cast as two brothers, each a representative character, choosing different paths—is much more convincingly portrayed in *A single man*, without any overt reference to spirituality and religion at all. The two sequences which speak to the relationship of the individual with the underlying, unifying matrix are the opening—as the protagonist emerges from sleep and more or less assembles himself to meet the day—and at the end of the story, as he goes to sleep, or dies (it is intentionally ambiguous). Even a reader unfamiliar with Vedanta will enjoy the humorous treatment of the character's gradual waking up:

> Waking up begins with saying *am* and *now*. That which has awoken then lies for a while staring up at the ceiling and down into itself until it has recognized *I*, and therefrom deduced *I am, I am now*. *Here* comes next, and is at least negatively reassuring; because *here*, this morning, is where it has expected to find itself: what's called *at home*. (*A single man*, p. 9)

The individual—referred to as 'it'—gets up, looks in the mirror, shaves:

> Obediently, it washes, shaves, brushes its hair, for it accepts its responsibilities to the others. It is even glad that it has its place among them. It knows what is expected of it.
> It knows its name. It is called George. (p. 11)

And: 'By the time it has gotten dressed, it has become *he*, has become already more or less George'. Faraone comments on this sequence:

> 'It knows its name. It is called George'. The identity of the individual is therefore seen as a product of its existence in space and time, and it must be reestablished immediately, continuously, every time it awakes, because every return to the world of reality constitutes for Isherwood a rebirth. (pp. 254–5)

A 'rebirth' into the awareness of separated, individuated existence: the personal self, I would say. After taking us through George's day, Isherwood puts George to bed:

> Meanwhile, here we have this body known as George's body, asleep on this bed and snoring quite loud. The dampness of the ocean air affects its sinuses; and anyhow, it snores extra loud after drinking. Jim used to kick it awake, turn it over on its side, sometimes get out of bed in a fury and go to sleep in the front room. (p. 183.)

So far, so ordinary. The domestic detail and other effects are humorous yet compassionately drawn. George is no spiritual warrior, resplendent with the effulgence of bliss. He gets drunk, and has a problem with his sinuses.

Then he poses the question: 'But *is* all of George altogether present here?' and segues into a sequence built around the image of a coastal rock pool, 'up the coast a few miles north, in a lava reef under the cliffs' (p. 183). Each of these pools is separate and different:

> Just as George and the others are thought of, for convenience, as individual entities, so you may think of a rock pool as an entity; though of course, it is not. The waters of its consciousness—so to speak—are swarming with hunted anxieties, grim-jawed deeds, dartingly vivid intuitions …' (p. 183)

'How can such a variety of creatures co-exist at all?' he asks, and replies:

> Because they have to. The rocks of the pool hold their world together. And throughout the day of the ebb tide, they know no other … But that long day ends at last; yields to the night-time of the flood. And, just as the waters of the ocean come flooding, darkening over the pools, so over

> George and the others in sleep come the waters of that other ocean—that consciousness which is no one in particular but which contains everyone and everything, past, present, and future, and extends unbroken beyond the uttermost stars. (p. 184)

The statement—'That consciousness which is no one in particular, but which contains everyone and everything'—is the pure expression of an Advaita position, yet here the religious teaching is subtly woven into the quotidian depiction of one unimpressive man's life. After creating George so convincingly between waking and sleeping as a kind of perplexed, shambolic anti-hero, Isherwood has earned the right, as it were, to press his point home:

> We may surely suppose that, in the darkness of the full flood, some of these creatures are lifted from their pools to drift far out over the deep waters. But do they ever bring back, when the daytime of the ebb returns, any kind of catch with them? Can they tell us, in any manner, about their journey? Is there, indeed, anything for them to tell—except that the waters of the ocean are not really other than the waters of the pool? (p. 184)

To visit that state unconsciously, asleep, probably allows for little to be brought back except in snatches of dream imagery; in a sense, Isherwood is providing us with an image in negative of what might be retrieved if one could reconnoitre the waters of the ocean in full consciousness. To know the waters of the 'pool' (could we equate this to the 'Atman'?) are of the same nature as the waters of the 'ocean' ('Param Brahman') is the beginning of enlightenment in this system.

I am not reading issues into the text that were not intended by Isherwood. He had used a similar image in *An approach to Vedanta*: 'there is a part of myself which, being infinite, has access to the infinite—as the sea water in a bay has access to the sea because it is the sea' (p. 20).

How disappointing then that DS Savage, so intent on the psychopathological reading, could write: '[Isherwood's] homosexual novel *A single man* (1964) contains not one reference to mysticism' (p. 83). S Nagarajan, on the other hand, was armed with the appropriate critical key to de-code the Vedantic vision informing *A single man*; and Terence Dewsnap's brief piece in *Critique* (1971), 'Isherwood Couchant', also could have provided an alternative reading. As both of these scholars published their articles in plenty of time for Savage's appraisal (Dewsnap in 1971, Nagarajan in 1972; Savage not until 1979) one can only assume he was so thoroughly and exclusively committed to the psychoanalytical approach—intent on superimposing that grid over Isherwood's personal psychology and reading his characterisations reductively—that he completely missed the mystic's insight.

One vision—the Advaita insistence on nonduality—is integrative; the other—the heteronormative, psychopathological pseudo-diagnostic—reinforces, even depends on alterity; relying as it does on constructions of difference and separation, using the reviled 'Other' to contrast with and coercively reinforce the privileged 'normal' imaginary. The homosexualist must remain a pariah for the psychological universe to retain its discursive shape, too.

Isherwood presents a fundamental Vedanta principle—of the underlying unity of all forms of life—concealed in an image from the natural world. This is the clearest indication of the integration of the non-dual Vedanta into Isherwood's descriptions of the self; he has drawn the tiny personal self in relation to the whole, without aggrandisement and without overt reference to religion. The irony comes from the fact that George has been getting by, in fact, without the spiritual resources to be consciously aware of the relationship; in effect, Isherwood has created an image in negative of the perfected 'saint hero' that he felt he lacked the requisite genius to write.

Isherwood was concerned, then, with integrating some of the insights of Vedanta practice into his texts. The earlier novel, *Prater Violet,* written while living in the Hollywood monastery and published soon after his departure, late 1945, concludes with the Christopher Isherwood character rejecting 'the way that leads to safety' (p. 126), the way out of the lonely valley of despair, as an implicit threat to the survival of the ego self. His protagonist ('Christopher Isherwood') pauses at the brink:

> It is that hour of the night at which man's ego almost sleeps. The sense of identity, of possession, of name and address and telephone number grows very faint. (p. 122)

But rather than surrendering the self, he wraps it around him:

> It was the hour at which man shivers, pulls up his coat collar, and thinks, 'I am a traveller. I have no home. (p. 122)

He has glimpsed another path, but it is distant, 'like the high far glimpse of a goat track through the mountains between clouds'. He briefly recognises that it might lead to safety, 'where there is no fear, no loneliness, no need of J, K, L, or M' but the clouds shut down and he feels a chill from the glacier, 'icy with the inhuman coldness of the peaks', and so that becomes the path not taken:

> To take that other way would mean that I should lose myself. I should no longer be a person. I should no longer be Christopher Isherwood. No, no. That's more terrible than the bombs. More terrible than having no lover. That I can never face. (p. 126)

Prater Violet was written during the period when his ambivalence about his renunciate experiment was at its strongest, and he was dallying with amatory liaisons outside the cloister. (His departure from the monastery virtually coincided with the surrender of Germany and Japan.)

While the book was well reviewed in the US, the British edition, the following year, was not—Isherwood was snubbed, punished for his war-time 'desertion'. A reviewer in *Horizon* complained:

> We had rather been given to understand that he had lately taken a long journey … far away from home. But can this be so? There is certainly no trace here of any pilgrimage having been taken since the production of his last work. (Strachey, p. 64; qtd Parker, p. 479)

We know that Isherwood was reluctant, due to the 'spiritual tact' discussed earlier in this chapter, to make any claims about his experiences in his spiritual praxis, and his ambivalence during this period, followed by the wild times that followed, certainly muddied the waters, even for himself. But the image of the mountain track and the choice it represents for his character is beautifully handled. Almost twenty years have passed by the time of *A single man*. His life had stabilised somewhat with the relationship with Don Bachardy and he had accepted the less than perfect aspects of his character, in the spirit of a non-judgemental religious philosophy, so his depiction of the everyman George reflects a wiser, more experienced sense of the real.

In *A single man* he was grappling with showing the contingent nature of identity as a secondary layer of being that can be taken up and can also be dropped (George may have died in his sleep). Identifying with the personal sense of self that forms in response to the world around it brings on a sort of amnesia whereby the individual loses awareness of the vast underlying field of consciousness/energy from which it springs—the unity among the diversity. This unitive awareness can be recovered through conscious technologies of introspection that are taught in the mystical traditions, as Isherwood had found. While his representation in this novel is indirect, yet Isherwood found a way of rendering states of mind not mediated by language into the text; paradoxically using language to evoke the zone of mystical experience—literally the 'no-man's land'—with this lovely image of the rock pools and the ocean. By asserting the reality of such experience, which is often ignored or dismissed or disputed by rational materialists, he subtly re-instates its validity, allowing the narrative to take up spaces and explore zones where language usually can't go (and which a British gentleman would certainly never claim any great success in accessing).

Far from taking an easy option, in seeking out a religion that would accept him as a homosexual, Isherwood used both the discomfiting perspective which meditation practice gives into the obsessive workings of the mind, and the acute awareness of the posturing 'performing self', as grist to the mill of his self-scrutiny, probing the very nature of being itself. If Wade has called for Isherwood to be re-evaluated as a serious religious writer, perhaps an age which has become sceptical of hagiography might recognise more truth in the fictional George, as well as the personally unflattering, non-confessional honesty of the 'Christopher Isherwood' of the diaries and the other life narratives, with all his flaws on show.

The diaries—and I include *Lost years*—stage a more direct delving into the self than the autobiographical novels such as *Down there on the visit*, where the focus is different. And it is as an inquiry—or even as a draft of an inquiry—

into the art of self-exposure that they should be read. Even while he is unapologetically examining his unabashed sexuality, Isherwood is paradoxically continuing the spiritual quest as I have configured it—i.e., probing the nature of being a self and the relation of that personhood to everything else.

To reprise the point from chapter two: the overriding point is not attainment of 'samadhi' or any *state*, for that matter; the goal is liberation—liberation from the delusion of a separate, alienated self—and this is why Isherwood's life narratives prove interesting to queer men and women, as well as so-called 'normal' folk (marginalisation is not an experience reserved only for queers).

The disillusionment queer folk might feel with societal grand narratives that privilege heterosexuality as the overriding project for humankind drops them out of identification with the received, normative assumptions about self and society. They may struggle for the freedom to express an alternative sexuality (and 'sensibility') but still have only begun on the path to 'liberation'. If disillusionment is the stripping away of illusions, either it can leave one depressed, or it can free one from unconscious identification with outmoded, pre-arranged roles and identities. The liberation process may continue beyond granting oneself the license merely to pursue an uninhibited sexuality, by persistently asking (in the best Heracleitian spirit) the penetrating question: 'Who am I?' If it is not 'straight', does it have to be 'bent'? Is that the most radical response we can come up with? How deeply do I dig in pursuing that enquiry? What level of 'I' identification truly corresponds to the existential reality of being here now?

If 'Yoga' is the re-alignment of the separate, anxious ego 'self' with the underlying ground of being, or the one 'Self' in all, Isherwood's spiritual preceptor provided a personalised form of yoga involving meditation, devotion and selfless service that perfectly fulfilled his quest for home. 'It is not Home that one cries for but one's home-self.' Spiritual practice challenges us: can we recognise this possibility, through the thicket of cultural differences, the egregious divisiveness of a simplistic morality and the reductive pathologies of drive theory? And can we grasp this re-union in spite of the manifold illusions of duality?

This is the ancient process that the great reformer of Hinduism, Shankaracharya, laid down, centuries ago. Michael Comans describes it this way:

> Sankara's method of yoga is a meditative exercise of withdrawal from the particular and identification with the universal, leading to contemplation of oneself as the most universal, namely, Consciousness. (1993, p. 26)

Comans emphasises that, in Shankara's formulation, this is not something 'to be acquired', since 'it is one's own nature, and one's own nature is not something that can be attained' (p. 26) and he characterises the yoga process as a method of 'negation':

> the removal of superimpositions in order to discover what is already there, although concealed as it were by all sorts of false identifications based ultimately upon the ignorance of who we really are. (p. 26)

It would follow, then, that *false* identifications would include the binarisms of gender. Prabhavananda recognised that homosexuals are neither more nor less likely or qualified to access these levels of awareness than those identifying around the 'hetero' pole. So, the Judaic—and modern Anglican and Vatican-led—teaching, that queer folk can't go there, is apparently wrong in this case. Isherwood's guru saw that it is *desire* that is the stumbling block, not queer or straight desire, and he provided a framework—even amidst the much touted distractions of his work in the Hollywood studios and a string of relationships—for Isherwood to find his way to the sublime awareness of inter-connectedness. Vrajaprana describes the process this way:

> Like a diamond buried in mud, the Atman shines within us, yet its presence remains obscured, its shining purity masked by countless layers of ignorance: wrong identifications, incorrect knowledge, misguided perceptions. It is important to emphasize that we are not trying to become something other than what we already are. (1999, p. 37)

If one is already united with the Godhead within, to continue to seek it as if it were only outside of oneself is to perpetuate delusion. Through theoretical study of an integrative philosophy it was possible for Isherwood to gain a deeper understanding of the relationship of the personal self to a deeper stratum of being. From time to time he was engaged in selfless service projects which, as I have indicated, work to dislocate the ego or personal self as the ruler of conscious awareness; this was deepened by his sustained practice of meditation techniques that bring the focal length of awareness into experiential contact with the deeper levels of being. So, I don't think it a stretch to claim that Isherwood was seriously engaged in seeking out his roots—not in the history of a personal, or familial, or national self but—in this truly universal leveler that Huxley posited as the purpose of human life:

> Man's life on earth has only one end and purpose: to identify himself with his eternal Self and so to come to unitive knowledge of the Divine Ground ('Introduction' to the Isherwood/Prabhavananda translation of the Bhagavad Gita, p. 13).

It was by re-locating his self in relationship to that Ground—rather than in London, Berlin or Santa Monica—that Isherwood found 'home'.

Further, as we have seen, in the Vedanta system as taught by his guru, Isherwood understood 'the phenomenal world of matter *and* of individualized consciousness—the world of things and animals and men [sic] and even gods', as the manifestation of 'a Divine Ground' within which 'all *partial* realities have their being, and apart from which they would be non-existent' (Huxley, again; p. 13). In an interview with Carolyn Heilbrun, Isherwood re-stated this principle in his explanation of Prabhavananda's attitude to 'homosexuality':

> [H]is view is that all attachment is attachment, that life exists only for God within one's self and that everything which hinders that is to be kept at a minimum, or sublimated. In a word, he said homosexuality is merely another form of attachment, neither worse nor better. (Heilbrun, p. 150)

Beyond this elementary principle, Isherwood adds the humorous rider:

> I've really come to the conclusion, in the wisdom of my seventy-one years, that there are even more beautiful and terrible obstacles to enlightenment than sex. And one of them is writing. (p. 150)

In a non-dual system, it matters not whether part of the personal, predicate self is classed as 'homosexual' or 'heterosexual', to use the now familiar binarism; the overriding journey proposed here is back towards a universal, unconditioned 'centre', and we are all equidistant from that. 'Samadhi', as Isherwood defined it, is 'the superconscious state in which man experiences his identity with the ultimate Reality. In Christian literature this is called the Mystic Union' (*Vedanta for the Western world*, p. 20). To the Taoists it might be called simply 'return':

> Plunge the finite into the infinite and, though only one remains, the finite, far from being diminished, takes on the stature of infinity ... the mind of one who returns to the Source thereby becomes the Source. (Blofeld 1979, pp. 163–4)

Whether he enjoys it or not, a queer protagonist finds himself cast as the existential hero of his own Absurdist drama, confronting a meaningless existence, thrown back again and again on his own resources, and forced to learn to trust in his own experience. Even when he accepts the help of a guru figure in his quest, what is given by the guru is not offered in the form of pre-ordained answers to his questions but as instruction in a useful set of tools to use to dig for his own answers, empirically, within the context of his particular life circumstances—which change, and will continue to change, and change again, as the years pass. The outcome of the research that he must conduct through his own lived experience is open-ended, rather than pre-ordained. Even with the theoretical framework provided by a system such as Vedanta, it can be approached as empirical research; which makes of this guru/guide a kind of co-researcher (albeit one with more experience)—travelling alongside, sharing insights and offering encouragement along the way—rather than a Patriarch handing down supernaturally inscribed, authoritative tablets in stone.

Carolyn Myss would frame this as an archetypal 'Hero's Journey' (a model she draws from the work of Joseph Campbell and others)—a journey, she writes, that:

> always begins with a process of separation or alienation from the tribe, followed by a series of difficult challenges that the hero must meet alone. The journey culminates in a descent into the abyss and a loss of faith in the Divine, but then results in a vital transformation and a renewal of trust, which in turn leads to a revelation of some new knowledge, insight or wisdom. The hero then returns to the tribe and imparts this insight—or tries to, since heroes, like prophets, are not always welcome in their hometown. (2002, pp. 65–6)

Perhaps this mythic framing speaks to the recent, renewed wave of interest in Isherwood that is focused on his much-misunderstood religious life. Through the texts that remain—especially those that were not welcome in his 'hometown', or home time—Isherwood the hero continues to speak to his 'tribe', and this makes him an interesting model for people engaged with their own inquiry into the nature of being but who are in a state of cognitive dissidence with conventional expressions of the religious life that position them at the margins.

There are indications that Isherwood was too unconventional a character for some later representatives of the Ramakrishna Vedanta Society to accept, as my own visit to the Center in 2005 confirmed. (In the respectable environs of the Center, I had the distinct impression that, were Ramakrishna to present himself, especially in one of his exalted *samadhi* states, or cross-dressed in the sari of the Mother, he might be found too disreputable to be allowed admission.) The Center's bookstore carried the Isherwood/Prabhavananda translations of the scriptures, but the manager took some pride in *not* carrying Isherwood's *My Guru*. However, this was not a unanimous view. The bookshop at the Santa Barbara branch does carry the autobiography and certainly Isherwood was remembered with great affection by some of the older associates. The publisher of Vedanta Press, himself a monk in the Center, remembers Isherwood well (after working on several publications with the writer while he was alive), and he was comfortable in describing himself and

Isherwood as 'mavericks'. He assured me, unprompted, that towards the end of his days Isherwood was 'illumined' (Bob Adjemian, in an unpublished interview with me, January 2005).

Perhaps the rascal and the saint were not so far apart, at all, and those not taken in by the external display of religiosity might see that Isherwood may have journeyed a least some of the distance that he recognised in his Swami. Isherwood, 'with his weaknesses *and* his virtues' was fading away, while this undefinable 'thing' was becoming more evident. Those mutually incompatible aspects of one life—what Forster's Margaret calls 'the beast and the monk'—connect, embrace each other and, 'robbed of the isolation that is life to either', die (Forster, *Howards end*, p. 188).

6

Changing trains: *Liberation and the 'disobedient' subject*

Out there beyond ideas of right and wrong, there is a field.
I will meet you there.

—Rumi

In my introduction, I expressed some discomfort with the terminology 'gay', 'homosexual' etc., and while I have focused my discussion since chapter two particularly on Christopher Isherwood, I now want to place the Isherwood material within a broader context of possibilities by returning to review some of the issues raised at the very beginning of this book. Underlying my discussion has been an interrogation of the suitability of sexuality as a taxonomic principle in organising human identities (and prescribing subject positionings). We could fruitfully ask: Who are these people known as 'homosexuals', anyway? (Who or what is a 'homosexual' when he is not 'having' sex?) In 1965, Gore Vidal opined that:

> there is, of course, no such thing as a homosexual ... Despite current usage, the word is an adjective describing a sexual action, not a noun describing a recognisable type. ('Afterword' *The city and the pillar*, revised edn, p. 157)

Vidal wrote this during the very early stages of the sexual revolution. Many men today would be disappointed that he refused to commit himself (and his weighty reputation) to the political cause of 'gay' rights, as a self-identified card-carrying *homo*: men who, today, are more than content to locate their subjectivity around this axis of identification—if not 'homosexual', then certainly 'gay', and for whom sexuality *does* entirely subsume identity. But each of these terms carries its own problematic baggage, laden down with assumptions and demands that, while each may have been appropriate for the historical circumstances operating at the time of its conception, as a marker of contemporary identity the terms cannot do the work they are required to do.

Since Vidal's disavowal, of course, an entire academic discipline has grown up around the issue of the constructed nature of identity. While I do not wish to resurrect the twenty-year long debate between 'essentialists' and 'constructionists' in regard to subject positioning, the field is still a rich source of discussion. Crudely put, the debate reduced around the question: is there some essential, transhistorical quality associated with this expression of sexuality? Did 'homosexuals' exist before the term was coined late in the nineteenth century or, as Michel Foucault suggests, is the notion of 'sexuality' itself, as a field of study—and the division between homo- and hetero- forms of that sexuality—a recent construction of modernism, an artefact of a particular set of historical circumstances, with dubious claims to universal, transhistorical status as 'truth'?

When Eva Cantarella's depiction of sex between men in Greece and Rome was published in English in 1992, as *Bisexuality in the ancient world*, Jasper Griffin, writing in *The New York Review of Books*, decried her book as 'a project of propaganda for homosexuality' (see 'The love that dared to speak its name' 1992). Cantarella's history was based on sources ranging from legal texts to medical documents, poetry and philosophy. Griffin's critique, perhaps inadvertently, relied heavily on the code of silence that had kept sexuality off the agenda for discussion, notwithstanding the massive studies by Alfred Kinsey et al., and any attempt to address socially unconventional modes of sexual behaviour was likely to be attacked as a form of 'recruitment'. Protecting the status quo required non-majoritarian forms of sexual expression to remain marginalised, demonised and covert—a source of shame and guilt, rather than a natural expression of human sexuality.

I don't have the space to do justice to all the claims and counter-claims that raged during the accompanying great debate between the essentialists—who supposedly argued for the presence of people we would identify using contemporary labels such as 'homosexual' or 'gay' at all times and in all places—and the social constructionists, who would argue that the division of people into 'heterosexual' and 'homosexual', even 'bisexual', is a recent phenomenon. This neat division of possibilities is impossibly crude and David Halperin's historicist analysis, in texts such as the watershed *One hundred years of homosexuality and other essays on Greek love* (1990), and the more recent *How to do the history of homosexuality* (2002), have refined discussion, and provide the issue continued intellectual currency.

But if you were to insist on asking whether there was, indeed, a 'homosexuality' before the term was coined, it would not be difficult for social historians, anthropologists and others to turn up evidence of male-male sexual couplings at various historical epochs. In his *Love stories: sex between men before homosexuality* (2001), Jonathan Ned Katz probed the historical record of some famous (and infamous) couplings in the United States, showing men struggling to find a language for the feelings they had. In a survey of famous criminal cases in Britain, stretching back centuries from the trials of Oscar Wilde, Montgomery Hyde concluded:

> At least four English kings have been inverts [he was writing in 1948], as have also been a number of distinguished soldiers, clergy, poets, peers of the realm, Members of Parliament and others prominent in one rank or another of English society. Further, the prevalence of homosexual conduct is attested by the fact that sodomy was regarded from early times as an ecclesiastical offence, although it did not become a felony and thus subject to ordinary criminal jurisdiction until the reign of Henry VIII. (p. 375)

So it should be fairly safe to say that sexual activity between men has occurred throughout history (and probably ought to be viewed as a normal variant of human sexual behaviour.) Yet it doesn't take much probing to realise that such behaviour was enacted differently in various eras, and the meaning, value and degree of social approbation it was accorded varied according to the formal rules and social expectations of different cultural and political settings. The most important point coming out of this work, then, is the recognition that the meanings and values ascribed to those acts and relationships continue to be constructed according to whatever set of evaluative concepts is embedded in the ideological discourses prevailing in any historical period. Our ideas of sex, and the identities we construct around it, have been demonstrated by this work by Foucault, Halperin, and others, to be quite particular configurations in culturally constructed spaces, to be read without the transcendental validities that previously might have been presumed from assumptions of a universalist 'human nature'.

If men have engaged in sexual and other intimate couplings with other men, the point should not be lost that to create an entire class of persons based on these acts—even to talk about 'sex', let alone 'sexual preference', 'sexual orientation', 'gender' and so on—is to use discursive constructions unconsciously. And the changing language both reflects and problematises the status and interpretation that applied in different eras. 'Sodomite' carries a different valency from a word such as 'invert'; and 'gay' has been differentiated from 'homosexual' since the late twentieth century, for example. Each of these terms carries considerable ideological baggage that reflects its temporal and ideological origins.

This shifting ground of language problematises attempts to transpose modern and postmodern language especially across to terms found in biblical texts recorded in ancient Greek. Is it valid, for example, to use terms such as 'homosexual' for 'malakoi' (from 'soft') and 'arsenokoitai' (1 Corinthians 6:9, 1 Timothy 1:10)—both used by St Paul? Such an exercise opens up a definitional can of worms, one sufficient to keep theologians and ethicists busy for decades. Each shift in language signals a shift in value systems, and thanks to the work of post-structural theorists the ground has been laid for a *conscious* interrogation of these constructions, a project that has produced a rich field for discussion, that is still being mined in countless scholarly studies. (Marjorie Garber, for example, analyses how 'bisexuality' problematises the binary logic embedded in dualistic discourses in her *Vice versa: bisexuality and the eroticism of everyday life*, 1995.)

De-stabilising the 'hegemony'

Deconstruction of the ideological substrates underlying prevailing discourse brings hidden assumptions out of the unexamined silence and into the public forum for analysis and discussion. Who authorises the production of meaning? By what mechanisms (Foucault's 'dispositifs') are those constructions defended, insitutionalised and policed? How far does such epistemic control penetrate the formation of identity and produce versions of selfhood acceptable to the supervisors of the normative template? What channels are available for voicing experience sequestrated in silence at the margins of authorised meaning?

This kind of interrogation challenges the epistemic control operated by powerful social, medical, religious, legal and political discourses that have relied on the untested assumption that the values and meaning systems of the dominant class are in some way 'natural' and even divinely ordained. Certain of the assumptions surrounding gender, especially, have been de-stabilised by recent criticism so that gender can no longer be reducible to prescriptions based on a binary logic. (In addition to its feminist deployments, such critiques have provided escape strategies for men, too, from the hegemonic masculinist constructions that would define and delimit their identities.)

While imprisoned in Fascist Italy, Marxist philosopher Antonio Gramsci developed a new usage for the term 'hegemony' to explain how 'the State' maintains political and social control using more than overtly coercive power. The term was originally used among ancient Greek states to refer to the leadership or dominance of one state over another (or others) but Gramsci applied it to the working of forces of social control internally, within a state. Hainsworth summarises the machinery of its operation thus:

> A ruling class forms and maintains its hegemony in civil society … by creating cultural and political consensus through unions, political parties, schools, media, the church, and other voluntary associations where hegemony is exercised by a ruling class over allied classes and social groups. (2000, np)

Beyond the crude and overt demonstration of such power—showing its muscle through the military and the police, say—social subjects can be controlled and manipulated by a combination of cultural instruments that promulgate and police the creation of authorised values and prescriptive life choices which ought to be followed. For Gramsci, religion was implicated in this political 'consensus' and therefore it was implicated in his analysis of the workings of the hegemon.

Later, Michel Foucault would investigate the mechanisms by which people 'governed' themselves (and others) according to notions of truth produced by certain discourses of knowledge that were the authorising source of domination and control. He questioned how 'knowledge' produced under the rubric of 'rationalism' enabled the exercise of particular mechanisms of power, for example. Foucault also discussed how notions of personal identity ('techniques of the self') were implicated in processes of government, and how institutions produce order within a society through the positioning of individual identity produced by these discourses. As Turner summaries this analysis, questions of politics and ethics operate through specific institutions and practices whereby powerful authorities, by 'justifying their actions according to specific discourses, install obedience in relatively powerless subjects' (p. 42).

The power of the name

So, we can ask: What happens when we use the typologies produced by the hegemon to define ourselves? How do we challenge the epistemic control of the dominant constructions that dictate who we are, what we can be and what we can know? Can we ignore or deflect the positioning of language if, following the French psychoanalyst Lacan, 'language exists before any of us is born, and we must locate ourselves in the field of language in order to take up a place in the human world' (Mansfield 2000, p. 39)? In accepting a culturally-assigned identity, whether positioned through language, per se, or through these politically powerful authorising discourses of knowledge, do we not accept a whole constellation of attitudes, judgments and possibilities for knowing, that come with the territory?

Our precise placement within a taxonomy of stigmatised types—Robb refers to this as 'the medical colonization which is homosexuality' (p. 63)—renders the wider field of possibilities of knowing and becoming unavailable to queer folk as socially marginalised undesirables. The production of the notion of the 'homosexual' in the nineteenth century was originally constructed to rescue sexual deviants ('inverts') from the punishments of criminal law, but that attempt to rescue men from harsh criminal punishments provided in its turn for some men to be defined and positioned as pathological specimens by the new discourse of psychological medicine. Individual freedom would thenceforth be bound more tightly into the control of an economy of power that controlled the production of meaning and identity itself. The further the 'individual' emerges as belonging to a type, class, or specimen, the more easily it is classified and controlled.

How could 'homosexuality' be acceptable to the wider community if it were constructed as a disease? More important: when, exactly, did any sexual act or set of acts become an entire identity—the 'homosexual'? It is my position that to defend such a narrowly conceived sense of self can operate to lock one into defending only a partially realised being. Let me illustrate from another autobiographical text. In his memoir, *The naked civil servant*, Quentin Crisp writes: 'As soon as I put my uniform on, the rest of my life solidified round me like a plaster cast' (p. 7). A plaster cast restricts movement in the interests of repair and healing but there is little sense of a healing as the narrative unfolds in Crisp's memoir. Perhaps there was nothing to repair in the first place, yet the protagonist's relationship with the wider matrix of social consensus *is* broken in Crisp's account. He exists in an uneasy relationship with a hostile audience for whom he must continually perform an identity. The mood of the text does not reflect any notion of 'gay pride'; and the wit is bitter.

To take on a persona and 'identify' with it could be seen, then, as suffocating the self; if subjectivity becomes a performance, that performativity controls and defines the performer himself. I am reminded, in contrast, of Isherwood's articulate discomfort with the performing self that coloured his early years; and how that dissatisfaction prompted his search for a subjectivity with deeper and more nurturing roots.

Psychology has moved forward from the alarmingly pathologist positionings of a Krafft-Ebing (whose classic tome *Psychopathologia sexualis* gave me a lot of grief in my youth) say, or even a Havelock Ellis and, in spite of the reactionary tactics of the 'reparative therapists' who persist in proposing the use of psychological techniques to 'cure' men of their 'sexual dysphoria' and 'gender identity disorder', many liberal therapists today would tend to see psychotherapy as an aid in adjusting to their 'orientation'. Some psychologists like to represent spirituality as a way of avoiding the difficulties of low self-esteem, emotional problems, etc., that psychological work could help them with (John Welwood 2000, calls it 'spiritual bypassing'). Welwood and others (see Ray 2006) like to present cases of Western practitioners of Eastern meditation who abjure the body in search of states of bliss and inner freedom, and they produce case histories to support their charge that spiritual practice can be used to bypass psychological work and an honest engagement with physical existence. But reading the autobiographies of Martin Duberman (*Cures*, 1991) and a Paul Monette (*Becoming a man,* 1992), it appears that even a sincere engagement with psychotherapy proved to be a pitiful, protracted struggle that came up somewhat short of their needs.

Isherwood was not one to deny the body; indeed, he instinctively sought a solution to his existential crisis that integrated all aspects of being. He *was* interested in psychological theory—initially under Auden's influence—but, as we have seen, he found the psycho-spiritual technologies for self-inquiry that were available within an ancient religious tradition more useful, and persevered with their use over a period of almost forty years.

Church leaders have been increasingly grateful for psychology's support in their campaign of moral persecution, almost as if the scientific taxonomies and diagnoses had been invented 'to allow prejudice and superstition to survive' in a new idiom, with a new respectability (Robb, p. 47). The result of this alliance that has the most relevance to my discussion is that unauthorised spiritual experience and religious beliefs are viewed as deeply suspect unless they result in a conversion satisfactory not only to some putative deity but also to the social canons of hetero-normativity, religiously blessed. Hence any statements, beliefs or experiences that fall outside this limited frame of authorised possibilities are easily dismissed, ignored, undermined, devalued, marginalised by hegemonically 'authorised' discourses.

Queer men might not all, like Isherwood, turn to the 'East' to seek out technologies of transformation but, to negotiate new possibilities for subjective identification, I propose that they will in all likelihood need to find effective ways to shake off the hegemonic control over meaning exerted by the Abrahamic traditions, adumbrated through systems of social, legal, philosophical and ethical norms, boosted by the selective application of psychopathology.

If this shakedown requires that each new generation will need to 're-invent the wheel', so be it. Religion is not the safety net against ontological doubt it might have been in some fondly imagined Golden Age of theological stability. Of course, people facing the existential fact of being without pre-ordained meaning might come to the same conclusions as their predecessors and find solace in the ancient formulae, but it must be allowed, too, that they might come up with startling new hybrid possibilities.

In the meantime, majoritarian and normative discourse still seems to require the alterity of the Queer, with its irreducible otherness, to maintain and coercively police its own proper boundaries, and to justify its continued practice of ostracism. To accept the rules of the naming game casts protagonists with a role in a script they have had little part in writing. I have to question whether shrugging off the pseudo-clinical 'homosexual' and calling oneself 'gay'—insisting that *The New York Times* should follow suit—was a truly effective move in the reclamation of equal rights before the law, full status as citizens and human beings. Certainly, to force a major newspaper to drop the pseudo-clinical terminology 'homosexual' (and everything that implies) was an effective strategy of resistance to the power of that discourse at the time; we simply cannot ignore the power of language, and to miss the chance to reorient the cultural debate would have been negligent; but how is 'gay' an effective alternative? Would it not be a more radical act of resistance to interrogate the taxonomical imperative itself? How is it 'we' can be constructed as a group or a type at all? And who benefits from the power embedded in the ideological discourse that drives this operation?

To make this kind of inquiry is a sign of the stirring—what Foucault called the 'insurrection'—of 'subordinated' or 'subjugated' knowledges. Postcolonial theorists speak of the 'colonising' power of discourse and it is not hard to recognise this process of colonisation occurring *within* a society—as any young queer man entering into the minefield of subjective identification soon discovers. Questioning the grip of 'science' as knowledge, for example, Foucault wrote that an alternative analysis would be opposed primarily:

> not to the content, methods or concepts of a science, but to the effects of the centralizing powers which are linked to the institution and functioning of an organized scientific discourse within such a society as ours. ('Two lectures' in Gordon, *Power/Knowledge*, p. 84; qtd Turner 2000, p. 60)

As Turner notes, the claim to the status of 'science' confers power on those who succeed in their claim, and I feel the same could be said where the authority of 'God' is invoked discursively. If the claim to the status of truth confers power on those who succeed in their claim, the claim to the status of religious truth confers power on those who succeed in their claim, just as medical science does; and so on. All such claims confer power on those who succeed in their claim. And all of them, in order to maintain their discursive authority, as Turner recognises, must suppress other expressions of meaning. But Turner also notes that this kind of analysis 'does not preclude critique and resistance' (p. 60). To resist the suppression is to participate in the kind of insurrection invoked by Foucault, and in his telling 'this task requires work on our limits, that is, a patient labor giving form to our impatience for liberty' (Foucault 1984, p. 50).

Spiritual practice, as a penetrating inquiry into the nature of being, does not necessarily lead to a kind of quietist renunciation of protest, then, and can be just as effective in wresting control, epistemologically, as a sit-down protest within a cathedral, say.

Taking Foucault's approach more broadly, as applicable to the operation of any organised discourse in a society (i.e., not only 'science'), Turner recommends paying attention to the 'the discursive constitution of subjects according to epistemic regularities'. This critique enjoins us:

> to pursue empirical, local, historical critiques of the specific *dispositifs*—the practices, discourses, architectures of the institutions in which we live daily—as the means of discerning the contingent and historical within what we perceive as natural and inevitable. (p. 60)

Perhaps it is clear why Foucault would term this kind of critique as 'insurrectionist'. As Turner notes, according to the common scientific explanations of the 1950s and 1960s, 'to ask after the stories of "homosexuals" as anything other than a compilation of case studies for psychological purposes would have been a waste of time; such stories possessed no other edifying value' (p. 61). Coming out of the set of assumptions that allowed such explanations to hold sway, queer theorists began to question the conceptual framework that enabled and justified the effects of power operating around claims to medical science as it was being applied to 'deviant', i.e. 'nonmale, nonheterosexual' identities (p. 61).

David Halperin, for example, has discussed how the political work around the AIDS epidemic has 'multiplied the sites of political contestation and resistance beyond such traditional arenas as the electoral process, the power structure, and the industrial economy' (1995, p. 28). Halperin agrees with Foucault's important insight that 'power's success is proportional to its ability to hide its own mechanisms' (1978, p. 86). I think it is high time to add to the multiplication of 'sites of contestation', then, and apply this kind of criticism to the unquestioned exclusivist claims to knowledge authorised by the hegemonic constructions of meaning operated by religion.

Interpellation, or the power of the name, continued

Recent theorists on gender, such as Judith Butler, draw on the notion of 'interpellation' proposed by the influential Marxist theorist Louis Althusser (1970). Althusser was referring to the police act of 'interpellating', or calling out to someone—'Hey you!'—with the 'guilty' subject or person turning back in response to the call. He saw the subject as an ideological and social construction produced by the discourses that precede it. Interpellation works because the subject identifies with a particular identity promoted by particular discursive formations that underpin such operations, and it depends both upon the supposed authority of the discourse (be it legal, medical, scientific, religious, or whatever) and the interpellation of the subject as an object upon which this discourse can be 'operated'. That is, it requires the subject to recognise him/herself in the naming and to accept the positioning implicitly offered in the ideology operating therein.

Judith Butler goes beyond Althusser by questioning the subject's willingness to participate in the operation; hence, the existence of what she calls 'failed' interpellations: 'there are any number of ways of turning around and responding to the call of the law' (Salih/Butler 2004, p. 212). Relating this back to her penetrating discussions of gender, Butler identifies a repetition of norms that necessarily precedes the emergence of the subject, and interpellates—or, as she terms it, 'initiates'—the subject into the symbolic order, which, for Butler, is constituted by the dominant norms circulating in society (see *Bodies that matter*, esp. p. 106).

According to her model, in order to remain viable within a hegemonic system following the initial interpellation, however, the subject must, in its turn, 'cite and mime' the very norms that created its 'intelligibility' in the first place [hence her idea of the re-iterative 'performativity' of gender]. If hegemonic norms are understood to be normative regulatory ideals, and if the subject's identification, as a subject, is dependent on reproducing already existing gender norms, then identifying with, or acceding to these norms, in her model, actually 'compels' bodies to act in ways that strive to act out, even embody the 'fantasy' of a coherent and 'natural' gender core. (Rottenberg, 2003.)

In *Excitable speech: politics of the performance* (1997), Butler analyses name-calling as both 'a social injury' and the way in which individuals are called into action for political purposes. She questions whether the subject can refuse the interpellating call—or repeated 'chain of calls'—outright, as it is through interpellation that the subject is constituted. According to Butler 'subject formation is dependent on the prior operation of legitimating norms' (1993, p. 232). Therefore, the 'I' who would oppose its own subjecting construction is always in some sense drawing from that construction to articulate its own opposition. That is to say, the 'I' draws what is called its 'agency' in part through being implicated in the very relations of power that it seeks to oppose, enmeshed by the very struggle to free itself.

Jonathan Luckhurst proposes a more active, positive role in subject positioning than the passive connotation of Althusser's model. Luckhurst argues that 'individuals continue to have significant capacity to constitute themselves through the articulation of subject-positions that they choose to adopt' (2008; online, n.p). He emphasises that 'subjectivation' implies active practices of the self, as opposed to the more passive connotation of Louis Althusser's 'interpellation'. Subjectivation concerns individuals' self-identification with certain subject-positions through their own volition, even though this might be a consequence of these subject-positions being suggested or advocated by others through relations of power. (n.p.)

Imprisonment and governance

Michel Foucault investigated the mechanisms by which people 'governed' themselves (and others) according to notions of truth produced by certain discourses of knowledge that were the authorising source of domination and control; mechanisms through which powerful authorities, by 'justifying their actions according to specific discourses, install obedience in relatively powerless subjects' (Turner, p. 42).

In his essay *Discipline and punish* Foucault enlisted the design principle from a certain type of prison building—the 'Panopticon'—designed originally by the English philosopher and social theorist Jeremy Bentham, in 1785. (It is often stated that Bentham never constructed an actual prison from his own design, but there is an example of one built in Tasmania, at Port Arthur.) The crucial principle in this design provides the prison guard with a position from which to observe all prisoners, without them being able to tell whether they are being watched. Foucault used this example as a metaphor for modern 'disciplinary' societies, describing the project operating not only to *observe* the behaviour of their citizens, but also to 'normalise' it. Foucault deploys this image as a metaphor for the power of government in modern states, to describe a kind of 'continuum of discipline' operating throughout modern society working not only within the prison but all the way into everyday lives, all connected by the supervision (from actual surveillance, to the application of norms of acceptable behaviour) of some citizens by others. In this model he was proposing that not only prisons but all hierarchical structures—such as the army, the school, the hospital and the factory—have evolved through history to resemble Bentham's Panopticon, with obvious implications for government and a template for the way other institutions function. The Panopticon, he writes:

> is an important mechanism, for it automatizes and disindividualizes power. Power has its principle not so much in a person as in a certain concerted distribution of bodies, surfaces, lights, gazes; in an arrangement whose internal mechanisms produce the relation in which individuals are caught up. (Foucault 1977, p. 202)

So, Foucault's analysis of 'governmentality' moves beyond mere electoral processes to focus on the regimens through which the conduct of subjects is regulated and regularised, rendering them docile. Apart from visible external mechanisms ('dispositifs'), if subjects of the State or any of its institutionalised discourses are to be kept in line, they must have internalised a regimen of *self*-government, in accordance with their training and indoctrination as good citizens so that governance becomes a self-regulating process. Such a process is 'especially important in the policing of sexual confession' (Dreyfus & Rabinow, p. 141).

In the name game, then, the effect of interpellation is not a singular act, but a continuous repetition of ideological interpellations, and subject-citizens are required—indeed, effectively coerced, in both positive and negative ways—to constantly demonstrate their 'innocence' through conformist practices. If I borrow from the Althusser/Butler analysis of how the (capitalist) society reproduces itself, and map that across the maintained landscape of heteronormative ideology, the coercive institutionalised apparatuses that reinforce its normative values are endlessly reiterated to produce the right degree of docility in its subjects, assuring their compliance within the dominant order.

According to this analysis, the policing effect of naming—categorising and placing the 'homosexual' subject in relation to the normative order—turns the individual into a certain type of subject, one that is answerable to the normative law and the ideological system behind it; this subject exists for the system (that needs it), and its reality is 'determined for it by the social apparatus that calls it into [this] certain type of being' (Mansfield 2001, p. 53).

For this system to operate and maintain its power, and its control over ways of being and knowing, the subject has to behave according to the rules in which it has been trained; if it moves outside that framework, in a very real sense the 'disobedient' subject threatens the system. As that oppositional system produces the parameters of meaning, and the possibilities of selfhood, it must maintain a model of human subjectivity that can be organised and measured according to its hegemonic constructions. And it must refuse to acknowledge the (liberated) subject as 'an irreducible field of differences that continually counter and defy reduction to a single description,' as Mansfield puts it (2001, p. 132). I can relate this back to earlier work done by the earlier sociologist of knowledge, Peter Berger (discussed in chapter two), who recognised that while 'it is possible to go against the social consensus that surrounds us,' there are 'powerful pressures (which manifest themselves as psychological pressures within our own consciousness) to conform to the views and beliefs of our fellow men' (p. 50). For a 'homosexual', with a very particular subject positioning inscribed by his/her culture, to step outside the powerful social order has powerful repercussions, then.

Given that background, to describe oneself based on one's erotic fixations would have to be a very particular and conscious choice as a strategy of positioning identity today, for it can, paradoxically, lock one into the very system of identification from which one is trying to liberate oneself. There are other concomitant costs, too. I have tried to show that, as constructed in the prevailing climate, part of the 'cost' has been not only for the churches to exclude religion as a source of knowledge about the self for 'deviants', but for non-conformists themselves to abjure the usefulness of spiritual resources in their own technologies of self, in many cases discarding the proverbial baby with the metaphorical bathwater.

This neglect has not been due solely to Western religious prejudice against certain forms of sexual practice; the scepticism also borrows heavily from the objectivist model of 'science', which rejects mystical practice and insight, privileging certain rationalist operations of mind above all others and presenting itself as the only reliable, authoritative tool for observing and interpreting experience, as if 'scientific objectivity' were itself uninflected by culture and politics. (Tom Beaudoin says, following Foucault, that 'psychology, religion, sexuality, and medicine: all have both freed *and* imprisoned us in new categories of self-definition' [2002, p. 344].) If I have questioned what pleasures and forms of relationship to oneself and others are denied us by the rigidity of 'modern confessions of sexual identity' (Beaudoin, p. 344), my focus has been on the subjugation of spirituality as a knowledge resource for men and women who love differently from the normative model. By engaging in a defensive struggle against the slander of religion and psychiatry, men wishing to assert a proud alternative identity may need to consider whether they are being driven into historicised subjective identifications that are in danger of ghettoising them. Foucault argued that:

> The notion of 'sex' made it possible to group together, in an artificial unity, anatomical elements, biological functions, conducts, sensations, and pleasures, and it enabled one to make use of this fictitious unity as a causal principle, an omnipresent meaning, a secret to be discovered everywhere. (1978, p. 154)

Holding close to the sexualised version of the self *as* the self compounds the problem, in my view, and reinforces the suppression of other sources of self-awareness that are neither valorised in the dominant hegemonic discourses, nor accessed using their methodologies.

Beyond 'liberation'?

Thus, as valuable as it can be as a stage of growth, even 'sexual liberation' can become an impediment if we wish to push the search for the self further than sexuality's ideologically produced parameters permit.

Before I pursue this point any further, I must emphasise that I am not arguing for men who love men to deny that love. Isherwood is the perfect case in point. Although his Vedanta practices continued for decades, that did not 'convert' him to a different form of sexual expression; nor did it need to, in order to demonstrate its efficacy, I would argue. His commitment to Don Bachardy was as important as his spiritual praxis; in fact he interpreted the relationship, and all its challenges, as integral to such praxis and rebutted the distinction between 'sacred' and 'profane' love. Even those holding only a cursory agreement with theories relating to psychological health would recognise that to be divided against oneself is an unstable basis for well-being, and to re-integrate sexuality into a holistic self-concept might be a good thing—unless they are still carrying unwieldy and outdated ideas of sexual morality bent into shape by the crassly normative teachings of religion as it is conventionally expressed, or by a psychology perversely inclined to want to 'repair' what is not broken. Nor do I intend to undermine the struggle for civil rights and equal justice before the law. But to accept that your sexuality has the last (or first) word in identity formation is to accept a bogus set of possibilities, in my view. To my mind, liberation must include the possibility of moving beyond 'gay', or 'queer'—let alone the toxic offerings embedded in terms like 'homosexual', 'invert', 'gender identity disorder', or 'abomination'—to take up less oppressive subject positionings and recover the fullness of being (or even the 'emptiness' of the whole construct, if we were to follow Buddhist logic).

It is worthy of note that Isherwood made his journey towards a unitive state of awareness in spite of the entrenched mid-century ideological discourses of shame that perpetuated the production and reproduction of the 'homosexual' as religious pariah, or as the bearer of a psychopathological condition—a developmental failure—or both, that were dominant in his time (see Carr 2006). It has not been difficult to demonstrate that these discursive formations have influenced evaluations of his work; but we should also be aware that these attitudes are not antique historical artefacts.

Latter day oppression

Religious discourse *continues* to use the figure of the 'homosexual'—straw man though it be—as a rhetorical weapon to de-authorise that which is construed as not in accord with its own beliefs and political interests. Witness Pope Benedict XVI's diatribe just two days before Christmas 2008, for example, when in the name of 'human ecology' he called for the protection of man [sic] from homosexuality ('Pope wants humanity "saved" from homosexuality', Reuters/AAP). Recommending that we should 'listen to the language of creation' and comparing behaviour 'beyond traditional heterosexual relations' as 'a destruction of God's work', he 'defended the Church's right to speak of human nature as man and woman, and ask that this order of creation be respected':

> '[The Church] should also protect man from the destruction of himself. A sort of ecology of man is needed,' the pontiff said in a holiday address to the Curia, the Vatican's central administration. 'The tropical forests do deserve our protection. But man, as a creature, does not deserve any less.' (Reuters/AAP 23 Dec 2008)

Perhaps such *ex cathedra* recommendations would carry more weight were the Church ready to acknowledge the deleterious effects on 'human ecology' of many of its own programs, including the pontiff's wrong-headed ruling (March 2009) against the use of condoms to control the spread of HIV/AIDS in Africa ('Pope in Africa reaffirms "no condoms" against AIDS.' Reuters 17 March 2009).

Were the Pope really listening for cues to 'the language of creation' he might have noticed, along with the more observant biologists, that so-called 'homosexual' behaviour occurs widely across the natural world, and has been described in literally thousands of species, from insects, to birds, to mammals (see Bagemihl, Bruce: *Biological exuberance: animal homosexuality and natural diversity*); that, in fact, such acts are normal variations of sexual behaviour. What kind of 'nature' was he referring to, then? Would that not be a construction that manipulates 'nature' in the service of church ideology?

Catholic theologian, priest and author James Alison notes how official Church teachings cast queer folk as the 'bad' other to contrast with the 'good' family values ('Collapsing the closet in the House of God', p. 10) in what he calls its 'totalizing moral ideology' ('Is it ethical to be Catholic?' p. 9), and he unmasks the danger to moral life in any society that comes from the very 'systems of goodness' themselves ('Collapsing the closet', p. 3).

I am not intending to target Catholicism unfairly here; the Pope's positions, as part of the wider public discourse on morality, are similar to public positions taken by leaders of other religious groups. Conservative Jewish rabbis are officially compelled, by their adherence to the Torah, to perpetuate toxic homophobic teachings. Steve Greenberg notes the refusal of Rabbi Moshe Feinstein—whom he calls 'one of the greatest and most innovative halakhic authorities of the last century' (2004, p. 136)—to consider questioning the prohibition in Leviticus against male-male sexual intercourse. In his refusal to take up the question, the revered 'Rav Moshe', as he is affectionately known in Orthodox circles, referred to 'the wicked ones who have this ugly craving', which is 'so detestable that even the nations of the world know that there are no abominations like it' (qtd in Greenberg, p. 137). When further pressed to consider the legitimacy of the prohibition, the Rabbi asserted: 'It needs no reason since it is an abomination despised by all the world. All understand that transgressors of this sin are corrupt and not members of civilizations at all' (p. 137).

There are signs of change in the Jewish context, of course, just as there are in some Christian faith communities. (See Yaakov Ariel, in Siker 2007, for a survey of positions in different Jewish communities.) Steve Greenberg is a rabbi, for example—a gay identified rabbi, at that. But the public discourse is still marked by toxic teachings hostile to men who love men.

Muslim mullahs continue to approve the executions of homosexuals under *shariah* law. In January 1990, Amnesty International protested the execution of at least five people convicted of 'homosexual tendencies' in Iran; and the practice has not died out. In December 2008, when sixty-six of the United Nation's one hundred and ninety-two member countries signed a nonbinding declaration calling for the worldwide decriminalisation of homosexuality (a measure that the US administration, under President George W Bush, refused to endorse), more than fifty nations—including members of the Organization of the Islamic Conference—opposed the declaration, according to a report from Associated Press. (The declaration was also opposed by the Vatican.) According to the AP coverage, seventy UN members outlaw homosexuality today and in several of these, homosexual acts can still be punished by execution. Islamic members of the UN were reported as saying that 'protecting sexual orientation could lead to "the social normalization and possibly the legalization of deplorable acts" such as pedophilia and incest.'

The imbrication of State and religious authority led to an Iranian MP in Britain (Mohsen Yahyavi) confirming—as late as November 2007—that Iran believes in the death penalty for homosexuality. According to this parliamentarian, gays 'deserve to be tortured, executed, or both' ('Gays should be hanged, says Iranian minister'; Timesonline.co.uk; 13 Nov 2007). In a speech at Harvard University, in September 2006, Mohammad Khatami, former President of Iran, justified his country's use of capital punishment for acts of homosexuality (*The Harvard Crimson*, 11 Sept 2006). In response to a question, President Khatami is reported to have said that the conditions for execution are so strict, however, that they are 'virtually impossible to meet,' apparently ignoring evidence reported in the press that these executions were still being carried out.

The documentary feature film *Be like others* (2008) records how, since the Iranian Islamic revolution firmly rejected corrupting Western influences, young men who find themselves attracted to other men, under the threat of a law that makes them liable to constant harassment by police, and even with execution, are persuaded into gender re-assignment surgery, with the approval of the mullahs. Sex changes have been legal in Iran since Ayatollah Khomeini, the spiritual leader of the 1979 revolution, passed a *fatwa*—a religious edict—authorising the surgery for 'diagnosed transsexuals', twenty-five years ago. With homosexuality punishable by death, according to Koranic teachings, this is seen as a perfect solution for, it is argued, nothing in the Koran specifically forbids the surgery. The Iranian cleric interviewed for the documentary, Hojatol Kariminia, says:

> Homosexuals are doing something unnatural and against religion … It is clearly stated in our Islamic law that such behaviour is not allowed because it disrupts the social order … Islam has a cure for people suffering from this problem. If they want to change their gender, the path is open.

Today, Iran carries out more sex change operations than any other nation in the world, except for Thailand. The government even provides up to half the cost for those needing financial assistance. Dr Mir-Jalali, the surgeon who carries out most of the operations, says he has performed over 450 operations in the previous twelve years. The operation is difficult, even brutal—a section of intestine (chosen for its texture and lubricating potential) is removed to fashion a vagina. Afterwards, the patient receives a new birth certificate with 'her' new gender. Yet, if the cases followed up in the documentary are representative, most of these new women are ostracised from their families and, even with the newly refashioned identities arranged to make them morally respectable, they become social outcasts. Rejected by their families, many of them work as prostitutes.

In the democratic state of Malaysia, the opposition of a political rival (Anwar Ibrahim) to the Prime Minister was effectively de-railed for years when he was jailed on charges of 'sodomy' (*The Economist*, 28 Aug 2008). Even today, to undermine the credibility of a position it is enough to reference (or in the Malaysian example, 'allege'—the man is conspicuously married, after all) a person's deviant sexuality.

I bring these examples into my theoretical discussion to remember that entrenched homophobic judgments have devastating real-world consequences. In case my personal position is misunderstood, I should state clearly that to teach a child shame about his/her sexuality is to drive a wedge into that child's heart and is a great crime, to my mind. Such a child will grow up with the idea that there is something fundamentally wrong with him/her and will carry that notion, as a deep psychic wound, into adulthood. That this is done in the name of a God figure, of any stripe, is a travesty. Religions that insist on carrying forward such toxic teachings into the twenty-first century should be resisted and challenged on every front. *When the sun shines it shines for all.* To carry the work of resistance forward it is high time that we follow the feminist lead and continue to 'talk back' to such homophobic 'Gods', on the one hand, and on the other, to throw off internalised complexes of shame by asserting newly won configurations of being and knowing.

To re-iterate my earlier position: the dominant cultural expectations of what it might be possible for a homosexual to know are part of a complex economy of power, produced by what Foucault calls 'regimes of truth'—power/knowledge relations that constitute 'a set of rules by which truth is produced' (Foucault 1994, p. 297). In Peter Berger's terms, any 'threat to the social definitions of reality' is neutralised by 'assigning an inferior ontological status, and thereby a not-to-be-taken-seriously cognitive status, to all definitions existing outside the symbolic universe' (Berger & Luckmann 1966, p. 133). Hence, within the hegemonic framework, any knowledge or insight gained by the notorious homosexual from his training in an alien religious tradition, has been dismissed too easily. By drawing on spiritual resources in the pursuit of self-knowledge, an independent thinker and writer such as Isherwood rehearsed those very 'unforeseen and unsanctioned modes of identity' proposed by Butler (Salih/Butler 2004, p. 10), effectively 'changing the subject' and disrupting authorised versions of masculinity and the disempowering construction of the 'homosexual' as religious pariah.

Political theorists such as Denis Altman fail to recognise the nature of Isherwood's achievement in this regard, but it should be clear that Isherwood has paved the way for more broadly based constructions of identity than those privileged by the now-familiar manouevres of identity politics; and he was engaged with this process long before it became 'fashionable', as implied by John Sutherland (2004).

My book has been about the almost complete invisibility of those forty valuable years in Isherwood's life and work, to offer a re-evaluation of Isherwood and to reclaim the important bridge-building work he did with little support from literary culture. For me, those bridges were built not only from East to West, but also for the maladaptive, bogus sub-species 'gay men', or 'homosexuals', to cross over and reclaim full status as human beings (without repudiating their sexuality—Isherwood persisted in using the term to identify himself, after all).

We have already seen that Isherwood was discreet about his long-term association with Vedanta. Even while he was writing his exegeses for Western readers, he didn't seek to recruit or convert friends and associates. To step away from the standard psychological theories of subjective development just for a moment, let me suggest an alternative way of thinking about the significance of this move that Isherwood made. I would propose a model in which the awareness of undifferentiated unity—what could be called the primary state—is the foundation of being and awareness. Gender can be read as a dislocation, in a sense, from the primary state (so, I term it a 'secondary' development); and sexuality a further, tertiary development. As a building could not be constructed in mid-air, with second and third storeys but no foundation, to construct an identity based on only secondary and tertiary levels, without the support of the foundation, would be a highly unstable enterprise, too. That foundational basis needs to be consciously recuperated, as Isherwood was able to do through decades of meditation practice. Let me be clear, I am not calling for infantile regression, an idea promoted by the neo-Freudians. This enterprise—to recover the lost parts of being—is work carried out consciously, in maturity. It has redemptive spiritual (and psychological) benefits and forms a solid basis for re-constructing subjectivity in more life-affirming ways.

Most analyses of the politics of identity deal with the complex web of social, familial, linguistic and political connections involved with the formation of identity that, following this model, are secondary and tertiary issues. Spiritual research, on the other hand, interrogates the reactive nature of the conscious awareness that has entered into the long and complex interaction with the worlds it encounters 'outside'. Whatever you think of this model, in my experience when the psyche recovers access to the underlying state of what I might call 'unity consciousness', personal subjectivity is enabled to re-connect with, or be re-absorbed by, a more deeply rooted ontological and psychological security—what Rumi described as the 'the root of the root of your own self'. (The model can rely only temporarily on this 'inside-outside' framing, of course, as the field of consciousness ultimately encompasses all.) To explore and to celebrate the reconciliation with the 'Divine'—to only connect with 'that thing' as it was called by Heard/Prabhavananda—is, if not a politically resistant act, certainly a thumbing one's nose at the hierarchy of official churches, all the ranks of bishops, rabbis, mullahs and the like, still actively promulgating the figuration of the homosexual as a religious pariah.

The stigmatising power of homophobia can drive shame so deep into a developing psyche that it takes a really radical re-alignment to bring the subject back into a healing, life-affirming integration. It would be difficult enough to overcome the insidious notion that one is a 'biological error'; but because the dislocation has ontological dimensions—the homophobia is authorised by the 'God' figure, after all—psychological work is often not enough to effect true healing. The subject must feel reconciled at the deepest levels of being. So I suggest that it is not enough to cluster together in 'intimate publics' (Berlant 2008), in the social groupings (the ghettoes: the Castro, the Village, West Hollywood, Darlinghurst) that provide a space of ersatz legitimacy not sanctioned by the dominant public. To me it isn't enough to act out some form of 'gay pride', thumbing the nose at external agencies, if that feeling isn't sourced from the deeply realised awareness of the whole being.

From dislocation to relocation

What some churchmen often fail to understand is that as human beings, we are all *already* members of the club. Any privileged social group, with its codes of inclusion/exclusion, might provide a certain socially-based amelioration of a sense of alienation and isolation, but when membership coalesces around reactionary or shallow resources of identification, these organisations are failing to meet a deeper need than social acceptability. So I am pointing a little further, a little deeper than the usual calls for self-respect and for liberal tolerance towards unconventional types. To be accorded tolerance by any socially favoured group is simply insufficient. My position is that the lost connection needs to be re-established within; if that is rooted in the deeper kind of re-alignment I discussed in earlier chapters, one has already reclaimed full membership of 'the kingdom'.

There is a Sufi teaching story that illustrates what I am reaching for (I first read a version of the story in *The exploits of the incomparable Mulla Nasrudin* by Idries Shah; Westerlund, 2004, cites it, without giving the main character a name, p. 136. My version has a woman protagonist):

> *A woman has lost her house keys. A neighbour notices the woman searching in the street outside her house and asks what she is doing and she explains that she is trying to find her lost keys. He offers to help her and they continue the search together. Before long, other people get involved, too, but in spite of all the help they are unable to locate the lost keys. Eventually someone asks her:*
> *'Are you sure you lost them here?'*
> *'Why no,' the woman replies, 'I lost them inside the house.'*
> *'Then why are you looking for them out here?' they demand to know.*
> *'Because the light is better out here, of course!' she says, as though it should be obvious.*

Sufi stories work on more than one level, but just to take up one aspect here: it is no use looking for what has been lost in places where it isn't. I will stretch this interpretation to offer that the quest for community, the search for a solution to so many problems—social, political, interpersonal—can easily be based on a misdiagnosis. If what has been lost is on the 'inside', what use looking 'outside'? As much as 'identity' is the product of 'one's place in the family, in society and in the social division of labour' (Zaretsky 2004, p. 5)—and even the position provided by one's religion—for some issues, the deeply felt 'disconnect' has occurred within. If that is the case, we can spend a great deal of time and energy trying to make connections by fixing the breaks, mending communities, comparing ideologies, building bridges, 'queering' religion—all repair work negotiated within the socio-political matrix and its economies of power—but if what has been unplugged is on the inside, those strategies will not be sufficient. The point is to find the plug, locate the socket, and re-connect. Working from that internal re-alignment, 'external' strategies will be based on the first-hand knowledge of an *underlying* matrix of unity, and the sense of mutual respect gained from a deeply realised recognition of a truly common source will better inform our efforts towards reconciliation. To win this level of understanding when the most influential and politically privileged forces of one's social setting are ideologically opposed to one reaching that insight still remains quite an achievement.

Once again, I am not trying here to proselytise for Eastern forms of religious beliefs and practices as *the* prescribed path for everyone locked inside oppressive institutional frames of understanding the self. But for Isherwood and men like him, who choose the resources of a 'psycho-spiritual' practice to reposition the moorings of identity, working with the different possibilities of meaning offered by such alternative systems can be a useful strategy in the reclamation of an integrative sense of being and becoming. As such it is a distinct alternative to banging at the doors of cathedrals demanding entry.

In my interpretation, this is what happens through meditation and other so-called 'spiritual' practices: the alienated, free-floating personal self re-locates the source of its own existence in a re-union with all that is, finding its root within a field of 'formless' consciousness energy that contains and enables all forms. Further, I would argue that this desire to re-connect with a matrix of inclusiveness is a primary urge, even if Freud, perhaps, didn't recognise it as such. The Viennese analyst preferred to characterise the 'oceanic feeling' that comes from this mystical re-union as 'regressive', associating it with the undifferentiated state of narcissistic absorption stemming from a failure to separate from one's mother. (Having killed off his image of a Father God in *Totem and taboo*, he had to do something about the residual Mother.)

Ramakrishna demonstrated a more fruitful approach to 'the Mother', in keeping with Indian mystical and devotional traditions (a pathway discussed by the mystic Andrew Harvey in several of his later books), and of course opened himself and his tradition up to reductive psychoanalytic putdowns. (Freud's primary informant was Romain Rolland, who wrote biographies of Ramakrishna and Vivekananda.)

In sleep, unconscious, we trust in something so deeply that we abandon all conscious defences, relinquishing of our very wits to sink into the arms of … what? Meditation could be seen as a *conscious* realignment with that deepest state of trust, a recovery of the *un*conscious layers of being, consciousness, bliss ('sat-chit-anand'). That is a process we can engage with whether we are male or female, so-called 'gay' or 'straight', Christian or Hindu, believer or agnostic, for even if it is practised within a particular philosophical framing, it is an empirical process. In a profound sense, we are all equidistant from that centre and intimately close to it. In effect, all the predicates of self are secondary aspects of being. Isherwood formally described the continuity in terms of ancient Vedantic philosophy:

> [T]hey drew no such crude dividing-line between Matter and Spirit. They explained the evolution of the universe as a projection of a series of coverings around the reality which is Brahman. Brahman itself is pure undifferentiated consciousness; but each of these coverings represents a stage in progressive differentiation, by which the One becomes seemingly many. (*Ramakrishna and his disciples*, pp. 14–15)

To build elaborate distinctions between the seemingly 'many' is to lose consciousness of reality:

> These coverings are therefore coverings of ignorance; they hide Brahman from us. The material universe which is known to our physical senses is the grossest manifestation of this ignorance, since it is the most outward covering, farthest from Brahman … Matter and Spirit are not divided; they are interrelated. The former is evolved from the latter, and the difference between them is only one of degree. When the meditative mind turns in upon itself, following a line of involution in its attempt to reach Brahman,

> it becomes aware of this truth. Beneath the gross elements of the material world it encounters the subtle elements which are their essences. (*Ramakrishna and his disciples*, p. 15)

Isherwood learned to relate his 'difference', then, within this integrative vision to an underlying matrix of unity. His 'home self' was not located, geographically, with his preferred residency in California, but in an interiorised psychological and ontological re-orientation.

This can be a healing journey, then, for someone whose predicate selves have controversial and political repercussions. And not incidentally, it may energise one to *continue* with the struggle for equal respect before the law (and the churches). Quietism is not the inevitable corollary of mystical experience. A personal, experiential taste of re-union may, in fact, make one more sensitive to injustice. I must say that all the really 'holy' men and women I have had the good fortune to work with have been highly energised beings, albeit with deeply peaceful hearts. One doesn't work on 'inner development' *instead* of working 'in the world'; as fearful as the activists might be, it is possible—even necessary—to work on *both* fronts.

Doubt and belief

The very forces that produce the kind of ontological dislocation that one experiences when one finds oneself marginalised by the dominator metanarratives that supervise being and knowing in queer-phobic societies, can lead to two areas of doubt that may prove to be unexpectedly useful: firstly, a deep questioning of the values embedded in the metanarratives themselves—the disenchantment, or disillusionment, to which I referred in the opening chapter—and second, a loss of faith in the models of a stable, discrete 'self' woven discursively from threads of the privileged socially and politically normative discourses. Doubt can be a very fertile ground for spiritual research, and this is one of the key features in my re-framing of spirituality-as-inquiry, as it can produce an awakening from the cosy sleep of unconscious belonging into a puzzled questioning which operates, deconstructively moreover, as a very different process from that of 'belief'.

Even in societies where religion has aligned itself with conventional heteronormative moral teachings; where men who love men become the sinful 'Other' by which the majority can define itself, and through whose exclusion from bonding rituals and myths (and by their condemnation as morally abhorrent) the majority can contrast and reinforce its superior values and beliefs (its 'plausibility structures', to refer back to Peter Berger; its 'discourses of legitimation', to Lyotard) there is this persistence of a desire to know, a longing to connect that will try to seek out alternative pathways of growth and discovery. The urge to 'connect'—which can be recognised in the desire for intimacy between human beings, from the most fleeting sexual encounter, to a more sustained expression in long-term relationship, or in the huddling together in group social and ritual events—can also be assuaged, deeply, by re-aligning the self of a separative, alienated subjectivity into a continuity of being with all that is, through disciplined spiritual praxis, those empirical transformational practices Isherwood learned from his guru that worked to re-align his small s personal 'self' within an all-embracing Self. Or, to use the metaphor proposed by Isherwood himself, the deep relief that might comes from finding the 'home self'. This 'homecoming' comes about, not through a reconciliation with a 'home' constructed filially, socially, geographically, politically and ideologically but, by a re-union of the separate, personal self with an underlying matrix, or 'ground', of being, at the deepest levels of conscious awareness.

Thus, while some activists have been working on the political and legal fronts to resist their marginalisation by the discursive operations and institutionalisation of heteronormative power, trying to force the powerful to allow them a 'place at the table' (to use Bruce Bawer's trope), other queer men and women have been working to reclaim technologies of the self recruited from mystical practice to realign marginalised subjectivities within a field of unity; and Isherwood continues to be seminally relevant to this struggle. If we are to accept the construction by the churches that queer intelligence and the religious life are antagonists, we will continue not only to accept a divisive and exclusivist imaginary of the spiritual life (and its hegemonic, exclusivist configuration by colonialist Christianity, and other traditions) but we will also continue to ignore the kind of information that spiritual practices can make available to our technologies of selfhood. In Isherwood we recognise the queer intelligence, liberated from an oppressive affiliation with the authorised religious teaching of his time, seeking out pathways for growth wherever it finds them.

Even while recognising that their 'type' is marginalised, then, ultimately queer children may learn to treasure their maligned 'sexuality', pleasantly surprised to discover that, in other cultures, at other points in history, outside the oppressive confines of religion as it is imagined and coercively and institutionally produced in their time, their androgyny might have been read as a marker of certain highly valued 'spiritual' gifts. If the first of their initiations is dis-illusionment, perhaps the second could be self-acceptance, a 'coming out' to themselves. They might learn to read the strictures derived from the particular forms of religious morality not only as deeply inimical to their survival, but also as seriously in error. A society whose principles of meaning and morality are based on a narrow binarist construction frames too much of complex reality outside of its scope, and is the poorer for doing so. To survive, such children will be forced to *un*-learn the pernicious homophobic interpretation of their place in the universe—ontologically, psychologically, politically—to recover a healing integration with the parts of being situated discursively out of bounds. (Anthony Venn-Brown uses this trope of 'un-learning' in his memoir of struggling to come to terms with his sexuality while serving as an evangelical preacher for the Assemblies of God Church.)

While the Christian churches have been, in relatively recent times, the 'primary institutional legitimator of discrimination' (Nelson & Longfellow, p. 357) against queer folk in Western culture (and increasingly, too, in recent years, in Africa), historian John Boswell claims that while those people we call gays and lesbians might be conspicuous outsiders from the churches today, they were often prominent *in*siders during the first twelve hundred years of Christian history (See *Same sex unions in premodern Europe*, pp. 361–73).

Knowledge sources that would position queer subjectivity within, rather than outside of, the cartography of spirituality have been strategically side-lined by the normative discourse of Western Christianity since that time. By stepping outside the frame, many writers in the past three decades have contributed to the effort to recuperate the lost resources. In addition to Boswell's work on Christian history, recent work by Michael Carden, particularly his *Sodomy: a history of a Christian biblical myth*, has also helped turn back the tide. Randy Conner's 1993 mythopoetic study, *Blossom of bone*, draws together accounts of gender-variant shaman figures, priests and artists—across cultures, and from widely different historical periods—to reclaim the connections between homoeroticism and the sacred. Similarly, Gilbert Herdt's study of the Chuckchi shamans of northeastern Siberia—from a society that otherwise disapproved of 'homosexuality'—is particularly telling. In his own classic study of shamanism, Mircea Eliade (1951) points to the Chuckchi as an example of a kind of divine or religious 'homosexuality'. I want to draw attention briefly to some of the ethnographic research giving insight into how other non-Western cultures framed the meaning of variance.

The berdache and the shaman

Walter Williams, an anthropologist at the University of Southern California, has done fieldwork among the surviving exponents of the cross-dressing 'berdache' tradition in indigenous American cultures. Approaching his informants as an 'out, gay' anthropologist, he earned their trust and, in some situations he was introduced to living exponents of the tradition who were otherwise hidden, denied or suppressed, post colonisation and the shame-filled impact of Christian missionaries. Such work in other cultures opens up the possibility that at different times in different cultures the value of such 'deviance' might have been construed in *positive* terms. Williams quotes an informant from this tradition, a Hawaiian *mahu*, as saying:

> On the mainland [referring to the United States] the religion doesn't allow a culture of acceptance. Gays have liberated themselves sexually, but they have not yet learned their place in a spiritual sense. (1992, p. 258)

From their own re-examination of shamanistic practices, Jenny Blain and Robert Wallis suggest:

> It may be that men whose sexuality is ambiguous, or who are marginalised because of sexuality, are in a position where they must attend to levels of meaning that escape from or that are not obvious to those privileged by dominant discourses of gender. (2000, p. 404)

In his study of the 'gynemimetic' shaman, William Dragoin writes of the 'associated talents' of sexual inversion, which include ecstatic trance, and he proposes that:

> contrary to the idea of illness or defect … such an individual might better be considered talented or gifted, with a readiness to learn to enter a trance state or a native ability to readily alter ordinary states of consciousness, and in so doing become the ecstatic visionary … to become the shaman for one's people. (1997, p. 247)

From his review of the ethnographic literature, Dragoin concludes that such individuals have been a part of non-literate societies for many millennia.

Ruth Benedict also considered the significance of the North American berdache, observing that a culture may 'value and make socially available even highly unstable human types' (1934, p. 27). If such a culture chooses to treat the 'peculiarities' of these types as *valued* variants of human behaviour, Benedict finds that the individuals in question might 'rise to the occasion' and perform useful social roles without reference to the 'usual ideas' of the types that can function in our society. Further, she points out, those who 'function inadequately' in any society are not those with 'abnormal' traits, per se, but may well be those 'whose responses have received no support' from the institutions of their culture; those whose 'native responses' were not reaffirmed by society (p. 27).

Obviously these few references are inadequate representation of an entire field of study, but perhaps they are enough to suggest that the constructions produced within the social and political contexts of one's time are ideologically charged and quite particular artefacts of culture, politically and epistemologically constructed at any point in history. They are not universal laws of some ideal 'human nature', channeled from some omniscient 'God' figure. To learn of other possibilities of meaning and knowing, constructed with different values by other human cultures, helps to destabilise the presumed authority of forms of knowledge that might be politically powerful now. Queer men have to dream their own mythologies.

I do not wish to contribute to the exoticisation of indigenous cultures, any more than I wish to appropriate practices and beliefs from cultures that spring from very different roots from my own; but from everything I have suggested to this point, for men whose political existence has been queered vis à vis dominant cultural orthodoxies, whose allegiance to the metanarratives embedded in the discourses of their own cultural setting has been problematised, and who have, as part of their own journeying, been 'border crossers', these concepts may resonate convincingly, and lead them to consider what knowledge resources might be available outside the framework of what was culturally permissible in their particular historical contexts. Reading of pioneer border-crossers like Isherwood, and recognising the value of the information they have been able to bring back and integrate into their own understanding and their felt experience, this work provides a kind of role modeling otherwise not available within the narrowly constructed set of morally-sanctioned codes of behaviour promoted in a homophobic society. In a secularised social setting, in which the Church no longer provides reliable ethical models for behaviour, and has eschewed, to a large extent, its mystical role in favour of policing a narrowly constructed set of approved moral behaviours, marginalised people continue to respond to the inner promptings to connect, and they find appropriate resources where they may.

Finessing Fromm's filter

Eric Fromm, who was one of the first in his field to address the relationship of psychoanalysis to the practices of Zen Buddhism, has helped me understand how these dominant, homophobic metanarratives participate in this process of occluding the possibility of queer spirituality, at the level of the individual. In his long essay 'Psychoanalysis and Zen Buddhism', Fromm wrote:

> [E]xperience can enter into awareness only under the condition that it can be perceived, related and ordered in terms of a conceptual system and of its categories. This system is in itself a result of social evolution. Every society, by its own practice of living and by the mode of relatedness, of feeling, and perceiving, develops a system of categories which determines the forms of awareness. This system works, as it were, like a socially conditioned filter … (p. 99)

And, he asserts, 'experience cannot enter awareness unless it can penetrate this filter'.

This is a related point to the one I raised earlier, when I referred to Peter Berger's 'plausibility structures' and the sociological function of religion as an inclusive/exclusive practice that positions queer men (and their spirituality) 'outside the fold'. Berger's analysis applies at the group level, but Fromm's insight—into how this filtering prevents certain experiences actually 'entering into awareness'—brings the analysis closer to how the occlusion works to produce or deny meaning at the level of individual subjectivities. Accordingly, Fromm's filter effect gives a clue to what is going on when queer folk feel compelled to reach outside the frame of the familiar coercive constructions of their own culture, where they are subject to the violence of exclusion, to find healing.

Queer folk still inclined to seek out an accommodation within the existential problematic of being in the world, but a world for which they have no culturally determined mindset (or 'system of categories', to use Fromm's term) that would allow them to recognise, or authenticate their experience, may find life narratives such as Isherwood's provide small bursts of inspiration to encourage them to persevere with their courageous explorations beyond the oppressive boundaries institutionally and coercively enacted in their own cultures.

In a kind of reverse colonisation, Isherwood turned 'East' to seek out practical technologies of introspection, namely meditation and other supporting tools, to turn within and examine the roots of self. The disciplined practices learned from his guru served to channel his earlier searches—through Socialism, and mid-century psychology—into a systematic transformational process. As I have tried to show, in the wrong-headed readings projected into the Isherwood *oeuvre*, the so-called 'weakness' which family, the prevailing religion and even scientific, psychological medicine would identify in him proves in many ways to have been a strength, but one that he had to reclaim with little support, save from his spiritual guide. The focus is a subjectivity in formation (or trans-formation), a protagonist in an existential present, surviving largely without the comforts of 'belonging'—a permanent, if willing, outsider.

I should stress that Isherwood was not inclined to play the 'victim' card as a homosexual. His early mentor, EM Forster, had something to contribute in this regard, in his description of the character of Wilby in *Maurice,* where he introduces the young man's conflicted sexuality as 'an ingredient that puzzles him, wakes him up, torments him and finally saves him'. (Forster describes it thus in a 'Terminal note' appended to the novel, p. 250.) I would say that this matches the attitude taken towards problematical issues in one's life that is common in the 'Eastern' outlook. On the spiritual path one should not shirk the difficulties one faces, for problems are like the gritty irritant in an oyster that might, eventually, produce a pearl.

This brings to mind a couplet from the Persian poet Rumi (it's from 'Divan-e Shams'), commonly cited as a proverb in everyday Farsi. The literal translation runs something like this: 'No physician gives medicines without sickness / I'll be all pain if it means I'll reach the healing'. I interpret this to mean 'the doctor won't prescribe for me unless I'm ill / So bring on the pain / It makes me seek out healing'. It is Rumi's heart that is in pain, yet he welcomes it, because it forces him to find the doctor who has the medicine he needs. Rumi's heart's desire was quenched in his relationship with his spiritual Master, Shams of Tabriz—his 'doctor'. William Chittick gives another translation:

> No physician gives pills and medicine without an illness—I will become totally pain that I may reach the Remedy. (Rumi/Chittick 1983, p. 209)

(As this is in everyday usage as a common proverb, I checked my interpretation with Iranian scholar Leili Golafshani and I thank her, and Raziye Salari, for drawing my attention to this saying and assisting me with drawing out its meaning.)

So, to hark back to the point made by Smith and Watson from my first chapter, people may 'choose not to narrate the stories that are prescribed for them', opting instead to 'reframe the present by bringing it into a new alignment of meaning with the past' (p. 12). 'Seizing the occasion and telling the story', say Smith and Watson, 'turns speakers into subjects of narrative who can exercise some control over the meaning of their lives' and this assertion, they say, is 'particularly compelling for those whose personal histories include stories that have been culturally unspeakable' (pp. 13–14). Writing autobiographically, then, as Isherwood was to do late in his life, in the testimonial *My Guru and his disciple*, is indeed a resistant strategy for re-narrativising the self, in an assertive recontextualisation that bypasses Fromm's 'filter', allowing breathing space for levels of experience—not otherwise permitted to enter into awareness—to re-surface, and be inscribed into the cultural record.

This subject—Christopher Isherwood—became an agent of free will (a 'disobedient' subject, as Gillian Whitlock [1996] terms it) rather than a puppet of contextualising forces, entirely a product of the social and political discourses operating on him (in a sense, *producing* him) in his time. Rather than the pejorative 'regression' of some of the psychoanalytic schools, then, such a process can provide one with a profoundly integrative experiential and theoretical understanding of what a man can become when he realises the limitations inherent in the dominant ideologies that are held in place by language itself and authorised through the hegemonic social and political institutions that dictate the meaning of his existence. First-person testimony, in the form of memoir and other autobiographical texts, challenges the 'discursive colonisation' (Stone-Mediatore, p. 122) that would position queer folk at the margins of a full humanity, and re-writes the myths that sustain the hegemonic control of dominant ideologies. Stone-Mediatore uses Anzaldùa's 'mestiza' trope, to describe how what she calls 'experience-rooted rewritings of identity' mount this challenge:

> We could say that stories that reckon with and publicize contradictory, hitherto muted aspects of experience are 'between past and future', in Hannah Arendt's sense: they are grounded in the world we have inherited from the past; yet by offering a new, creative perspective on that past, they enrich our experience of the present, thereby interrupting the seeming momentum of history and enable us to envision and work toward alternative futures. (p. 122)

She sees Anzaldua's 'mestiza' consciousness linked with a rewriting of myths newly understood, not in exclusivist terms of inclusion/exclusion, nor even of hybridity, but a deeply humanitarian inclusivity.

Some literary scholars will wonder at so much attention paid to what many of them regard after all as a 'major minor' writer, of only moderate interest in the history of English literature. I have tried to show how and why a third wave of interest in Isherwood has emerged, especially among groups of young men engaged in a struggle for more life-affirming subject positions in the face of toxic, hostile forces that would deny them full humanity. In chapter two I argued for the dis-illusionment process that they often go through as a first 'initiation' into a spirituality that concerns itself with a searching inquiry into the nature of being. If this 'initiation' model were more fully developed, perhaps it would read the 'coming out' process as another in a series of important initiations in that inquiry. Certainly, it has become a rite of passage for men who refuse not only to internalise the rejection by Church, Law, Medicine, and Family (and the Military!) but, also, refuse the invitation to performative respectability as a mask for socially sanctioned hypocrisy, that was offered to and conscientiously rejected by Isherwood in Edwardian times. To own one's differently ordered erotic nature in the face of such opposition requires overcoming the shame internalised by powerful and insidious forces of socialisation. Courage is not just a military virtue.

Others have noted (see McColly, 2006; and medical studies by Cotton et al. 2006, for example) the awakening of spiritual awareness during the AIDS crisis, and so on—the existential encounter with death has often worked as such a call. But as each individual comes into awareness, the recognition of others who face similar sets of problems offers not only a fraternal bond but also the possibility of a more affirmative way of viewing their non-conformist loving. Christopher Isherwood, who quit country, family and religion, and refused to accept the humiliating diagnosis of alterity and the prognosis of shame and eternal damnation, and who sought out and pursued life-saving strategies of spiritual and ontological healing, stands out as a beacon for those who hope for wholeness and aspire to love. In his disobedience was the seed of his liberation. In his long apprenticeship with a spiritual Master he found the submission that brought that seed to fruition.

Bibliography

ABC TV. 2002. 'Christian meditation'. *Compass.* Producer: Peter Kirkwood. 20 Oct. Online: http://www.abc.net.au/compass/s706523.htm

Adam, Lucy 2003. 'Fear kept author's desires secret'. *The Australian,* 6 Jan: 7.

Adjemian, Robert (ed.) 1987. *The wishing tree: Christopher Isherwood on mystical religion.* San Francisco: Harper & Row.

Alison, James 2005. 'Collapsing the closet in the house of God: opening the door on gay/straight issues'. Cardoner Lecture at Creighton University. Omaha, USA, 27 Sep. Online: http://www.jamesalison.co.uk/pdf/eng16.pdf

——2006. 'Is it ethical to be Catholic? Queer perspectives'. Presentation at a discussion hosted by the University of San Francisco 'Communities in conversation' Project, Most Holy Redeemer Parish, 12 Feb. Online: http://www.usfca.edu/lanecenter/pdf/Alison_Presentation_USF.pdf

Allen, Brooke 2004. 'Isherwood: The uses of narcissism'. Rev. of *Isherwood: A life revealed,* by Peter Parker. *The New York Times,* 19 Dec: 20.

Als, Hilton 2005. 'I, me, mine'. Rev. of *Isherwood: A life revealed,* by Peter Parker. *The New Yorker,* 17 Jan: 87–90.

Althusser, Louis 1971. 'Ideology and ideological state apparatuses'. In *Lenin and philosophy and other essays.* Trans. Ben Brewster. New York and London: Monthly Review Press.

Altman, Dennis 1972. *Homosexual oppression and liberation.* Sydney: Angus & Robertson.

——1992. 'What price gay nationalism?' In *Gay spirit: myth and meaning.* Ed. Mark Thompson. New York: St Martin's Press (Stonewall Inn Editions): 16–19.

——2002. *Global Sex.* Chicago: U Chicago Press.

——2004. 'One snap too many of Isherwood the camera'. Rev. of *Isherwood: A life revealed,* by Peter Parker. *The Age* (Melbourne) Review 26 Jun: 4.

Alvarado, Manuel & Oliver Boyd-Barrett (eds) 1992. *Media education: an introduction.* London: BFI/Open University.

Anzaldùa, Gloria 2001. 'Borderlands/la frontera'. In *Literary theory, an anthology.* Eds Julie Rivkin & Michael Ryan. Malden: Blackwell: 887–902.

——2003. 'La conciencia de la mestiza: towards a new consciousness'. In *Feminist theory reader: local and global perspectives*. Eds Carole R McCann & Seung-Kyung Kim. New York: Routledge: 179–187.

Arendt, Hanna 1959. *The human condition*. Chicago: Chicago U P: 1998. [DoubleDay, 1959].

Ariel, Yaakov 2007. Entry on 'Judaism', *Homosexuality and religion: an encyclopedia*, ed. Jeffrey S Siker. Westport CT, London: Greenwood Press: 138–45.

Arnold, Edwin 1917. 'The Light of Asia'. *The Oxford book of English mystical verse*. Eds DHS Nicholson & AHE Lee. Oxford: Clarendon Press.

Atmajnanananda, Svami (Stuart Elkman) 1997. 'Scandals, cover-ups, and other imagined occurrences in the life of Ramakrsna: An examination of Jeffrey Kripal's *Kali's child*'. *International Journal of Hindu Studies* 1, 2: 401–20.

Bachardy, Don 1990. *Last drawings of Christopher Isherwood*. London: Faber & Faber.

Bagemihl, Bruce 1999. *Biological exuberance: animal homosexuality and natural diversity*. New York: St Martin's Press.

Barthes, August Roland 1975. *The pleasure of the text*. Trans. Richard Miller. New York: Hill & Wang.

Barzan, Robert. *Sex and spirit: exploring gay men's spirituality*. San Francisco: White Crane Press.

Batchelor, Stephen 1997. *Buddhism without beliefs: a contemporary guide to awakening*. New York: Riverhead Books.

Bawer, Bruce 1994. *Place at the table: the gay individual in American society*. New York: Touchstone Books.

Beaudoin, Tom 2002. 'I was imprisoned by subjectivity and you visited me: Bonhoeffer and Foucault on the way to a postmodern Christian self'. *Currents in Theology and Mission* 29.5: 341–61.

Beckett, Samuel 1954. *Waiting for Godot: tragicomedy in two acts*. New York: Grove Press.

Be Like Others 2008. Documentary film. Dir. Tanaz Eshaghian. Forties B/Necessary Illusions Productions. Prods: Christoph Jörg, Tanaz Eshaghian, Peter Wintonick. Executive producers: Richard Shaw, Sally Jo

Fifer. Ed: Jay Freund. Cinematographer: Amir Hosseini. http://www.belikeothers.com/

Benedict, Ruth 1934. *Patterns of culture*. Boston: Houghton Mifflin.

Berg, James J & Chris Freeman (eds) 2001. *Conversations with Christopher Isherwood*. Jackson, MI: UP of Mississippi.

——2001. *The Isherwood century: essays on the life and work of Christopher Isherwood*. Madison, WI: U of Wisconsin P.

Berger, Peter 1969. *A rumour of angels: modern society and the rediscovery of the supernatural*. London: Allen Lane Penguin Press; Garden City, New York: Doubleday & Co.

Berger, Peter & Thomas Luckmann 1966. *The social construction of reality: a treatise in the sociology of knowledge*. New York: Doubleday.

Berger, Peter, Brigitte Berger & Hansfried Kellner 1973. *The homeless mind: modernization and consciousness*. New York: Random House.

Berlant, Lauren (ed.) 1998. 'Intimacy: a special issue'. *Critical Inquiry* 16.2.

——2008. *The female complaint: the unfinished business of sentimentality in American culture*. Durham, NC: Duke UP.

Bhattacharyya, Somnath n.d. '*Kali's child*: psychological and hermeneutical problems'. Online: http://www.infinityfoundation.com/mandala/s_rv/s_rv_bhatt_kali_frameset.htm. Accessed: 23 Jun 2005.

Blackmore, Susan 1986. 'Who am I? Changing models of reality in meditation'. In *Beyond therapy: the impact of Eastern religions on psychological theory and practice*. Ed. Guy Claxton. London: Wisdom Publications: 73–85.

Blain, Jenny & Robert J Wallis 2000. 'The 'Ergi' Seidman: contestations of gender, shamanism and sexuality in Northern religion past and present'. *Journal of Contemporary Religion* 15.3: 395–411.

Blair, Ruth 2003. 'Logging Melville'. Rev. of *Herman Melville a biography Vol I & II* by Hershel Parker. *Australasian Journal of American Studies*. 22.2: 79–91.

Blofeld, John 1979. *Taoism: The quest for immortality*. London: Unwin/Mandala.

Bolt, Robert 1965. *Doctor Zhivago*. Prod. Carlo Ponti. Dir. David Lean. Videorecording . Turner Entertainment Company.

Booth, Howard J 2002. 'Same-sex desire, ethics and double-mindedness: the correspondence of Henry Graham Dakyns, Henry Sidgwick & John Addington Symonds'. *Journal of European Studies*, 32: 283–301.

Bouldrey, Brian (ed.) 1995. *Wrestling with the angel: faith and religion in the lives of gay men*. New York: Riverhead Books.

Boswell, John 1980. *Christianity, social tolerance and homosexuality: gay people in Western Europe from the beginning of the Christian era to the fourteenth century*. Chicago: U of Chicago P.

——1989. 'Revolutions, universals, and sexual categories'. In *Hidden from history: reclaiming the gay and lesbian past*. Eds Martin Duberman, Martha Vicinus, & George Chauncey Jr. New York: Meridian/Penguin: 17–36.

——1994. *Same sex unions in premodern Europe*. Random House. paperback edn New York: Vintage, 1995.

——1997. 'Concepts, experience, and sexuality'. In *Que(e)rying religion: a critical anthology*. Ed. Gary David Comstock & Susan E Henking. New York: Continuum Publishing: 116–29.

Boyarin, Daniel 1994. 'There is no male and female: Galatians and gender trouble'. In *A radical Jew: Paul and the politics of identity*. Berkeley: U of California P: 180–200.

——1997. *Unheroic conduct: The rise of heterosexuality and the invention of the Jewish male*. Berkeley: U of California P.

Boyd, Malcolm 1978. *Take off the masks*. Garden City New York: Doubleday.

——1986. *Gay priest: an inner journey*. New York: St Martin's Press.

Bravmann, Scott 1997. *Queer fictions of the past: history, culture, and difference.* (Cambridge Cultural Social Studies). Cambridge: Cambridge UP.

Joseph Bristow 1995. *Effeminate England: homoerotic writing after 1885*. New York: Columbia UP.

British Broadcasting Corporation 1979. *Interview with Christopher Isherwood.* Audio tape. BBC Radio 2, Sunday Night: 1 Jul 1979.

Brodzki, Bella & Celeste Schenck (eds) 1988. *Life/Lines: theorizing women's autobiography*. Ithaca: Cornell UP.

Bruner, Jerome 1987. 'Life as narrative'. *Social Research* 54: 13–32.

Bucknell, Katherine (ed.) 2000. 'Introduction'. *Lost years: a memoir, 1945–1951*. New York: Harper Collins: vii-xxxiii.

——(ed.) 1996. 'Introduction'. *Christopher Isherwood diaries volume one: 1939–*

1960. London: Methuen: VII-XLIX.

Butler, Judith 1990. *Gender trouble: feminism and the subversion of identity*. New York: Routledge.

——1993. *Bodies that matter: on the discursive limits of "sex"*. New York: Routledge.

——1997. *Excitable speech: politics of the performance*. London: Routledge.

——2004. *Undoing gender*. New York: Routledge.

Butler, Peter 1990. 'Diagnostic line drawing, professional boundaries, and the rhetoric of scientific justification: a critical appraisal of the American Psychiatric Association's DSM Project'. *Australian Psychologist* 34.1: 20–29.

Campbell, Colin 1999. 'The Easternisation of the West'. In *New religious movements: challenge and response*. Eds Bryan Wilson & Jamie Crosswell. London: Routledge: 35–48.

Canning, Richard 2007. 'A Passage to England'. Review of *A Spiritual Bloomsbury: Hinduism and homosexuality in the lives and writings of Edward Carpenter, EM Forster, and Christopher Isherwood* by Antony Copley. *Gay and Lesbian Review Magazine Worldwide* 14.3. Accessed online: http://www.glreview.com/article.php?articleid=56

Cantarella, Eva 1992. *Bisexuality in the ancient world*. Trans. Cormac Ó Cuilleanáin. New Haven: Yale UP.

Carden, Michael 2004. *Sodomy: a History of a Christian Biblical Myth*. London; Oakville, Conn.: Equinox Pub.

——2006. 'Enchanting camp: ritual, the sacred and queer politics of resistance and affirmation'. In *Popular spiritualities: the politics of contemporary enchantment*. Eds Lynne Hume & Kathleen McPhillips. Aldershot, England and Burlington, VT: Ashgate Press: 78–89.

Carr, Jamie M 2006. *Queer times: Christopher Isherwood's modernity*. New York and London: Routledge.

——2007. Review of *Kathleen and Christopher: Christopher Isherwood's letters to his Mother*. Ed. Lisa Colletta. Minneapolis: U Minnesota Press, 2005. *Modernism/Modernity* 14.1: 170–1.

Carrette, Jeremy R 2000. *Foucault and religion: spiritual corporality and political spirituality*. London and New York: Routledge.

——(ed.) 1999. *Religion and Culture*. New York: Routledge.

Carroll, John 2007. 'Jesus, the Essence of Being'. *The Australian Literary*

Review 7 Mar: 14–15.

——2007. *The existential Jesus.* Melbourne: Scribe.

Cavalcanti, Cynthia 1997. Rev. of *Homosexuality and world religions.* Ed. Arlene Swidler. *International Gay & Lesbian Review.* Accessed Online: http://gaybookreviews.info/review/2849/714

Chandler, Daniel 1994. 'The Sapir-Whorf hypothesis.' University of Wales. Accessed. 20 Jul 2005. Online: <http://www.aber.ac.uk/media/Documents/short/whorf.html>.

——2000. 'Marxist media theory.' Accessed 15 May 2007. Online: http://www.aber.ac.uk/media/Documents/marxism/marxism10.html

Charpentier, Sari 2000. 'Gender, body and the sacred: heterosexual hegemony as a sacred order'. *Queen: A Journal of Rhetoric and Power* 1.1. Online: <www.ars-rhetorica.net/Queen/ Volume11/Articles/charpentier.html>.

Chris & Don: A love story 2007. Documentary on Christopher Isherwood and Don Bachardy. DVD. Prod./Dir./Eds Guido Santi & Tina Mascara. Exec. Prod. James White. Distr. Zeitgeist Films. Los Angeles: Asphalt Stars Productions.

Clendinnen, Inga 2000. *Tiger's eye: a memoir.* Melbourne: Text Publishing.

Colletta, Lisa (ed.) 2005. *Kathleen and Christopher: Christopher Isherwood's letters to his Mother.* Minneapolis: U Minnesota Press.

Comans, Michael 1993. 'The question of the importance of samadhi in modern and classical Advaita Vedanta'. *Philosophy East & West* 43.1: 19–38.

Conner, Randy P 1993. *Blossom of bone: reclaiming the connections between homoeroticism and the sacred.* San Francisco: Harper San Francisco.

Conrad, Peter 2000. 'Tom, Dick and Christopher'. *The Observer Review* 2 Jul: 13.

Conradi, Peter J 2004. *Going Buddhist: panic and emptiness, the Buddha and me.* London: Short Books.

Copley, Antony RH 2006. 'Isherwood and Swami Prabhavananda'. In *A Spiritual Bloomsbury: Hinduism and homosexuality in the lives and writings of Edward Carpenter, EM Forster, and Christopher Isherwood.* Lanham, MD: Lexington Books.

Cotton, Sian, et al. 2006. 'Changes in religiousness and spirituality attributed to HIV/AIDS'. *Journal of General Internal Medicine* 21, Supplement 5:

S14–S20.
Craft, Robert 2000. 'Andrew, Barry, Brad and Cliff'. *The Times Literary Supplement*, 18 Aug: 13.
Craig, Mickey & Jon Fennell 2005. 'Love in the age of neuroscience'. *The New Atlantis* 10: 59–71. The Ethics and Public Policy Center, Washington DC. <http://www.thenewatlantis.com/archive/10/craigfennell.htm>.
Crisp, Quentin 1968. *The naked civil servant.* London: Jonathan Cape. Fontana/Collins, 1977.
Dalziell, Rosamund 1996. 'The bastards Smith and Jones: Illegitimacy, shame and Australian autobiography'. In *Shame and the modern self.* Eds Rosamund Dalziell, Iain Wright & David Parker. Melbourne: Australian Scholarly Publishing: 130–47.
——1999. *Shameful autobiographies: shame in contemporary Australian autobiographies and culture*. Carlton, Vic: Melbourne UP.
Damasio, Antonio R 1999. *The feeling of what happens: body and emotion in the making of consciousness.* New York: Harcourt Brace.
Deikman, Arthur J 1996. 'Intention, self, and spiritual experience'. In *Toward a science of consciousness: the first Tucson discussions and debates*. Eds S Hameroff, A Kaszniak, & A Scott. Cambridge MA: MIT Press: 695–706.
——1997. 'The spiritual heart of service'. *Noetic Sciences Review* Winter: 30–35.
De Kock, Leon 1992. 'Interview With Gayatri Chakravorty Spivak: New Nation writers conference in South Africa'. *Ariel: A Review of International English Literature* 23(3): 29–47.
De La Huerta, Christian 1999. *Coming out spiritually: the next step*. New York: Jeremy P Tarcher/Putnam.
Dennis, Oliver 2009. 'Prose a virtue of poetic necessity'. Rev. of *The complete works of WH Auden: prose volume three, 1949–1955*. *Australian Literary Review* 4.3: 21.
Dessaix, Robert 1994. *A mother's disgrace.* Sydney: Flamingo/Harper Collins.
Dragoin, William 1997. 'The gynemimetic shaman: evolutionary origins of male sexual inversion and associated talent'. In *Gender Blending*. Eds Bonnie Bullough, Vern L Bullough & James Elias. Amherst, NY: Prometheus Books: 227–247.
Drescher, J & Jospeh P Merlino (eds) 2007. *American psychiatry and*

homosexuality: an oral history. Binghamton NY: Harrington Park Press.

Dreyfus, Hubert L & Paul Rabinow 1982. *Michel Foucault: beyond Structualism and Hermeneutics*. Chicago: The University of Chicago Press.

Duberman, Martin 1991. *Cures: a gay man's odyssey*. New York: Dutton.

Dunaway, David King 1998. *Aldous Huxley recollected. An oral history*. Lanham, MD: Rowman & Littlefield/AltaMira Press.

Duran, Isabel 2003. 'Autobiography, 2000 BCE'. *The Literary Encyclopedia*.Accessed 8 April 2005. <http://www.litencyc.com/php/stopics.php?rec=true&UID=1232>.

Eakin, Paul John 1988a. *Fictions in autobiography: studies in the art of self-invention*. Princeton, New Jersey: Princeton UP.

——1988b. 'Narrative and chronology as structures of reference and the new model autobiographer'. In *Studies in Autobiography*. Ed. James Olney. New York: Oxford UP: 32–41.

——1992. *Touching the world: reference in autobiography*. New Jersey: Princeton UP.

——1999. *How our lives become stories: making selves*. Ithaca: Cornell UP.

——2004. 'What are we reading when we read autobiography?' *Narrative* 12.2: 121–32.

——2008. *Living autobiographically: how we create identity in narrative*. Ithaca: Cornell UP.

Ehrenstein, David 2004. 'Everywhere man'. Rev. of *Isherwood: A Life Revealed* by Peter Parker. *The Advocate*. Issue 929, 21 Dec.

Eliade, Mircea 1964. *Shamanism: archaic techniques of ecstasy*. Trans. Willard R Trask. London: Routledge & Kegan Paul.

Eliot, TS 1943. *Four Quartets*. Harcourt (London: Faber & Faber, 1944).

Ellwood, Robert 1994. *The sixties spiritual awakening: American religion moving from modern to postmodern*. New Brunswick NJ: Rutgers UP.

Eribon, Didier 2004. *Insult and the making of the gay self*. Trans. Michael Lucey. Durham and London: Duke University Press. [*Réflections sur la question gai*. Fayard, 1999.]

European Graduate School website 2008. 'Biography. Judith Butler.' http://www.egs.edu/faculty/butler.html. Accessed June 2008.

Fallowell, Duncan 2004. 'Life was no Cabaret for Isherwood'. Rev. of *Isherwood: A Life*, by Peter Parker. Daily *Express*, 28 May: 50.

Faraone, Mario 2000. 'The path that leads to safety: spiritual renewal and autobiographical narrative'. In *The Isherwood century: essays on the life and work of Christopher Isherwood.* Eds James J Berg & Chris Freeman. Madison, WI: U of Wisconsin P: 247–58.

——2010. 'Staring and staring into the mirror, it sees many faces within its face': Images and reflections of the spiritual self in Christopher Isherwood's narrative'. *Postscripts: The Journal of Sacred Texts and Contemporary Worlds.* Forthcoming 2010; pp t.b.c.

Finney, Brian 1979. *Christopher Isherwood: A critical biography*. London: Faber & Faber.

Forster, EM 1924. *A passage to India*. London: E Arnold & Co.

——1927. *Aspects of the novel.* New York: Harcourt Brace.

——1971 *Maurice: a novel.* Paperback re-issued. New York and London: WW Norton & Company.

——1989. *Howards end.* Penguin Books [London: Edward Arnold, 1910].

Foucault, Michel 1977. *Discipline and punish: The birth of the prison (Surveiller et punir: Naissance de la prison.)* Trans. Alan Sheridan. London: Allen Lane, Penguin.

——1978. *The history of sexuality. Volume 1: An introduction*. Trans. Robert Hurley. London: Penguin.

——1980. *Power/Knowledge: selected interviews and other writings, 1972–1977.* Trans. Kate Soper. New York: Pantheon: 82.

——1984. 'What is enlightenment?' ('Qu'est-ce que les lumières?') In *The Foucault reader.* Ed. P Rabinow. New York: Pantheon Books: 32–50.

——1988. 'Politics and reason.' In *Politics, philosophy, culture: interviews and other writings,1977–1984.* Ed. Lawrence D Kritzman. Trans. Alan Sheridan et al. London: Routledge: 57–86.

——1994. 'The ethics of the concern for self as a practice of freedom'. In *Ethics: subjectivity and truth.* Ed. Paul Rabinow. Trans. Robert Hurley et al. New York: New Press: 281–301.

——1999. 'Michel Foucault and Zen: a stay in a Zen temple'. In *Religion and culture*. Ed. Jeremy R Carrette. New York: Routledge: 110–14.

——2000. 'Sexuality and solitude'. In *Michel Foucault, Ethics: essential works of Foucault 1954–1984, Vol. 1.* Ed. P Rabinow. London: Penguin Books.

Fraser, Andrew 2009. 'What would Jesus do?' *The Weekend Australian*

Magazine, 21–22 Feb: 19–23.

Freud, Sigmund 1953–1974. 'Introductory lectures on psycho-analysis (1916–17)'. *The standard edition of the complete psychological works of Sigmund Freud*, Vol. 16. Trans. and ed. J Strachey et al., London: Hogarth Press, and Institute of Psychoanalysis.

——1953–1974. 'Totem and Taboo (1912)'. *The standard edition of the complete psychological works of Sigmund Freud*, Vol. 13. Trans. J Strachey et al. London: Hogarth Press, and Institute of Psychoanalysis: 1–131.

——1992. *Letters of Sigmund Freud*. Ed. Ernest L Freud. Trans. Tania & James Stern. New York: Dover Publications [Basic Books, 1960].

Fromm, Erich 1960. 'Zen Buddhism and Psychoanalysis'. In *Zen Buddhism and Psychoanalysis*, by DT Suzuki, Erich Fromm & Richard De Martino. New York: Harper & Row.

Gagnier, Regenia 1986. 'Art as propaganda in wartime: the Pemberton-Billing trials on *Salome*' (Appendix A). In *Idylls of the marketplace: Oscar Wilde and the Victorian public*. Stanford: Stanford UP: 199–204.

Galin, David 2003. 'The Concepts 'Self,' 'Person,' and 'I' in Western psychology and in Buddhism'.In *Buddhism and science: breaking new ground*. Ed. B Allan Wallace. New York: Columbia UP: 107–142.

Garber, Marjorie 1992. *Vested interests: cross-dressing & cultural anxiety*. New York, London: Routledge.

Geherin, David J 1972. 'An interview with Christopher Isherwood'. *The Journal of Narrative Technique*. 2.3: 143–158. (Reprinted in *Conversations with Christopher Isherwood*. Eds James J Berg & Chris Freeman. Jackson: U Press of Mississippi, 2001: 74–89.)

Gilmore, Leigh 1994. 'The mark of autobiography: postmodernism, autobiography, and genre'. In *Autobiography & Postmodernism*. Eds Kathleen Ashley, Leigh Gilmore & Gerald Peters. Amherst: U of Massachusetts Press.

——2001. *The limits of autobiography: trauma and testimony*. Ithaca: Cornell UP.

Glaser, Chris 1975. *Uncommon calling: A gay man's struggle to serve the church*. Harper Collins (San Francisco: Harper & Row, 1988).

Goodheart, Adam 2004. 'The age of Uranians'. Rev. of *Strangers: homosexual love in the nineteenth century* by Graham Robb. *New York Times:* Sunday, 7

March.

Gramsci, Antonio 1971. *Selections from the prison notebooks*. London: Lawrence & Wishart.

Greenberg, Gary 1997. 'Right answers, wrong reasons: revisiting the deletion of homosexuality from the DSM'. *Review of General Psychology* 1.3: 256–70.

Greenberg, Joel 2004. 'A life without secrets'. Rev. of *Isherwood: A life* by Peter Parker. *Weekend Australian* (Review) 10 Jul: R8–9.

Greenberg, Steven 2004. *Wrestling with God and men: homosexuality in the Jewish tradition*. Madison: University of Wisconsin Press.

Griffin, Jasper 1992. 'The love that dared to speak its name'. Rev. of *Bisexuality in the ancient world* by Eva Cantarella. *New York Review of Books* 39.17 (22 Oct).

Griswold, Alexander B 1957. 'King Mongkut in perspective'. *Journal Siam Society*, XLV: 16–18.

Gunn, Robert Jingen 2000. *Journeys into emptiness: Dogen, Merton, Jung, and the quest for transformation*. New York: Paulist Press.

Gunn, Thom 1990. 'Christopher Isherwood: getting things right'. *P.N. Review* 17.1: 35–43.

Hainsworth, Stuart 2000. 'Gramsci's hegemony theory and the ideological role of the mass media'. Online: http://www.cultsock.ndirect.co.uk/MUHome/cshtml/contributions/gramsci.html [accessed 25 Jun 2007].

Halperin, David M 1990. *One hundred years of homosexuality and other essays on Greek love*. New York: Routledge.

——1995. *Saint Foucault: towards a gay hagiography*. NY: Oxford University Press.

——2004. *How to do the history of homosexuality*. Chicago: University Of Chicago Press.

Hamilton, Malcolm 2002. 'The Easternisation thesis: critical reflections'. *Religion* 32: 243–58.

Hamilton-Merritt, Jane 1976. *A meditator's diary: a western woman's unique experiences in Thailand monasteries*. London: Souvenir Press. (Paperback edn. London: Mandala/Unwin Paperbacks, 1986.)

Hanegraaf, Wouter 1999. New Age spiritualities as secular religion: a historian's perspective'. *Social Compass* 46.2: 145–60.

Harvey, Andrew 1994. *Way of passion: a celebration of Rumi*. Hardcover edn. Berkeley, California: Frog Ltd.

Hatcher, Brian A 1999. 'Kali's problem child: another look at Jeffrey Kripal's study of Sri Ramakrsna'. *International Journal of Hindu Studies* 3.2: 165–82.

Hawthorne, Mark 1999. 'Vedanta's western poet'. *Hinduism Today*. Himalayan Academy. Accessed 11 Nov. 2005. Online: http://www.hinduismtoday.com/archives/1999/9/1999-9-12.shtml

Heelas, Paul 2006. 'The infirmity debate: on the viability of New Age spiritualities of life'. *Journal of Contemporary Religion* 21.2: 223–40.

Heelas, Paul & Linda Woodhead 2005. *The spiritual revolution: why religion is giving way to spirituality*. London: Blackwell Publishing.

Heilbrun, Carolyn 1970. *Christopher Isherwood*. New York: Columbia UP

——1976. 'Christopher Isherwood: an interview'. *Twentieth Century Literature* 22: 253–63. Reprinted in *Conversations with Christopher Isherwood*. Eds James J Berg & Chris Freeman 2000. Jackson: U Press of Mississippi: 141–51.

Hensher, Philip 2004. 'Christopher and his kind'. Rev. of *Isherwood: A life*, by Peter Parker. *The Spectator Online*. 15 May. <http://www.spectator.co.uk/bookreview.php?table=old§ion=current&issue=2004-09-11&id=2272&searchText>.

Herdt, Gilbert 1997. *Same sex different cultures: exploring gay & lesbian lives*. Boulder, Colorado: Westview Press/Harper Collins.

Highwater, Jamake 2001. *The mythology of transgression: homosexuality as metaphor*. Bridgewater, NJ: Replica Books. (Originally New York: Oxford UP, 1997.)

Hitchens, Christopher 1997. 'The long littleness of life'. *The New York Review of Books* 44.8 (15 May).

Hodge, Dino 1996. *The fall upward: spirituality in the lives of lesbian women and gay men*. Casuarina, NT: Little Gem.

Holleran, Andrew 1995. 'The sense of sin'. In *Wrestling with the angel: faith and religion in the lives of gay men*. Ed. Brian Bouldrey. New York: Riverhead Books: 83–96.

Hollinghurst, Alan 2004. 'Wrestling with destiny'. Rev. of *Isherwood: A life*, by Peter Parker. *The Guardian* Saturday Review Book of the Week. 29 May:

9.

Hooker, EA 1957. 'The adjustment of the male overt homosexual'. *Journal of Projective Techniques* 21: 18–31.

hooks, bell 1990a. 'Talking back'. *Out There.* Ed. Russell Ferguson et al. New York: New Museum of Contemporary Art: 337–39.

——1990b. 'Marginality as a site of resistance'. *Out There.* Ed. Russell Ferguson, et al. New York: New Museum of Contemporary Art: 341–344.

Houlbrook, Matt 2005. *Queer London: perils and pleasures in the sexual metropolis, 1918–1957* (The Chicago series on sexuality, history, and society). Chicago: U Chicago Press.

Hume, David 1740. *A treatise of human nature.* Oxford: Oxford University Press edition, 1967.

Huxley, Aldous 1944. 'Introduction'. *The song of God: Bhagavad Gita. The Hindu epic translated by Swami Prabhavananda and Christopher Isherwood.* New York: Mentor/New American Library.

——1945. *The perennial philosophy.* New York: Harper.

Hyde, H Montgomery (ed.) 1948. *The trials of Oscar Wilde.* London: William Hodge.

Inden, Ronald 1986. 'Orientalist constructions of India'. *Modern Asian Studies* 20.3: 401–446.

Irigaray, Luce 1993. 'Divine Women'. In *Sexes and genealogies.* New York: Columbia Press [1987].

Isherwood, Christopher 1928. *All the conspirators.* London: Jonathan Cape.

——1932. *The memorial.* London: Hogarth Press.

——1935. *Mr Norris changes trains.* London: Hogarth Press.

——1935. *The last of Mr Norris.* New York: William Morrow.

——1937. *Sally Bowles.* London: Hogarth Press.

——1938. *Lions and shadows.* London: Hogarth Press.

——1939. *Goodbye to Berlin.* London: Hogarth Press.

——1939. *Journey to a war.* London: Faber; New York: Random House.

——1945. *The condor and the cows.* New York: Random House; London: Methuen.

——1946. *Prater Violet.* London: Methuen.

——1951. *Vedanta for modern man.* New York: Harper.

——1952. 'Address to the Vedanta Society of NY. March 26. Huntington: CI 1014.

——1954. *The world in the evening*. London: Methuen.

——1962a. 'Biographical introduction'. In *What religion is in the words of Swami Vivekananda*. Ed. John Yale. London: Phoenix House: i-xxi.

——1962b. *Down there on a visit.* London: Methuen.

——1963. *An approach to Vedanta*. Hollywood, CA: Vedanta Press.

——1964. *A single man*. New York: Simon & Schuster.

——1965. *Ramakrishna and his disciples.* London: Methuen. [Calcutta: Advaita Ashrama, 1980.]

——1966. *Exhumations.* London: Methuen.

——1966. 'The problem of the religious novel'. In *Exhumations.* London: Methuen; New York: Simon & Schuster: 136–40. [*The wishing tree: Christopher Isherwood on mystical religion*. Ed. Robert Adjemian. San Francisco: Harper & Row, 1987: 164–8.]

——1967. *A meeting by the river*. New York: Simon & Schuster.

——1969. *Essentials of Vedanta.* Hollywood: Vedanta Press.

——1971. *Kathleen and Frank*. London: Methuen.

——1977. *Christopher and his kind*. New York: Avon.

——1980. *My Guru and his disciple*. London: Eyre Methuen.

——1986. *The wishing tree.* Ed. Robert Adjemian. New York: Harper & Row.

——1998. *Diaries, volume one, 1939–1960*. Edited with an introduction by Katherine Bucknell. US paperback edn: Michael di Capua Books/Harper Flamingo.

——2000. *Lost Years: A Memoir 1945–1951*. Ed. Katherine Bucknell. New York: Harper Collins.

——n.d. 'Girish Ghosh, playwright'. Lecture. Audio CD. Hollywood: Vedanta Press.

Isherwood, Christopher & Swami Prabhavananda 1944. *The Song of God: Bhagavad Gita.* Los Angeles: Marcel Rodd.

——1947a. *Crest jewel of discrimination by Shankara.* Hollywood: Vedanta Press.

——1947b. 'What is evil? In *Crest jewel of discrimination by Shankara.* Hollywood: Vedanta Press. Also in *Parabola* 24.4 (1999): 55–58.

——1953. *How to know God: The Yoga aphorisms of Patanjali.* New York: Harper; London: Allen & Unwin.

Isherwood, Christopher & Don Bachardy (eds) 1989. *Where joy resides: A Christopher Isherwood reader.* Farrar Straus & Giroux.

Johnson, Toby 2004. *Gay spirituality: gay identity and the transformation of human consciousness.* New York: White Crane [Los Angeles: Alyson Books, 2000].

Joy, Morny 2006. *Divine love: Luce Irigaray, women, gender and religion.* Manchester & New York: Manchester UP.

Jung, Carl G 1959. 'Conscious, Unconscious and Individuation'. *Collected Works,* vol. 9.1 *The Archetypes and the Collective Unconscious.* Trans. RFC Hull. Bollingen Series XX. Princeton U P.

Kabirdas 2006. *The thirsty fish: poems of Kabir.* Trans. Sushil Rao. NY, Miami: Hrdai Press.

Kakar, Sudhir 1985. 'Psychoanalysis and religious healing: siblings or strangers?' *Journal of the American Academy of Religion,* LIII/3: 841–53.

——1991. *The analyst and the mystic: psychoanalytic reflections on religion and mysticism.* Chicago: U Chicago P.

Kamel, Rose 1982. 'Unraveling one's personal myth: Christopher Isherwood's autobiographical strategies'. *Biography* 5.2: 161–75.

Kaplan, Morris B 2005. *Sodom on the Thames: sex, love, and scandal in Wilde times.* Cornell University Press.

Karr, Mary 1995. *The liars' club: a memoir.* London: Picador; New York: Viking.

Katz, Jonathan Ned 2001. *Love stories: sex between men before homosexuality.* Chicago: U Chicago P.

Kelly, Michael Bernard 2007. *Seduced by grace: contemporary spirituality, gay experience and Christian faith.* Melbourne: Clouds of Magellan.

King, Anna S 1996. 'Spirituality: transformation and metamorphosis'. *Religion* 26.4: 343–51.

King, Richard 1999. *Orientalism and religion: postcolonial theory, India and 'the Mystic East'.* London: Routledge.

Kinsey, Alfred C, Wardell B Pomeroy & Clyde E Martin 1948. *Sexual behaviour in the human male.* Bloomington: WB Saunders [Indiana University Press, 1998].

Kohn, Rachael 1991. 'Radical subjectivity in 'self religions' and the problem of authority'. In *Religion in Australia.* Ed. Alan Black.London: Allen & Unwin: 133–50.

——2003. *The new believers: re-imagining God.* Sydney: Harper Collins.

von Krafft-Ebing, R 1924. *Psychopathia Sexualis, with especial reference to the Antipathic Sexual Instinct. A Medico-Forensic Study.* English adaptation of the twelfth German edn. New York: Physicians and Surgeons Book Company.

Kripal, Jeffrey J 1998a. *Kali's child: the mystical and the erotic in the life and teachings of Ramakrishna.* Chicago: U of Chicago P.

——1998b. 'Mystical homoeroticism, reductionism, and the reality of censorship: a response to Gerald James Larson'. *Journal of the American Academy of Religion* 66.3: 627–35.

——2007. *Esalen: America and the religion of no religion.* Chicago: U of Chicago P.

Lachance, Paul 1990. *The mystical journey of Angela of Foligno.* Toronto: Peregrina.

Lake, Catherine (ed.) 1999. *Recreations: religion and spirituality in the lives of queer people.* Toronto: Queer Press.

Lane, Christopher 1995. *The ruling passion: British colonial allegory and the paradox of homosexual desire.* Durham: Duke UP.

Larson, Gerald James 1997. 'Polymorphic sexuality, homoeroticism, and the study of religion: a review of Jeffrey J Kripal's *Kali's Child*'. *Journal of the American Academy of Religion* 65.3: 655–65.

Lehman, John 1987. *Christopher Isherwood: a personal memoir.* NY: Henry Holt.

Leyland, Winston (ed.) 1998. *Queer dharma: voices of gay Buddhists.* San Francisco: Gay Sunshine Press.

Literary Encyclopedia. 'Judith Butler'. Online: http://www.litencyc.com/php/speople.php?rec=true&UID=5173 [accessed 6 Jun 2005]

Locke, John 1997. *An essay concerning human(e) understanding.* Ed. Roger Woolhouse. New York: Penguin Books [1690].

Lohrey, Amanda 2006. 'Voting for Jesus: Christianity and politics in Australia'. *Quarterly Essay* 22 June.

Lucas, Phillip Charles 1996. Rev. of *The sixties spiritual awakening: American religion moves from modern to postmodern* by Robert S Ellwood. In *Church History* 65.1: 149.

Luckhurst, Jonathan 2008. 'A constructivist approach to identity and how to combine different levels of analysis'. Conference paper. International Studies Association Annual Convention, San Francisco, 26–29 March. Accessed online: http://www.allacademic.com//meta/p_mla_apa_research_citation/2/5/2/1/6/pages252167/ p252167-1.php

Lyotard, Jean-Francois 1986. *The Postmodern condition: a report on knowledge*. Manchester: Manchester UP.

—— 1989. *The Differend: phrases in dispute.* Trans. Georges Van Den Abbeele. U of Minnesota P. Theory and History of Literature Series, vol 46.

McCleary, Rollan Richard 2004. *A special illumination: authority, inspiration and heresy in gay spirituality.* London: Equinox Publishing.

McClure, John A 1995. 'Postmodern post-secular: contemporary fiction and spirituality'. *Modern Fiction Studies* 41.1: 141–163.

McColly, Michael 2006. *The after-death room: the journey into spiritual activism.* NY:Soft Skull Press.

McDonough, Joshua 2003. 'Nagarjuna as philosophical reformer'. *Religious Studies* 460: 5 Dec.

McNeill, John J 1998. *Both feet firmly planted in midair: my spiritual journey.* Louisville, Kentucky: Westminster John Knox Press.

Malamud, Margaret 1996. 'Gender and spiritual self-fashioning: the master-disciple relationship in classical Sufism'. *Journal of the American Academy of Religion* 64.1: 89–117.

Malcolm, Janet 1984. *In the Freud archives.* London: Jonathan Cape (Fontana, 1986); New York: Alfred A Knopf.

Mansfield, Nick 2000. *Subjectivity: theories of the self from Freud to Haraway.* St Leonards, NSW: Allen & Unwin.

Marcus, Laura 1994. *Auto/biographical discourses: theory, criticism, practice.* Manchester: Manchester UP.

Marsh, Victor 2005a. 'The journey of the queer 'I': subjective dis-location and re-location in the life-writings of Christopher Isherwood'. *Queen* 5 (special issue). Online: <http://www.ars-rhetorica.net/Queen/VolumeSpecialIssue5/Articles/Marsh.pdf>.

——2005b. Rev. of *Isherwood: A life revealed*, by Peter Parker. *White Crane Journal*. Online: <http://www.whitecranejournal.com/64/art6411.asp>.

——2006/07. 'Portrait of an artist as a Zen monk: a White Crane conversation with Don Bachardy'. *White Crane Journal* 71: 13–26. Online: http://whitecrane.typepad.com/journal/

——2007a. 'Border crossings? Queer spirituality and Asian religion: a first person account'. *Gay and Lesbian Issues and Psychology Review* 3.2: 97–108.

——2007b. '*The boy in the yellow dress*: Re-framing subjectivity in narrativisations of the queer self'. *Life-writing* 4.2: 263–286.

——2008. 'The disobedient subject: disrupting authorized versions of masculinity and spirituality in Christopher Isherwood's life-writing'. *Ariel* 39.1/2: 71–88.

——2009. 'Advaita Vedanta and the repositioning of subjectivity in the life-writing of Christopher Isherwood, 'homosexualist'. *Theology & Sexuality* 15.2: 93–116.

Mason, Eric D 2004. 'Border building: cultural turf and the maintenance of hybridity'. *M/C: A Journal of Media and Culture* 7.2. Queensland University of Technology. Accessed 6 Jun 2006. <http://www.media-culture.org.au/ 0403/03-border-building.php.

Masson, Jeffrey Moussaieff 1974. 'Sex and yoga: psychoanalysis and the Indian religious experience'. *Journal of Indian Philosophy* 2: 307–320.

——1980. *The oceanic feeling: the origins of religious sentiment in ancient India*. Eds Bimal K Matilal & J Moussaieff Masson. Dordrecht, Holland: D Reidel Publishing.

——1984. *The assault on truth: Freud's suppression of the seduction theory*. New York: Farrar Strauss and Giroux [Penguin 1985].

Matousek, Mark 1998. 'Interview: Ken Wilber. Up close and transpersonal with the philosopher king of consciousness'. *Utne Reader* (Jul–Aug): 50–55, 106–07.

Mayes, Bernard Duncan 2001. *Escaping God's closet: the revelations of a queer priest*. Charlottesville and London: UP of Virginia.

Meeks, Wayne A 1973. 'The image of the androgyne: some uses of a symbol in earliest Christianity'. *Journal of the History of Religions* 13.1: 165–208.

Maurice 1987. Prod. Ismail Merchant. Dir. James Ivory. Screenplay James Ivory & Kit Hesketh-Harvey. Merchant Ivory Productions.

Merton, Thomas 1975. *The seven storey mountain*. New York: Harcourt Brace Jovanovich. (1st publ. London: Sheldon Press, 1948.)

——1958. *Thoughts in solitude*. Boston: Shambhala Publications.

——1992. *The Way of Chuang Tzu*. Boston and London: Shambhala.

Milk 2008. Feature film. Dir. Gus van Sant. Writer Dustin Lance Black. Prod. Dan Jinks & Bruce Cohen. Focus Features.

Mol, Hans 1976. *Identity and the sacred: a sketch for a new social-scientific theory of religion*. Oxford: Blackwell.

Molleur, Joseph 2008. 'A Hindu monk's appropriation of Eastern Orthodoxy's Jesus prayer: the 'inner senses' of hearing and seeing in comparative perspective.' Conference paper. American Academy of Religion Annual General Meeting, Chicago, 3 Nov.

Monette, Paul 1992. *Becoming a man: half a life story*. San Francisco: Harper Collins.

Montaigne, Michel de 1987. *The Complete Essays*. Transl. and ed. MA Screech. London: Penguin.

Murphy, Susan 2004a. *Upside down Zen: a direct path into reality*. South Melbourne: Lothian Books.

——2004b. 'Minding Zen'. Interview Rachael Kohn. *The spirit of things*. Prod. Rachael Kohn & Geoff Wood. 18 Jul. Transcript. ABC Radio National. 20 Jul. 2004. <http://www.abc.net.au/ rn/spiritofthings/ stories/2004/1152163.htm>.

Murray, Stephen O 2002. *Homosexualities* (Worlds of desire: the Chicago series on sexuality, gender, and culture). Chicago: U Chicago P.

Musil, Robert 1953–54. *The man without qualities*. Trans. Eithne Wilkins & Ernst Kaiser. London: Secker & Warburg. (*Der Mann ohne Eigenschaften*, 1930, 1933, 1943).

Myss, Caroline 2002. *Sacred contracts: awakening your divine potential*. New York: Random House.

Nagarajan, S 1972. 'Christopher Isherwood and the Vedantic novel: a study of *A single man*'. *Ariel: A Review of International English Literature* 3.4: 63–71.

Nederveen Pieterse, Jan 2000. 'Hybridity, so what? The anti-hybridity backlash and the riddles of recognition'. *Theory, Culture & Society* 18.2/3:

219–245.

Nelson, James B & Sandra P Longfellow 1994. *Sexuality and the sacred: sources for theological reflection*. Westminster John Knox Press.

Nicholson, Susan 1995. 'The narrative dance—a practice map for White's therapy'. *ANZ JournalFamily Therapy* 16.1: 23–28.

Nussbaum, Felicity A 1988. 'Toward conceptualizing diary'. *Studies in Autobiography*. Ed. James Olney. New York: Oxford UP: 128–40.

O'Byrne, Robert 2004. 'A fraudulent rebel'. Rev. of *Isherwood: A life*, by Peter Parker. *The Irish Times*, 26 Jun: 13.

Osborne, Arthur (ed.) 1972. *The collected works of Ramana Maharshi*. New York: Samuel Weiser.

Osborne, Charles 1995. *WH Auden: The life of a poet*. London: Michael O'Mara Books. (1st edition 1980.)

Paine, Jeffery 1989. *Father India: how encounters with an ancient culture transformed the modern West*. New York: Harper Collins: 178-226.

—— 2004. *Re-enchantment: Tibetan Buddhism comes to the West*. New York & London: WW Norton.

Parker, Peter 1998. 'Christopher's kind and other Berliners'. Rev. of *Auden and Isherwood the Berlin years*, by Norman Page. *Times Literary Supplement*, 25 Dec: 32.

——2004. 'A writer's life'. Interview with Lewis Jones. *The Telegraph* (Arts) 8 May: 12. <arts.telegraph.co.uk>.

——2004. *Isherwood: A life*. London: Picador.

——2004. *Isherwood: A life revealed* (US edition) New York: Random House.

Parsons, William B 1999. *The enigma of the oceanic feeling: revisioning the psychoanlytic theory of mysticism*. New York, Oxford: Oxford UP.

Pearson, Christopher 2009. 'A Church collapsing without foundations'. *The Weekend Australian* Inquirer, 28 Feb: 28.

Phillips, Adam 1988. *Winnicott*. Fontana Modern Masters. Ed. Frank Kermode. London: Fontana Press.

——2004. 'Setting the record straight'. Rev. of *Lost years: a memoir 1945–51*, by Christopher Isherwood. *The Guardian online*. 29 Jun. Guardian Unlimited. 9 Nov. 2000. <http://books.guardian.co.uk/lrb/articles/0%2C6109%2C395280%2C00.html>.

Phillips, Timothy & Haydn Aarons 2007. 'Looking "East": an exploratory

analysis of Western disenchantment'. *International Sociology* 22.3: 325–341.
Piazza, Paul 1978. *Christopher Isherwood: myth and anti-myth*. New York: Columbia UP.
Prabhavananda, Swami 1957. 'What is true mysticism'. Lecture recorded in Santa Barbara. CD reproduction of audio recording. The voice of Vedanta series. Hollywood, CA: Vedanta Press. 13 Oct: 13.
Prabhavananda, Swami & Christopher Isherwood (trans.) 1978. *Shankara's crest jewel of discrimination (Viveka-Chudamani)*. Third edn. Hollywood, CA: Vedanta Press.
——1989. *How to know God: the yoga aphorisms of Patanjali*. Paperback edn. New York: New American Library.
Raab, Kelley Ann 1995. 'Is there anything transcendent about transcendence? A philosophical and psychological study of Sri Ramakrishna'. *Journal of the American Academy of Religion* 63.2: 321–41.
Radstone, Susannah 2006. 'Cultures of confession / cultures of testimony: turning the subject inside out'. In *Modern confessional writing: new critical essays.* Ed. Jo Gill. London: Routledge: 166–179.
Ray, Reggie 2006. 'Touching enlightenment'. *Tricycle: The Buddhist Review*. Online:
http://www.tricycle.com/-practice/touching-enlightenment.
Reese, William L 1980. *Dictionary of philosophy and religion: Eastern and Western thought*. New Jersey: Humanities Press.
Reid, Lucy 2005. *She changes everything: seeking the divine on a feminist path.* NY, London: T & T Clark.
Reuters 2009. 'Pope in Africa reaffirms "no condoms" against AIDS'. 17 Mar 2009. Online:
http://www.reuters.com/article/homepageCrisis/idUSLH936617._CH_.2400
Reuters/AAP 2008. 'Ecology of man: Pope wants humanity "saved" from homosexuality'. 23 Dec.
Richardson, Owen 2004. 'His life through the lens'. Rev. of *Isherwood: A life*, by Peter Parker. *Spectrum. Sydney Morning Herald* 24–5 Jul: 10.
Rinpoche, Sogyal 1994. *The Tibetan book of living and dying*. Ed. Patrick Gaffney & Andrew Harvey. San Francisco: Harper Collins.
Robb, David 1984. 'English expatriates and spiritual consciousness in modern

America'. *American Studies* 26: 45–60.

Robb, Graham 2004. *Strangers: homosexual love in the nineteenth century*. NY: WW Norton & Company.

Robinson, Paul A 1999. *Gay lives: homosexual autobiography from John Addington Symonds to Paul Monette*. Chicago: U of Chicago P.

Rogers, Eugene F (ed.) 2002. *Theology and sexuality: classic and contemporary readings*. Blackwell readings in modern theology. Oxford, Malden MA: Blackwell.

Rohr, Richard 2006. Interview with Stephen Crittenden. *The Religion Report* 15 Nov. Transcript. ABC Radio National. 17 Nov. 2006. Online: <http://www.abc.net.au/rn/religionreport/stories/2006/1788767.htm>.

Roland, Alan 1998. 'Ramakrishna: mystical, erotic, or both?' *Journal of Religion and Health* 37.1: 31–35.

Rolland, Romain 1970. *The life of Ramakrishna*. Trans. EF Malcolm-Smith. Calcutta: Advaita Ashrama (1929).

Roof, Wade Clark 1998. 'Modernity, the religious, and the spiritual'. *Annals of the American Academy of Political and Social Science* 558: 211–224.

——1999. *Spiritual markeplace: baby boomers and the remaking of American religion*. Princeton: Princeton UP.

Rosenberg, Harold 1946. Rev. *The perennial philosophy*, by Aldous Huxley; and *Vedanta for the Western world*, by Christopher Isherwood. *Commentary*, 1946. Online: http://www.commentarymagazine.com/viewarticle.cfm/the-perennial-philosophy--by-aldous-huxley--and-vedanta-for-the-western-world--by-christopher-isherwood-226

Rosenthal, Michael 1994. 'Isherwood, Huxley, and the Thirties'. In *The Columbia history of the British novel*. Ed. John Richetti et al. NY: Columbia UP: 740–64.

Rossi, John 2009. 'Evelyn Waugh's neglected masterpiece – Put out more flags'. *Contemporary Review*. Nov, 2002. Online: 21 Apr 2009. http://findarticles.com/p/articles/mi_m2242/is_1642_281/ai_94775541/

Rottenberg, Catherine 2003. 'Judith Butler'. Literary Encyclopedia online. http://www.litencyc.com/php/speople.php?rec=true&UID=5173. Accessed June 26, 2005.

Rowbotham, Sheila 2008. *Edward Carpenter: A Life of Liberty and Love.* London, Brooklyn: Verso.

Rumi, Jalāl al-Dīn & William C Chittick 1983. *The Sufi path of love: the spiritual teachings of Rumi.* Trans. William C Chittick. NY: SUNY Press.

Sacks, Oliver 1993a. *The man who mistook his wife for a hat.* Picador.

——1993b. 'Making up the mind'. *The New York Review of Books* 8 Apr: 42–49.

Said, Edward 1995. *Orientalism.* London: Penguin (London: Routledge & Kegan Paul, 1978).

Salih, Sara (ed.) with Judith Butler 2004. *The Judith Butler reader.* Malden MA and Oxford UK: Blackwell.

Sands, Kathleen 2008. 'Mixing it up: religion, lesbian feminism, and queerness'. Conference Paper. American Academy of Religion Annual Meeting, Chicago. 3 Nov.

Saul, Joanne 2001. 'Displacement and self-representation: theorizing contemporary Canadian biotexts.' *Biography* 24.1: 259–272.

——2006. Writing the roaming subject: the biotext in Canadian literature. Toronto: U of Toronto P.

Savage, DS 1979. 'Christopher Isherwood: the novelist as homosexual[ist]'. *Literature and Psychology* 29.1/2: 71–88.

Savastano, Peter 2007. 'Gay men as virtuosi of the holy art of bricolage and as tricksters of the sacred'. *Theology & Sexuality* 14(1): 9–28.

Schneiders, Sandra M 2003. 'Religion vs. spirituality: A contemporary conundrum'. *Spiritus: A Journal of Christian Spirituality* 3.2: 163–85.

Schuhmaker, Stephan & Gert Woerner (eds) 1994. *The encyclopedia of Eastern philosophy and religion* (Trans. of *Lexicon der ostlichen weisheitslehren*) Bern & Munich: Otto-Wilhelm-Barth Verlag, 1986). Trans. Karen Ready, Michael H Kohn & Werner Wunsche. Boston: Shambhala.

Shah, Idries 1989. *The exploits of the incomparable Mulla Nasrudin.* London: Octagon Press.

Shallenberger, David 1998. *Reclaiming the spirit: gay men and lesbians come to terms with religion.* New Brunswick, New Jersey: Rutgers UP.

Siker, Jeffrey S 2007. *Homosexuality and religion: an encyclopedia.* Westport, CT & London: Greenwood Press.

Sil, Narasingha P 1991. *Ramakrsna Paramahansa: A psychological profile.*

Leiden: EJ Brill.
——1993. 'Vivekananda's Ramakrsna: An untold story of mythmaking and propaganda'. *Numen* 40: 38–62.
——1997. 'Is Ramakrishna a Vedantin, a Tantrika, or a Vaishnava? An examination'. *Asian Studies Review* XXI, 2/3: 212–224.
——1998. *Ramakrishna revisited: a new biography*. Lanham: University Press of America.
Smith, Sidonie 1993. *Subjectivity, identity, and the body: women's autobiographical practices in the twentieth century*. Bloomington: Indiana UP.
Smith, Sidonie & Julia Watson 1996. *Getting a life: everyday uses of autobiography*. Minneapolis: U of Minnesota P, 1996.
Sokefeld, Martin 1999. Debating self, identity, and culture in anthropology'. *Current Anthropology* 40.4: 417ff.
Spender, Stephen 1953. *World within world*. London. Readers Union.
——1962. 'Confessions and autobiography'. *Autobiography: Essays theoretical and critical*. Ed. James Olney. Princeton: Princeton UP: 115–22.
——1980. 'Issyvoo's Conversion. Rev. of *My Guru and His Disciple*, by Christopher Isherwood'. *The New York Review of Books*. 27.13: 18–21.
Spivak, Gayatri Chakravorty 1985. 'Three women's texts and a critique of Imperialism.' *Critical Inquiry* 12.1: 243–261.
——*Other Asias* 2007. Malden, MA: Blackwell.
Stanley, Liz 1992. *The auto/biographical I: The theory and practice of feminist auto/biography*. Manchester and NY: Manchester UP.
Stewart, Christopher Buren 2002. 'In paths untrodden: queer spiritual autobiography.' PhD thesis. Case Western U.
Stone-Mediatore, Shari 2000. 'Chandra Mohanty and the revaluing of experience'. In *Decentering the center: philosophy for a multicultural, postcolonial, and feminist World*. Ed. Uma Narayan & Sandra Harding. Indiana University Press: 110–127.
Strachey, Julia 1946. Review of *Prater Violet. Horizon* 14.79: 60–4.
Strawson, Galen 2004. 'Against narrativity'. *Ratio* 17.4: 428–452.
Sullivan, Andrew 2002. 'Alone again, naturally: the Catholic Church and the homosexual'. In *Theology and sexuality: classic and contemporary readings*. Ed. Eugene F Rogers. Oxford: Blackwell. 275–288.
Summers, Claude J 1981. *Christopher Isherwood*. New York: Ungar.

Sutherland, John 2005. 'Outsider, vagabond, and "objective narcissist".' Rev. of *Isherwood: A life*, by Peter Parker. *The Boston Globe*. 2 Jan: C9.

——2004. 'I am a cactus'. Rev. of *Isherwood: A life*, by Peter Parker. *London Review of Books*. 26.11: 23–24.

Sweasey, Peter 1997. *From queer to eternity: spirituality in the lives of lesbian, gay and bisexual people*. London: Cassell.

Swidler, Arlene (ed.) 1993. *Homosexuality and world religions*. Valley Forge, Pennsylvania: Trinity Press International.

Tacey, David J 1985. 'Patrick White's *Voss*: the teller and the tale'. *Southern Review* 18.3: 251–71.

——1990a. 'Reconstructing masculinity: a post-Jungian response to contemporary men's issues'. *Meanjin* 49.4: 781–92.

——1990b. 'The politics of analysis: psychology, literary culture and Australian innocence'. *Meanjin* 49.1: 123–33.

Tambiah, Stanley Jeyaraja 1990. *Magic, science, religion, and the scope of rationality.* Cambridge and NY: Cambridge UP.

Teachout, Terry 2000. 'England's greatest composer'. *Commentary* 109.6: 58–62.

Thanissaro Bhikkhu (trans.) 1994. *Buddhist Monastic Code.* Online: accessed 2007 http://www.accesstoinsight.org/lib/authors/thanissaro/bmc1/bmc1.intro.html

Thompson, Mark 1987a. 'Double reflections: Isherwood and Bachardy on art, love, and faith'. In *Gay spirit: myth and meaning*. NY: St Martin's Press: 36–48.

——1987b. *Gay spirit: myth and meaning*. NY: St Martin's Press.

——1995. *Gay soul: finding the heart of gay spirit and nature.* San Francisco: Harper San Francisco.

The times of Harvey Milk 1984. Documentary feature film. Dir. Rob Epstein. Prod. Richard Smiechen. Black Sand Productions and Pacific Arts and WNET.

Toibin, Colm 2001. *Love in a dark time: gay lives from Wilde to Almodovar.* London: Picador.

Trapnell, Judson B 2000. Rev. of *Ramakrishna revisited: A new biography* by Narasingha P Sil,1998. *International Journal of Hindu Studies* 4.1: 101–2.

Trilling, Lionel 1972. *Sincerity and authenticity*. London: Oxford UP.

Trinh, T Minh-Ha 1992. *Framer framed*. NY & London: Routledge.

Turkle, Sherry 1995. 'Aspects of the self'. In *Life on the screen: identity in the age of the internet.* NY: Simon & Schuster.

Turner, William B 2000. *A genealogy of queer theory*. Philadelphia: Temple University Press.

Tweedie, Irina 1986. *Daughter of fire: a diary of a spiritual training with a Sufi master*. (Previously publ. as *The chasm of fire*, 1979). Nevada City, CA: Blue Dolphin Publishing.

Tyagananda, Swami 2004. 'Kali's child revisited, or, didn't anyone check the documentation?' Review article. Infinity Foundation (The educational council on Indic traditions). Online: 4 May 2004 http://www.infinityfoundation.com/ECITkalichildframeset.htm

Ulanov, Ann Belford 1981. *Receiving woman: studies in the psychology and theology of the feminine.* Philadelphia: Westminster Press.

Vanita, Ruth & Saleem Kidwai 2000. *Same-sex love in India: readings from literature and history*. NY: St Martin's Press.

Van Ness, Peter H (ed.) 1996. *Spirituality and the secular quest*. NY: Crossroad.

Varela, Francisco 1999. *Ethical know-how: action, wisdom, and cognition.* Stanford: Stanford UP.

Varela, Francisco & Natalie Depraz 2003. 'Imagining: embodiment, phenomenology, and transformation'. In *Buddhism and science: breaking new ground.* Ed. B Alan Wallace. Columbia UP: 195–232.

Vedanta Society of Southern California. *Fequently asked questions* 1. Pamphlet. <http://www.vedanta.org>.

Venn-Brown, Anthony 2004. *A life of unlearning: coming out of the Church.* Sydney: New Holland.

Vidal, Gore 1972. *The city and the pillar.* Revised edn London: Panther/Granada, [Heinemann 1965].

——1976. 'Art, sex and Isherwood'. Rev. of *Christopher and his kind:1929–1939*, by Christopher Isherwood. *The New York Review of Books.* 9 Dec: 10–18.

Vidyatmananda, Swami (John Yale) n.d. 'The devotee as disciple'. In *The making of a devotee*. Ramakrishna Order of India. Accessed 12 May 2004. http://world.std.com/~elayj/Chapter4.html.

——2001. *A Yankee and the Swamis: a westerner's view of the Ramakrishna order*. Chennai: Sri Ramakrishna Math, 2001 [George Allen & Unwin Ltd, 1961].

Vivekananda, Swami & Christopher Isherwood 1976. *Meditation and its methods according to Swami Vivekananda*. Los Angeles: Vedanta Press & Bookshop.

Vrajaprana, Pravrajika 1997. Rev. of *Kâlîs child: the mystical and the erotic in the life and teachings of Ramakrishna* by Jeffrey J Kripal. *Hindu-Christian Studies Bulletin* 10: 59–60.

——1999. *Vedanta: a simple introduction*. Hollywood: Vedanta Press.

Wade, Stephen 1991. *Christopher Isherwood*. London: Macmillan.

——2001. 'Christophananda writes his religion: Isherwood's purgatory (Religion and self in the works of Christopher Isherwood)'. *Critical Survey* 13.3: 3–18.

Watts, Alan 1989. *The way of Zen*. NY: Vintage Books (1957).

——1973. *The book on the taboo against knowing who you are*. London: Abacus [1969].

Waugh, Alec 1917. *The loom of youth*. London: Richards.

Waugh, Evelyn 2000. *Put out more flags*. Penguin Modern Classics. [London: Chapman & Hall 1942.]

Webster, Len 1971. 'A very individualistic old liberal: interview with Christopher Isherwood'. Reprinted in *Conversations with Christopher Isherwood*. Eds James J Berg & Chris Freeman. Jackson: U Press of Mississippi, 2001: 57–71.

Weinraub, Bernard 2004. 'A tribute to Isherwood in the land he loved'. *The New York Times*, Sec. Arts: D5. 7 Jul.

Welwood, John 2000. 'The psychology of awakening'. *Tricycle: The Buddhist Review*, Feb.
Online: http://www.tricycle.com

West, Donald James & Richard Green (eds) 1997. *Sociolegal control of homosexuality: a multi-nation comparison*. NY: Plenum Press

Westerlund, David (ed.) 2004. *Sufism in Europe and North America.* NY: Routledge Curzon.

White, Edmund 1980. 'A sensual man with a spiritual quest'. Rev. of *My Guru and His Disciple*, by Christopher Isherwood. *New York Times Book Review* 1 Jun: 9.

——(ed) 1991. 'Foreword'. *The Faber book of gay short fiction.* London, Boston: Faber & Faber Limited: ix-xviii.

——2002. 'Writing gay'. *Michigan Quarterly Review* 41.3: 369–87.

——2004. 'Tale of two kitties: how Christopher Isherwood was defined by his mother and his lover'. Rev. of *Isherwood: A life* by Peter Parker. *Times Literary Supplement* 4 June: 3–4.

Whitlock, Gillian (ed.) 1996. 'Introduction: Disobedient subjects'. *Autographs: contemporary Australian autobiography.* UQP Australian authors. St Lucia: U of Queensland P: ix-xxx.

Wickes, George 1965. 'An interview with Christopher Isherwood'. *Shenandoah*: 22–52. Reprinted in *Conversations with Christopher Isherwood.* Eds James J Berg & Chris Freeman. Jackson: U Press of Mississippi, 2001: 24–44.

Wilde, Alan 1971. *Christopher Isherwood.* New York: Twayne Publishers.

Wilber, Ken 1980. 'The pre/trans fallacy'. *ReVision* 3: 51–73.

——2000. *One taste: daily reflections on integral spirituality.* Boston: Shambhala.

Wilhelm, Amara Das n.d. 'Presenting the third gender as described in ancient Vedic (Hindu) texts'. The gay and lesbian Vaishnava association. 30 Mar 2005. Online: <http://groups.yahoo.com/group/galva108/>

Williams, Walter L 1986. 'Persistence and change in the Berdache tradition among contemporary Lakota Indians'. In *The many faces of homosexuality: anthropological approaches to homosexual behaviour.* Ed. Evelyn Blackwood. NY: Harrington Park Press: 191–200.

——1992. *The spirit and the flesh: sexual diversity in American Indian culture.* Boston: Beacon Press.

Woodhead, Linda, Paul Heelas & David Martin (eds) 2001. *Peter Berger and the study of religion.* London and New York: Routledge.

Worthington, Kim L 1996. *Self as narrative: subjectivity and community in contemporary fiction.* Oxford: Clarendon Press.

Yale, John 1961. *A Yankee and the Swamis. A Westerner's view of the Ramakrishna Order*. Chennai: Sri Ramakrishna Math [re-issued 2001].

Yale, John (ed.) 1962, with a biographical introduction by Christopher Isherwood. *What religion is in the words of Swami Vivekananda*. London: Phoenix House.

Yip, Andrew KT 2002. 'The persistence of faith among nonheterosexual Christians: evidence for the neosecularization thesis of religious transformation'. *Journal for the Scientific Study of Religion*. 41.2: 199–212.

Zaehner, RC 1960. *Hindu and Muslim mysticism*. University of London: Athlone Press.

Zaretsky, Eli 2004. *Secrets of the soul: a social and cultural history of psychoanalysis*. New York: Knopf.

After previous careers in television (*Beyond 2000*, *Young Talent Time*) and theatre (The Australian Performing Group at the Pram Factory), Victor Marsh received his PhD in literary studies from the University of Queensland in 2007. A student of comparative religion for four decades, he has taught meditation in a dozen countries in Asia and the Pacific rim.